A MIDSHIPMAN'S WAR

A Young Man in the Mediterranean Naval War 1941 - 1943

Frank Wade

CORDILLERA PUBLISHING COMPANY
VANCOUVER, B.C.

Copyright 1994 © Frank Wade

Canadian Cataloguing in Publication Data

Wade, Frank, 1921-
  A Midshipman's War

  Includes bibliographical references and index
  ISBN 1-895590-06-X

  1. Frank Wade, 1921- 2. World War 1939-1945 — Personal
narratives, Canadian. 3. World War, 1939-1945 — Campaigns-
-Mediterranean Sea. I. Title
D766.W32 1994   940.54'23   C94-910329-2

Cover Artwork by Wendy C. Mars
Typesetting by
    J. & P. Gunderson
    263 210th Street
    Langley, B.C. V3A 7R2
Printed and bound by
    Friesen Printers
    P.O. Box 720, Altona, Manitoba
    Canada, ROG 0B0
Published by
    Cordillera Publishing Company
    8415 Granville Street, Box 46
    Vancouver, B.C.
    Canada, V6P 4Z9

*The cover picture is reproduced from an original by Ken Gibson, artist of West
Vancouver, B.C.*

Contents

Frank Wade, taken in 1944 on his return to Canada.

Acknowledgements

One is helped by so many kind people in preparing a detailed work of this nature, and I am very much in their debt. I would like to first thank Peter Colenbrander for editing the manuscript and helping me reshape it. Also Hal Lawrence, the dean of Canadian naval writers, who read the first draft and encouraged me to finish it.

Thanks also go to Larry Milberry of Canav Books who was very helpful and encouraging, and to my readers Jim Murray, a retired Canadian army officer, Tom Hoeflok (Dutch army) and Gordon Stead, ex-Lt.-Commander RCNVR who wrote a book on his experiences in MLs in Malta.

John Morrison, an RCNR Lieutenant clearance diver, discussed the Italian mini-submarine attack in Alexandria harbour with me and made helpful technical comments. Ken Gibson, a *Barham* survivor, went over his experiences in great detail and provided the art work. Friend Evelyn Robbins, a cartographer, did the maps.

Desmond Hagan of Bligh Park, New South Wales, Australia, an ex RAN telegraphist, kindly provided me with books, magazines and photographs on RAN ships in the Med war. Joan Humphries, an archivist of the Burns, Philp shipping company sent information and a photograph of *Bulolo*.

Commander Phil Booth RCN discussed his experiences in *Eskimo* during the Sicilian landings and let me use some excellent photographs. Hans Von Tiesenhausen, the Captain of U331, now a Canadian citizen, discussed his attack on the *Barham* with me. Old friend Dr Burton Yuill also told of his experiences in the Sicilian landings.

The Imperial War Museum in London, England, the Italian Navy Museum — Museo Storico Navale, in Venice, Italy and the Vancouver Maritime Museum were very helpful.

Bob Symons, an ex-RN lieutenant living in South Africa; Commander W.M. Bisset SAN, Director of the South African Naval Museum, Simonstown, South Africa; John Duffell-Canham, Ben Darby, D.E., Clapham, V. Harrington and E.V. Corbishley, National Chairman of the MOTHs (Members of the Tin Hat) the equivalent of our Legion; all South African naval and army vets, were particularly helpful sending me books, articles, magazines and photographs on the SA ships in the Med war.

Captain Russel, an old Conway master mariner, helped me with the merchant ship identification.

Don McGill and Paul Pidcock, both ex-RCNVR Lieutenants told me their stories and provided me with interesting photographs. Ex-Petty officer Wren Edythe Amoore RN, now a Canadian, also did the same thing.

I am extremely indebted to all these people. They helped me try and tell the interesting story — not well-known, of one Canadian and others who served with the Royal Navy in concert with the Australian and South African navies in the Mediterranean theatre in World War II.

I would also be remiss if I did not thank the helpful reference librarians in the Vancouver Public Library and the West Vancouver Public Library.

I am also grateful to my wife Ruth, and sons George and Alan for their input, assistance and encouragement.

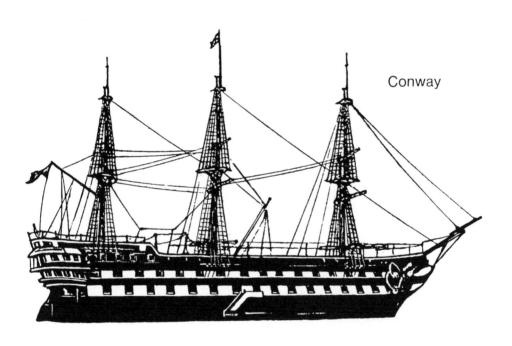

Conway

CHAPTER ONE

My First Ship
Training Ship HMS Conway

Old Ship who cradled us and gave us friends
And sealed us to the service of the Sea.
John Masefield

By Command of the Commissioners
for executing the office of the
Lord High Admiral of the United
Kingdom, etc.

To. Mr. F.E.Wade, Paymaster Midshipman R.C.N.

The Lord Commissioners of the Admiralty hereby appoint you
Paymaster Midshipman R.C.N. of His Majesty's Ship *Queen
Elizabeth,* additional for training and to obtain a ledger certificate, and direct you to repair on board that ship at Rosyth on
1st January 1941.

Your appointment is to take effect from that date.

You are to acknowledge the receipt of this appointment forth-
with, addressing your letter to the Commanding Officer HMS
Queen Elizabeth taking care to furnish your address.

BY COMMAND OF THEIR LORDSHIPS

The great news had arrived at last. It was something that I had been waiting
for these many long years. "Additional for training" sounded all right but I
didn't like "to obtain a ledger certificate". It sounded boring.

I met Tyndall at Euston Station in London. He took the officer's new entry
training course at Dartmouth Royal Naval College with me and had also been
appointed to *Queen Elizabeth.* We travelled up to Scotland overnight in the
same compartment. We were so damned excited that I'm afraid we had hardly
any sleep. He had half a bottle of sherry which we finished very slowly, talking
about the course and what we thought the ship was going to be like.

After twenty-four hours onboard I found her to be a wonderful ship; very
modern and majestic and giving a great sense of power and security. She was
just what I wanted. She had completed a two-and-a-half year modernization
in the Portsmouth Naval Dockyard and was now the most up-to-date battleship in the fleet. Who would have thought that, when I was shipped off to
England from Canada by my parents to attend a school run by my great uncle,
I would end up joining this mighty ship?

My adventure started many years previously when I was put on a train in Winnipeg in the charge of a kindly black porter. I can't remember being homesick. It all seemed like a great adventure. I travelled across the Atlantic in the *Duchess of York,* a fine Canadian Pacific liner. On arrival in England I was looked after by adoring grandmothers and aunts.

I attended a preparatory school in England: a boarding school for boys from eight to fourteen. It was located in Hove, next to Brighton, a seaside resort on the south coast of England. It was an attractive place of old Victorian houses, high trees, substantial walls and wide avenues. The school was originally started by my uncle and another man. When uncle died, my family continued to have an association with it.

My great aunt Stella, a large jolly woman, was matron and kept a close eye on me. There were two headmasters, Mr. Carson and Mr. Jamieson, while I was there, and they ran the school benignly but effectively. We studied all the regular subjects plus Latin and Greek and, as a result, acquired a good knowledge of Mediterranean names and places especially when following Hannibal's march through Spain and France into Rome. In addition to our school work, other activities were afforded almost equal importance. Sport was stressed — soccer and cricket — and we always seemed to be listening to visiting speakers: a clergyman who had worked with the poor, or a young pilot from the Fleet Air Arm. They all spoke to us as if we were grown-ups. A regular lecturer came on Sunday nights, bringing an ancient magic lantern and hundreds of large coloured glass slides of pictures of the great masters. On Sunday afternoons, while we rested in our wooden cubicle, an old boy who lived in Hove played classical music records to us on a wind-up victrola. Current affairs were stressed and we often discussed the rise of the Fascist dictators Hitler and Mussolini, the Spanish civil war and the League of Nations.

It was a happy time for me with many wonderful memories: cricket in white flannels on green playing fields below rolling Sussex Downs with lemonade and buns afterwards; idyllic country picnics in summer; our annual cadet corps route march, all of us dressed in First World War uniforms with khaki shorts and puttees. Several evenings each week we listened spellbound as boy's adventure books were read to us.

Once when we went to play cricket we found a tramp sleeping on the grounds. I always remember that Mr. Carson, instead of waking him and asking him to leave, diverted us to some other activity and left him in peace. He even undertook to get cook to prepare him a meal when he awoke. This was one of our few encounters with the reality of the Depression, which was at its height.

Before I left Belvedere school, I began devouring books at a great rate, especially books about naval life by "Bartimeus" and "Taffrail", and by the American Lowell Thomas on Lawrence of Arabia and Count Luckner, the First World War German commander of a sailing ship sea raider. Not surprisingly my grandmother decided that I should try for the navy.

Arrangements were made for me to attend the Training Ship *HMS Conway,* then lying at anchor on the Merseyside near the great seaport of Liverpool. I was to be a cadet in the navy class. The *Conway* was a unique ship and was similar in many ways to Nelson's *Victory* but smaller. She was launched at Plymouth on 28 June 1839 as *HMS Nile:* and was one of the wooden walls of England. In 1854 she was fitted with an engine and, after further service in the

Training ship HMS *Conway* in Liverpool harbour in September 1938.

HMS *Conway* lying aground, her back broken, in the Menai Strait on 14 April 1953 in her 114th year. She was the last floating "wooden wall of England" but was sadly left to rot as a derelict.

navy, became a training ship for Merchant Marine officers and Royal Navy applicants and was renamed *Conway.*

The 150 cadets onboard lived in primitive conditions. Despite this, life aboard was somehow enjoyable. There was very little bullying and what there was ceased when the ringleader was expelled, an experience which we would never forget. We fell in on parade to witness the unfortunate cadet having his brass buttons cut from his uniform and his cap badge removed. Then he was marched over the side, down the gangway to a waiting boat, never to return.

The discipline was strict but not overdone. Our officers and masters were good-humoured and appeared to be enjoying working with young cadets. They were all connected with the merchant service, and I suppose it was a nice break for them being able to stay at home with their families instead of being on long voyages.

There was plenty of good fellowship and joking. There were humorous traditions which illustrated this. On Sundays an old sailor would come aboard and played the harmonium for the hymns. We would sing them fast so that it would be very difficult for him to keep up with us. This came from the singing of the school song which was sung after the service. The words and melody were excellent but the composer was rather eccentric when it came to the tempo. The chorus was sung slowly, then very quickly and then slowly.

> *(Slowly)*
> Carry on, carry on, till the last days gone,
> and the old ship knows you no more.
>
> *(Quickly)*
> O East and West and North and South,
> From Rio Bay to Mersey mouth.
> From ev'ry distant sea and shore,
> You'll hear the cry.
>
> *(A little slower)*
> "Ship ahoy, Ship ahoy!"
> and you'll find on the bridge a Conway boy,
> So for the love of the ship that sends us forth,
> Till last tide turns and the last days gone,
> Carry on, Carry on, Carry on."

We were kept busy with academic work, including navigation and engineering, and learned seamanship from firsthand experience by actually handling small boats in all kinds of weather. I soon discovered that I was red-green colour-blind, so I could never be a deck officer. I decided to apply for a job as a paymaster officer, an ancient and honourable position in the Royal Navy. One of my heroes, "Bartimeus", the naval writer, whom I later met on *Queen Elizabeth,* was a retired Paymaster Captain. The title paymaster is deceptive because this branch of the navy looks after the administration of the fleet and shore establishments, including not only pay, but also victualling, stores, accounting, legal and personnel matters.

We lived like sailors in the days of Nelson, each of us slinging a hammock on the orlop deck, in the bowels of the ship. Awakened early in the morning, we would lash our hammocks and stow them in racks. After washing we would change into our uniforms which were kept in wooden sea chests. Then to the main deck, where metal tables were set for breakfast by duty messmen. After breakfast the tables were cleared and we mustered for divisions (parade) and prayers on the lower deck. Then back to the main deck, where we let down partitions which were hooked to the deckhead. The deck was now changed into classrooms. In the afternoons we would row or sail or go ashore to our excellent playing fields. The evenings were our own except for a study period.

The main deck could be cleared for church or assembly by returning the dividers to the deckhead and by folding and clearing the tables. Thus we were able to make the utmost use of the very limited space, and soon grew used to living together in the confined area of a ship.

The Mersey was alive with shipping, from large liners, visiting warships, and all types of cargo ships down to harbour dredgers. We even caught sight of the ancient but still working windjammer *Pamir* on her annual visit to the port. Nearby, Cammell Lairds shipways were jammed with merchant and naval ships under construction.

A particularly memorable day for us was Sunday 11 September 1938 when a new figurehead for the *Conway* was unveiled. It depicted Nelson and was a fine work of carving. The ship was towed to the Liverpool Prince's ferry landing stage for the ceremony. We mustered on the upper deck, facing a large crowd on the dockside. My job was to play the bugle. The figurehead was unveiled by none other than the Poet Laureate, John Masefield — himself an old *Conway* man. Apparently he harboured great affection for his old ship, having written two books about her. On this occasion he read a poem to the crowd about the ship, and the figurehead was officially unveiled.

Later in the day we were each introduced to him and given an autographed copy of his poem. The ceremony over, we marched to the cathedral to commemorate the "Masting of Nelson on the School Ship *HMS Conway*". The Dean was keen on ceremony, and this was not the first service in which we had participated; we had led the bishop's procession into the church on several occasions. Once our bugle band, led by myself, took station high in an upper gallery and when we played our call, it reverberated around the great modern building, the largest cathedral in England, with great effect.

Towards the end of my time on *Conway* I had to prepare hard for the Royal Navy entrance exams. During the summer of 1939 I was sent to a cram school in the heart of London, near Lincoln's Inn Fields and much enjoyed getting to know the narrow streets and monuments in the area.

I took my exams and was, unfortunately, unsuccessful. However the competition had been very tough and I had almost made it. Soon after, the war started and in September 1939 I went back to the ship for my last term. Everyone had known that war was bound to come despite the efforts of Neville Chamberlain. The ambitions of the Germans seemed to know no bounds. Even in September 1938, when Chamberlain returned from Munich, we had been issued with gas masks and continued to dig bomb shelters.

My first personal experience of what was going on was when my great aunt Stella came back from Germany very upset. She had close ties with several German families and spoke German and would always spend part of her summer holidays there. She wouldn't speak too much about what was worrying her, but it concerned the treatment of the Jews.

I was staying with grandmother on the day that war was declared. We sat

13

THE COMMON WEAL

Then the Lord Lieutenant, the Earl of Derby, shall speak to the people.

WE OF THIS BRITISH NATION
FOUNDED IN SEA TRADITION
OF THIS CITY
ITSELF BORN OF THE SEA
ARE GATHERED IN OUR CATHEDRAL CHURCH
TO REMEMBER BEFORE GOD

our Merchant Navy, its ships, and the men who sail them through all the seas and oceans of the world, through the hazards of tempest, climate, reef and shoal, to all harbours, all ports, in the progress of their lawful occasions, effecting the steady interchange of the world's resources, the fuller understanding of its peoples and nations: and

TO PRAY

for the continuing of their spirit of ungrudging service with our Sovereign Lord the King.

Then shall all the people sing

"GOD SAVE THE KING!"

Which done, the Lord Lieutenant of the County shall continue

THUS MAY WE OF THIS COMMONWEALTH BE FOUND STRENGTHENING HUMAN UNDERSTANDING BETWEEN THOSE ON SEA AND THOSE ASHORE

And all the people shall sing

ONE realm of races four,
Blest more and ever more,
  God save our land!
Home of the brave and free,
Set in the silver sea,
True nurse of chivalry,
  God save our land!

Of many a race and birth
From utmost ends of earth,
  God save us all!
Bid strife and hatred cease,
Bid hope and joy increase,
Spread universal peace,
  God save us all!

8

A page from the programme of "The masting of Nelson" on the schoolship
HMS *Conway*, Liverpool Cathedral, 11 September, 1938.

in the living room, listening to Chamberlain's fateful radio speech. Immediately he had finished, the air raid sirens began to wail. Both grandmother and my aunt appeared unconcerned, perhaps because the gravity of the situation had not yet sunk in. And indeed the circumstances quickly turned to comedy. Our elderly neighbour was the local Air Raid Warden, and was wearing every piece of kit he had: oilskin jacket and trousers, rubber boots, tin helmet and a gas mask over his face. He hastened by frantically waving at us to get away from the windows but all we could do was laugh.

My last term on *Conway* coincided with the Phoney War, the calm before the storm. But the inactivity was punctuated by three major events; the totally unexpected Ribbentrop-Molotov Pact, the sinking of the *Graf Spee,* and, in February 1940, Commander Vian's dashing rescue, in *Cossack,* of the British prisoners taken by the *Graf Spee* and held aboard the *Altmark* in Norwegian territorial waters. Nelson's tradition of attacking despite the cost was clearly still alive and well in the Royal Navy.

During the holidays at Christmas time, I went up to Canada House to see if I could join the Royal Canadian Navy. A Mr. Mcleod, a kindly gentleman, took note of my marks and sent them on to Ottawa. By the end of January I had received word that I had been accepted as a permanent officer with the rank of cadet. I would be officially appointed on 22 August 1940 and was to take an entry course at the Dartmouth Naval College in Devon.

I was therefore at a loose end for six months with nothing to do but see the sights of London and follow the war, such as it was at this time. One of my most vivid memories of this period was the march past of the officers and men of the victorious cruisers *Ajax, Exeter* and *Achilles* which had forced the sinking of the *Graf Spee.* It was held on a cold wintry day on Horse Guards Parade behind the Admiralty. The King and Winston Churchill, the First Lord of the Admiralty, a determined bulky figure in his heavy overcoat and bowler hat took the salute.

Then on 9 April 1940 the Germans unexpectedly invaded Norway, by sending naval forces and troops to four centres spread out along the length of the country. Oslo, Bergen, Trondheim and Narvik were overcome with little resistance. Our response in sending troops to relieve Trondheim and Narvik was relatively quick in the circumstances.

Unfortunately things did not turn out well. Two naval actions were fought at Narvik with severe losses on both sides, though the Germans lost more destroyers than we did. On 1 May our troops were withdrawn from Trondheim and a dramatic debate followed in the House of Commons after which Chamberlain resigned and a new coalition government was formed under Churchill.

One of the highlights of the debate was the speech of Sir Roger Keyes, Admiral of the Fleet and a Conservative member of the House.

He was a naval hero of the First World War, having led the attack to block Zeebrugge. He came into the house wearing his uniform and his medals the better to make his point. During all the recriminations and soul-searching that went on, the press report of his speech seemed to bring back a spark of self-confidence to many including myself. I kept the copies of the debate from the "London Times."

Keyes was the first to indicate openly in the debate that the country needed Churchill to lead it. He went on to deliver a fighting speech, full of support and admiration for Churchill and praise, albeit qualified, for the Royal Navy's recent exploits in the South Atlantic and especially off Norway. He felt that the British troops should have been taken directly up the fiord into Trondheim instead of to the north and south. The admiral finished off resoundingly by urging more vigorous naval action in Norwegian waters and by quoting Nelson's dictum, "I am of the opinion that the boldest measures are the safest." His speech was met with prolonged cheers.

Then, before the Norwegian campaign had ended, Hitler launched his *blitzkrieg* against Holland and Belgium. Each day the map of the front depicted in the press moved further to the west. The British army retreated to Dunkirk about fifty miles across from Dover, and was evacuated by some miracle and the strenuous efforts of the navy.

At this time I had the chance to go down to work on a farm near Christchurch in Hampshire. At least I felt I was helping the war effort while waiting to join the navy. I took the train down from Victoria station, right in the middle of the Dunkirk evacuation. When I was waiting outside the platform, a train from one of the south coast ports slowly came in and dishevelled soldiers began to get off and head for the barriers. One scene stands out. A commotion developed near one the compartments where a senior French officer was getting off attended by a young aide. He was wearing a French pillbox hat with plenty of gold braid, but wore no trousers, only his underpants and a shirt. Luckily it was beautiful warm day, so he wasn't too cold. But clearly the poor man must have gone through some truly dreadful experience.

On the way down to Hampshire my train came slowly to a stop. After awhile another northbound train stopped right beside us. We looked across at it to realise that though it was as silent as an empty train, it was in fact crowded with soldiers, everyone one of whom was dead asleep. They lay across each other in every kind of position and yet had the look of complete contentment on their faces. Their uniforms were filthy and most of them needed a shave. They must have just been taken off the beaches and were utterly exhausted. No noise came from our train as we looked at them in awe. The war was getting close to home. Thank God we still had the Channel; the Germans would never be able to cross it.

The farm where I worked was located in the lush countryside of Hampshire on the edge of the New Forest, within a mile of the coast. It was large by English standards, with hundreds of acres. Like most of the property in the area, it belonged to the local landowner, being on long lease to the farmer. It had originally been two separate farms and had two dairy herds each with their own milking barns. There was also a flock of sheep, and the fields carried a variety of crops. The labourers, dairymen and the shepherd were simple men living in farm cottages and could have come straight out of a Thomas Hardy novel, even the Middle Ages. One of my jobs was to pay their meagre weekly wages. They would lay their caps on a table in one of the barns, into which I would then count the coins.

I lived with the farmer and his wife in an attractive farmhouse and was immediately accepted as one of the family. The farmer was a bluff hardworking man and his wife was very motherly and attentive. The summer of 1940 was one of the best in years, and if it hadn't been for the war, reaping the crops would have been an idyllic pastime. I seemed to spend most of my time working on the top of hay stacks, helping the hayrick maker to construct them. The hay was cut by a horse-drawn cutter, raked by a horse-drawn rake, made up into sheaves by hand and then piled into clumps and left to dry. The sheaves were then pitched on to horse drawn carts before being taken away to the haystacks. Slowly the stacks rose above the green hedgerows as the sheaves were carefully laid one on top of another.

Although we all worked hard, every waking hour was taken up in thinking about the war as we listened to the radio and read of the sudden collapse of the allied armies in France, of Italy's declaration of war and invasion of the south of France, of the fall of Paris and the retreat of our remaining troops into the Cherbourg peninsular to await evacuation. By this time we could actually hear the noise of the guns rolling across the Channel as we bathed off Whitecliff.

Then finally on 25 June 1940 as we were building a haystack near one of the dairy barns, an agitated head dairyman came and announced in a quavering voice, "The French 'ave ceased hostiles." We were now on our own just as in the days of the Armada and of Napoleon.

The pitiful state of our army was revealed soon after when we went to the small, picturesque town of Ringwood on market day. The battalion of troops billeted there — no doubt evacuees from Dunkirk — were actually drilling in a field with wooden dummy rifles.

Word now came that we must form a Local Volunteer Defence unit. The farmer and I immediately volunteered, along with several of our farmhands. Our Commanding Officer was a recently arrived member of the local gentry. Right from the start he was the object of fertile suspicions, as he was an Irish lord and had only moved into the village two years before. Any newcomer, especially an Irish one, was definitely suspect, even when, as in this case, he had served in the Irish Guards, and seemed a decent enough type. He had to drive around the area at night to visit his men, and the villagers soon concluded that the blackout slits on his headlights were incorrrectly set and that he was perhaps signalling to the enemy.

There wasn't much formal organisation in the unit. Guns of any sort were collected from the village and issued. We were each given a shotgun and ten rounds of buckshot. There were no parades but we were gathered together periodically and given pep talks. Most of the work was done during weekends because we were so busy with the harvest. Defensive points around the village were planned. Our farmhouse was set back from the road and across from it was a large barn. The latter we turned into a defensive point by knocking firing ports in all the four walls. This was done without the permission of the landlord, and his bailiff was far from pleased about it. One Sunday a group of us was sent round to dig trenches on some privately owned property. The owner met us with a shotgun under his arm. He was not a volunteer and didn't think too much of us. We were not allowed to dig the trench and were smartly told to get off his land. Our leader then went to the local policeman to sort things out, but this didn't help matters and we never did get to dig the trench.

Another of our duties was to strew old farm equipment and any kind of vehicle that was not needed and could be moved, across the fallow fields. The idea was to deter troop-carrying gliders from landing. Our headquarters was the local pub, "The Carpenters Arms," where we always posted someone on the end of a phone during the night. In the event of invasion the watch would receive word and relay the message to the rest of us. We were then to repair to our designated defensive points and await instructions. I have often wondered how we would have fared if the Germans had indeed come.

Dartmouth Naval College.

The public signal for invasion was to be the ringing of bells. No church bells were rung and even automatic clock chimes were shut off. One balmy summer night I was awakened by bells ringing in the distance across the English countryside, and I could hear the farmer's wife, much disturbed, trying to wake her husband and calling out to me. The faroff eerie sounds were riveting and deeply unsettling. Thoughts of all the bloodshed and disruption that an invasion would bring coursed through my mind. Finally the farmer got up and tried to phone the pub to find out what was going on. This was a waste of time because everybody else had the same idea. We went outside to see if we could hear or catch a glimpse of anything happening but all was quiet and peaceful. The farmer's wife was by now in a terrible state and resorted to the inevitable pot of tea. We could do little else but sit and wait. Eventually we received a phone call to the effect that it was all a false alarm; an automatic tower clock in a manor house in the next village had suddenly started to ring.

After the fall of France, the German air force started to soften up the country for the intended invasion. Large centres, particularly London, experienced almost continuous day and night bombing. Right from the start there was news of large numbers of enemy aircraft being shot down by our fighters. This was very encouraging and boosted our morale, especially as we could hear the low humming of German bombers at night as they flew over us to targets farther north.

One day in broad daylight we actually witnessed a dogfight when a Hurricane dived at a German bomber right overhead. We were working in the centre of a field and saw the German plane being hit. Smoke started to pour from its tail and it went out of control and dived steeply towards the sea. It was all over in a matter of two minutes and then, after a very slight delay, empty shell cases began raining down around us.

Finally the time arrived for me to collect my new uniforms and report to Dartmouth Naval College for training. The college was situated 160 miles west of London on a river up from the English Channel. It was a large, well-built building with several wings, located on a hill behind the town. Quickly we were caught up in a busy round of lectures and training. I now met up with other Canadians from every part of Canada. There were twenty of us, and we immediately fitted in well with the English cadets.

We were formed into a cadet battalion with an eye to the invasion. Our equipment was an improvement on the Local Defence Volunteers but hardly the latest issue. We were given Canadian Ross rifles, which although of First World War vintage were still serviceable. Rifle drill, target shooting and hand to hand bayonet fighting were taught to us. Our instructor was a typical Gunnery petty officer with all the characteristic quips and bellowing. He had quite a job trying to whip us into shape and gave up on our bayonet charge, dismissing it as " a bloody ballet dance". We also had an ancient water-cooled Maxim machine-gun and a Heath Robinson contraption called a Holman Projector that catapulted hand-grenades into the air. I felt sorry for the cadets manning it, as it seemed to be very dangerous to operate. It was implied that we were being trained to hold our ground and fight to the last man.

Finally, on one weekend toward the end of September, we were all drawn up on parade in full battledress, feeling very awkward and constricted. Our equipment included heavy boots, puttees, bayonet belt, bulky webbing ammunition shoulder pouches, and our rifle and tin hat. Our captain — R.L. Cunliffe — addressed us dramatically saying that the invasion was expected that weekend and that Devon could be a prime target. All shore leave was cancelled and we were put on standby until further notice. We waited with bated breath but nothing happened, and after a few more weeks the invasion scare receded, never to be thought about again.

Time seemed to fly and within a few weeks our course was over and we were sent on a month's leave before joining our ships. I went back to London to stay with my grandmother and experienced my first real air raid. By this time, the Germans had stopped their daylight raids because of their severe losses and resorted to night attacks. In early December I went up to the West End to meet a friend of mine from the course. After dinner we went to a show at the Windmill theatre, which was the only one which had remained open. After the heavy night raids had started, most people just would not go to the theatre district. There was a strict blackout everywhere, which made it difficult to get around, and most restaurants closed early so there was also the problem of getting a meal. That particular night was not too dark and the weather was quite mild.

The Windmill theatre was noted for its risque musical shows which included nude women onstage. The Lord Chamberlain allowed theatres to do this provided the nudes did not move. The show ran on a continuous basis, and we entered as a comic was putting on his act. About halfway through, a noise could be heard from the front foyer and there seemed to be a commotion going on outside, followed by the sound of a fire engine driving by. The comic continued his spiel and with typical cockney quickness quipped that the milkman had come too early, which got a good laugh. This was followed by the nude tableau, but noises were still coming from the street. Then we heard anti-aircraft guns in the distance. Members of the audience began to look at one another, wondering what was going on and why the performance wasn't stopped, and whether or not to leave right away for the bomb shelters. There was no movement onstage. The naked chorus girls, in true British spirit, kept their composure.

Then in the middle of the act and the singing, the curtains suddenly dropped and the manager, in dinner jacket, came slowly on to the stage from the side. With dramatic flair he paused and then said quite slowly that, as there was an air raid now taking place, the show must unfortunately be stopped and that we could pick up tickets for another show at the box office in the lobby. Then he paused again and said that as a matter of fact a fire bomb had hit the building next door and the place was on fire. There immediately followed a most unceremonious rush for the exits.

When we got outside, several fire engines were right alongside the theatre with their hoses spread all over the street and spraying water into the building next door. There was a little smoke coming from the upstairs windows, and we decided to move away. The "all clear" signal had not yet been sounded, but nothing was going on, so we decided to have a look around.

The streets were almost deserted but there were still a few people walking about. Several bombs had been dropped on Piccadilly street, and from the Circus to Green Park, past the Royal Academy and Fortnum and Mason, the street was covered with broken glass. A bomb had dropped right on the edge of a corner building about eight storeys high. The walls from the top of the building to the bottom had been stripped away as well as some of the floors. However, some surviving floors hung precariously at a angle. The side of the building looked like an open, damaged doll's house. On one of the floors a bed stood intact with pictures hanging askew on the walls and clothes and other objects lying about the floor.

When I finally got home I found quite a hubbub as several incendiaries had been dropped on our street. My dear grandmother, who was a granddame in the best Victorian tradition, showed no signs of distress. Later, my aunt Enid and I went up to the top storey of our house and to the east could dimly see some flames and a great pall of smoke. We could just make out the black buildings silhouetted against the flames. Luckily, although bombs were dropped around it, the great cathedral of St Paul's remained untouched.

The night raids persisted but on a lesser scale, and there was no more excitement in Wimbledon before I left to join my first fighting ship soon afterwards.

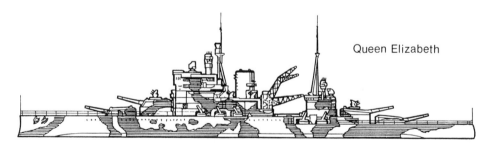

Queen Elizabeth

CHAPTER TWO

Atlantic Capers and Gibraltar

The Laws of the Navy

*Now these are the laws of the navy
Unwritten and varied they be,
And he that is wise will observe them,
Going down in his ship to the sea.
As naught may outrun the destroyer,
Even so with the law and its grip.
For the strength of the ship is the service,
And the strength of the service, the ship.*

Ronald A. Hopwood

After my arrival onboard the *Queen Elizabeth,* my first project, along with everyone else, was to find my way around her. There were so many decks and compartments it was easy to get lost. The ship's bridge and the admiral's bridge, below it, were high up in the forward superstructure — six decks above the upper deck. Below this a number of decks stretched down to the bilges where the storerooms were, and where I would probably be working from time to time. Also down at this level were the four anti-aircraft control room Transmitting Stations (TS); four tiny separate compartments which controlled the four batteries of 4.5 inch guns.

Queen Elizabeth was commissioned in 1915 but did not fight in the Battle of Jutland in May 1916, although she did become the flagship of the British Home Fleet later on. She was used for bombardment at Gallipoli in 1915. After the war she continued as the flagship of the Home Fleet during the twenties and thirties before going in for a major refit. Her forward superstructure was completely altered and her two original funnels were replaced with one. Her main armament of four twin 15 inch gun turrets was left but with improved control facilities. The major modification was the removal of her 6 inch guns along each side on the forecastle deck, and their replacement by ten twin 4.5 inch batteries, which had a wide angle of elevation and could be used against aircraft or for surface or shore bombardment.

Battleships such as *QE* had enormous destructive power. Our 15 inch guns could fire heavy projectiles to a range of twenty miles, and these could penetrate thick armour plating. If they hit a ship's ammunition magazine, the ship could blow up. Our 4.5 inch had a range of ten miles, our 1.5 inch anti-aircraft (AA) Pom-Poms, two miles, and the smaller AA Oerlikons, one mile.

Our new secret equipment was a brand new device to warn us of impending attack and also to control our guns. It was called RDF (Radar Direction Finder) which was just then being fitted in the fleet. The equipment had been used to direct our fighters in the Battle of Britain and, for obvious reasons, was not known to the public.

Walrus aircraft being catapulted from HMS *Queen Elizabeth*.

The principle behind it was that an object coming into the path of a transmitted radio wave reflects waves back which can be picked up and tracked by a receiver.

We had four different types of RDF. Type 271 could pick up small objects on the surface of the sea, such as a submarine, at a range of two miles. Type 279, also a warning system, could track aircraft up to forty miles away and surface ships at twenty-five miles. We also had two more precise sets for tracking at closer range and controlling our guns; Type 284 for surface ships up to eleven miles, and 285 for aircraft up to eight miles.

On our masts and superstructure we had an array of interesting looking aerials which transmitted and received these radio waves. Signals received were passed down to RDF offices where they were monitored on cathode ray tubes. Ranges and bearings were passed to gun control rooms where calculations were made and passed to the gun crews to enable them to fire at the moving targets.

Abaft the funnel were two hangars to house two Walrus aircraft, small, old fashioned biplane flying boats manned by a pilot and a navigator. They were catapulted off the ship by a hydraulic launcher situated abaft the hangars, and were used for reconnaissance or air-sea rescue work only since, they could never be used against modern aircraft. However, they might be useful on certain occasions. All midshipmen were required to take a flight in them, presumably to interest them in becoming Fleet Air Arm aircrew. They shook terribly before take-off when they revved up their engine and, I would think, put anyone off the idea.

There were nineteen midshipmen aboard, of which six were Polish and one, myself, Canadian. The Poles had escaped from Danzig in Polish Navy ships and had many interesting stories to tell of their adventures. Several came from the area which the Russians had occupied.

The ship had a company of eighty-two officers and around 1400 petty officers and sailors. There were Free French and Newfoundland seamen aboard. We, the midshipmen, had a pleasant separate mess just about big enough to accommodate all of us at one time. Our sleeping quarters were terrible and bore out what Charles Laughton said in his role as Captain Bligh, "Midshipmen are the lowest form of animal life in the British Navy." We could sleep in a hammock or a camp-bed in a small cramped compartment without port holes. I preferred to sleep on a camp-bed in the flats (space) leading to the officers' cabins, because this area was not so enclosed. Each of us had a steel locker for our clothes and there was a large washroom next door.

We were all aboard for training and were rotated through various departments and given periodical tests. "Snotties," we were called presumably after snot-nosed youths, and had a "Snotties' nurse" — a senior Lieutenant Commander who supervised our training and lectured us from time to time about the ship and the war situation.

The ship had sailed north from Portsmouth very hastily, before the refit was finished, because of the increasing frequency of night air raids. Three hundred dockyard maties (workmen) had come to finish the job in Rosyth. As a result, conditions in the ship were chaotic, with crew and workmen getting in each other's way. However, there was no trouble as everyone was too busy learning their tasks, finding out about the huge ship and carrying out those drills that could be undertaken with the ship alongside. All leave was cancelled except for a wonderful variety show in a huge dockyard shed where Vera Lynn was a big hit.

I was also able to visit a Canadian midshipman named Baird, who had taken the course with me, and who was now on the mighty *Hood* which was lying astern of us. It was interesting to see another type of capital ship and meet old friends. *Hood* seemed so much larger than us, although our armaments were similar. She was undoubtedly one of the most beautifully proportioned warships ever built. Being a battlecruiser she was therefore faster than us. However we could crank it up too: the *QE* class was noted for speed. We could steam at twenty-five knots, which amounts to 100 miles in four hours. Their gun-room (midshipmen's mess) was cavernous and rather dingy with no outside ports. *Hood* had not had the benefit of a recent refit like *QE* and her quarters were thus not nearly as modern.

After two weeks in Rosyth, we sailed for Scapa Flow in the Orkneys. This has to be one of the loneliest and dreariest places in the world. The Flow comprises a group of low-lying scrubland islands formed in a rough circle. Inside lies a large natural harbour which can accommodate a huge fleet and this was why it was used as the base for the Home fleet in both wars. All the various inlets allowing access from the open sea, had been blocked. As we entered the main channel leading to the anchorage, heavy wire nets strung across the gateway were pulled back to let us in. These nets blocked the harbour off completely from the open sea.

The anchorage was always assumed to be completely impregnable until, on 14 October 1939, Captain Gunther Prien ran his U-boat on the surface at night over the obstacles blocking a small inlet. He managed to sink the battleship *Royal Oak,* lying in the middle of the anchorage, before escaping through the same inlet. Quite a stir erupted in the papers. Presumably high

Mediterranean Fleet flagship HMS *Queen Elizabeth*.

tides had enabled him to get over these obstacles, but what incompetence on the part of the local naval authorities.

Our stay at Scapa was not too long, but long enough. We hoped for a quick transfer to another fleet, anywhere else but this God-forsaken spot. However we were still kept very busy practising every conceivable type of drill — gunnery battle stations (all done in harbour without the guns being actually fired), seamanship drills, and the testing of all types of engines and equipment. It was a great challenge and our technical staff seemed to be thoroughly enjoying learning about all the new equipment aboard. Groups of officers and petty officers, working day and night, were all over the ship, huddled in earnest discussion over their manuals and drawings.

A great proportion of the ship's company were regulars and specialists with a sprinkling of "hostilities only" officers and ratings. Everything was being done in great haste so that all of us would quickly have some kind of idea as to our battle station duties, as the German Navy could come out to sea at any moment. This seemed unlikely as they hadn't been very active since the Norwegian campaign nearly a year earlier.

The only recreation was a walk on the rocky tundra shoreline. Several large ships lay at moorings — the battlecruisers *Repulse* and *Hood* and the battleship *Nelson* plus some cruisers and destroyers. Large fishing boats called drifters, which carry about 150 men, each day would ferry hundreds of restless officers and ratings ashore to stretch their legs. There were no pubs or cafes, just the bare tundra.

The need for battleworthiness and to learn our jobs as quickly as possible seemed to keep us in good spirits despite the dreary weather and location. Our officers — the captain, Claud Barry, and the commander (second in command), R. Gotto, and our department heads — seemed to be very energetic yet reasonable men. In the gun-room, all of us midshipmen were getting along well, and

ORKNEY

Kirkwall

Hoy

Scapa Flow

S Ronaldsay

Atlantic

North Sea

Pentland Firth

our sub lieutenant in charge was a decent sort who had the necessary self-confidence to control our youthful unruliness.

*****

We had sailed very suddenly in the early morning — 12 March 1941 — I was told when I awoke in the morning. I had heard the restless sounds of activity throughout the ship all through the night and had subconsciously thought that there was a "flap" on. When I entered the gun-room, I found the mess full of rumours and ideas as to where we were going. Everyone was aglow with restrained excitement. This was the first time that we had gone to sea on business. I gulped my breakfast, and rushed on deck to see what was going on.

The mighty *Hood* was crashing along ahead of us, with the cruiser *London* well astern, zigzagging to protect us from behind, and of course the usual anti-submarine (A/S) escort of destroyers in formation far out ahead of us. It was a typical misty Atlantic day. The visibility was fairly good, but sometimes a heavy patch of mist and rain suddenly descended, all but cutting out the

Queen Elizabeth taking water over her bow in the North Atlantic.

screen from our view. There was a heavy swell, the sea being rough enough to cover the quarterdeck with stinging wisps of spume and spray. Not what you would call a nice day, but an exhilarating one. We all stood up on the after boat-deck to keep out of the wet of the quarterdeck and discussed the situation with infectious enthusiasm.

I went down to the cypher office and found out what was going on. THE SCHARNHORST AND GNEISENAU WERE OUT. Big stuff and on our first real trip to sea. It was no wonder we got rid of those 300 dockyard maties within half an hour before leaving Scapa. Evidently the first indication we had that the two German battle-cruisers were at sea was a message from the battleship *Malaya* which was escorting a convoy steaming north from Trinidad. From what I could gather, these two enemy ships had been in contact with this convoy for some time, but had now disengaged and were lost. We, in company with *Hood,* were steaming northwestward for the Denmark Strait between Iceland and Greenland to stop the enemy from escaping through there northward to Norway. We were still two days sailing away, so no fun was to be expected for a while yet.

The Admiralty was beginning to redeploy naval forces in the Atlantic. Force H from Gibraltar, composed of the battlecruiser *Renown* and the aircraft carrier *Ark Royal,* was at sea in the Atlantic many hundreds of miles to the south. It was beating northwestward to try and intercept.

The *Scharnhorst* and *Gneisenau* were German battlecruisers which were faster than us and, although about the same tonnage, 33,000, carried smaller guns. Whereas we carried eight 15 inch guns they carried nine 11 inch; so we could outrange them.

*****

The captain made a speech to the ship's company in the evening over the Sound Reproduction System (SRE) and told us what was happening — that the two enemy battlecruisers were out commerce raiding; that they must have left Germany, crept northward close to the Norwegian coast and then sailed back down into the Atlantic; that contact with them had been lost for the moment and that *Hood* and ourselves would steam as fast as possible to the Denmark Straits where we would patrol in wait for them. He added that Commander-in-Chief (C-in-C) Home Fleet had sailed in *Nelson,* a much slower ship, and was toddling along behind us.

If the enemy steered for France, Force H would be in a position to its westward to block its passage. If they turned south then there was all the more chance of their being caught, and if they headed directly north toward the Denmark Strait we could intercept them. Notwithstanding all this, the Atlantic was a vast area with varied and unpredictable weather and it might be difficult for us to find them. Apparently in the First World War, German ships would wait until the weather deteriorated before trying to get through past our patrols. However, in those days there were no long-range reconnaissance aircraft.

*****

Still there was no sign of the enemy. Not a word had been received for twenty-four hours. We continued to steam northwest at full speed. The weather had become very dirty — overcast, with heavy seas keeping the whole upper deck awash. The ship had begun to pitch up and down gently and had developed a slight pausing roll. Pausing because, like all big ships, she rolled over very slowly until she had gone as far as she wanted to and then, instead of swinging back gently, she held that position for a few seconds before she finally decided to swing back again. Many of us felt a little squeamish, facing our first pangs of seasickness.

Everyone was now in watches and each day went by like the last until one fell into a soothing routine. You took your watch, grabbed a meal, caught up a bit on your work if you could, lost yourself in a book for a short while, got some sleep and took your watch again. People were moving around the huge ship quietly day and night, opening and closing watertight doors, nodding to one another politely as they crossed in passageways. And always in the background the low persistent hum and vibration of the main engines, driving the ship forward at full speed. We received no outside news and became very aware that we were on our own in this vast ocean. One day seemed to blur into the next and we lost track of time. As everyone seemed to be on a different watch schedule, I didn't get to see my friends very often.

One evening a drowsy gun-room mess was awakened by the ominous sound of splashing water cascading down from the hatch outside the door. It was too late for the eight midshipmen to do much about it before the place was a quarter-inch deep in water. Someone had forgotten to close a hatch-cover properly and the next big sea did the trick. Loud and long was the swearing and complaining before the place was cleaned up and things settled down again.

Arguments were running high as to what direction the enemy was heading. The conclusion was that they would either be returning home, having realized that the cat was out of the bag, in which case we would get them, or else they were headed south. It was agreed that while the present weather continued, there was little hope of the reconnaissance planes picking them up.

*****

There was still no news next morning, but the weather was decidedly better. The wind had dropped and the seas had calmed considerably, with wispy clouds and the odd patches of blue sky occasionally evident. The previous suppressed excitement had now changed to disappointment that we were going to be done out of a fight. However, we still hoped for the best. It was probably a good thing that we weren't going into action, bearing in mind that we had never done any proper work up trials. They say that in peacetime it takes three months to shake a ship down to get its crew properly trained. The crews in these German battle-cruisers were seasoned veterans.

The captain addressed us again over the SRE, and said that we were not to get too depressed because nothing had been heard for over thirty-six hours. He had every confidence that the two truant ships would be found. The *Ark* had her aircraft up searching and Coastal Command of the RAF was co-operating to the full.

*****

At last there was news and it was good. In the evening when just about everyone had given up hope, at about 1800, the ship suddenly went to action stations. I closed up to the cypher office where I found the Paymaster Commander (Pay) and the Accountant Officer (AO), his assistant, self-consciously adjusting their life-jackets. These were very light, and consisted of a rubber inner tube, which was inflated by blowing into it, and was secured around the waist and over the shoulders. Pay seemed to be having trouble with his, but when it was finally adjusted, it looked unconvincing on his portly frame. We were supposed to wear them all the time at sea, but they were only donned at action stations, and then only reluctantly. Tyndall, my midshipman friend, was huddled over the long desk which ran down one side of the office, working on a message with the Chief Writer's assistance. We found out from the W/T (Wireless Telegraph) office next door that the admiral in *Hood* had ordered the force to close up at action stations, turn south, and increase to full speed. Something was in the wind but we had received no word by cypher. Perhaps the enemy was in the immediate vicinity, who knew?

There was a clattering, clanking, and shouting from inside the 4.5 inch turret across the passageway outside the office. The Marine gun crew was getting the guns ready for action. We watched the white deck-head and waited. The dull throb of the engines from below changed in pitch and tempo as we increased speed. The deck lurched up at us, causing books to slide, as we sharply altered course. The air was tense and there was nothing else to do but sit and chat. We all leant back against the edge of the other empty desk and watched Tyndall finish his work. The message wasn't too exciting, concerning as it did something from C-in-C Western Approaches (in Liverpool) about redisposing convoys in the Atlantic. Pay slowly settled into a chair and we continued our discussion. He looked tired, dissipated under the harsh artificial light. After a while he became expansive and, nervously slapping his anti-flash gear (a flannel hood and gloves to prevent flash burns in case of explosions) on his knee, told us how he had spent four years at sea in the last war and had never seen a shot fired in anger. Things were going to be different in this war, he thought.

Then word came. Our first very urgent message was being received. The Chief Telegraphist stuck his wizened head through the small connecting window between the two offices and informed us dramatically that the message

Battle cruiser HMS *Hood* in heavy weather in the Atlantic.

was now being received. Tyndall immediately stopped what he was doing and waited expectantly. The Accountant Officer told him to carry on, saying that he would deal with it when it was sent in. Pay opened his eyes and began to take notice again. Finally a scrawny arm thrust the long-awaited message through the connecting hole and the AO grabbed it. A hectic argument ensued as to who would do it. The AO had possession but Pay insisted that, as Chief Cypher Officer, he had the priority. Seniority prevailed and we watched as the meaning was teased out. "To: Admiralty . . . From. S.O.(Senior Officer) Force H . . . *Ark Royal's* aircraft sighted enemy in position . . . " etc.,etc.

The enemy were some hundreds of miles to the south of us and were steering due north right towards us. As the position stood, Force H was close behind them and had them under surveillance somewhere off Portugal. The Admiralty was ordering changes to convoy routes to divert them well clear and sending all available warships to sea to intercept. We were steaming south in their direction at full speed. To the east of us, but well astern, *Nelson* was doing the same. The battleship *King George V*, which had been escorting a convoy off Canada, had been detached and was heading southeast. The 2nd Destroyer Flotilla under Lord Louis Mountbatten was leaving Plymouth and the battlecruiser *Repulse* was steaming southeast from a position off Ireland. We now seemed to have them in a trap. Aircraft from *Ark Royal* might be able to attack the next morning and slow them down so that the whole of Force H could make contact. Then perhaps we could get down to be in on the kill. If the German ships kept on the same course at their same speed we should be in contact with them within twenty-four hours.

The captain made a rather bombastic, overconfident speech but I'm afraid he simply reflected the mood of the crew. He proclaimed that at that very moment he would not like to be the captains of either *Scharnhorst* or *Gneisenau* as he thought that *Hood* and the old *QE* would be more than a match for

29

both of them. Although both *Hood* and *QE* outgunned them — *Hood* carried the same 15 inch guns as we did, we — *QE* — were still very wet behind the ears.

There were great dissertations on the situation in the gun-room. A definite exhilaration was sweeping through the ship. Everyone you passed in the passageways had an understanding grin on their face. Most of us seemed to be lapping up the excitement of war with apparent enjoyment, probably because most of us had never eaten a slice of this deadly cake. For more than 90 per cent of the ship's company this would have been their first experience of a sea battle.

There were last minute exchanges and gossip before we all went off for a restless night before the impending battle. Apparently the skipper had got mad at the pilot (Navigating Officer) when he had said that possiby we would not intercept them. Others thought that the action would be over before we got there.

Dawn came up on the great day, revealing another cold, misty Atlantic, not at all what we wanted. With this kind of weather it would be difficult for aircraft to seek out and attack the enemy. There were no new signals indicating that Force H was still in contact.

That morning I met a civilian on the quarterdeck. He certainly was an incongruous sight to see on a battleship going into action, as he stood in the wind in an old, brown raincoat with a battered grey hat pulled down heavily on his head. When I got talking to him, I discovered that he had been left behind when we got rid of the dockyard types. He seemed to be taking things very calmly, and was keenly observing how a battleship prepares for a sea action.

*****

Later in the day we were still battling along at full speed to the south. Latest information indicated that Force H had lost touch with the enemy. *Ark Royal* had sent up air patrols and strike forces but they could find nothing. The weather was still poor, with mist and low clouds. There was a chance that the Germans had made a dramatic change in course. It was now 19 March 1941, and at 1100 a message was received from *Hood* visually by Aldis lamp. The gist of it was that if contact were made with enemy surface ships, destroyers were to concentrate in two divisions and act as circumstances dictated. Whilst torpedo attack was the primary object, flank marking (spotting fall of shot) for the heavy ships should be borne in mind. A number of messages of this type were sent as the admiral made his last minute preparations for action by 1800 that evening.

We closed up at action stations at 1700 that evening and patiently awaited a sighting of the enemy. As we had the most modern RDF of any ship in the squadron, we expected advance notice and would inform the others. The atmosphere in the cypher office was proverbially tense. There was an uncomfortable silence as we waited for something to happen. Pay made a few forced jokes as we gazed at the tattered map of the Atlantic pinned to the bulkhead, trying to estimate where all the ships and squadrons on both sides of the action were. The minutes passed slowly until half an hour had gone and there was still no action. I looked in at the W/T office to see if any important messages were coming in. The place was quiet except for an overalled operator, a pair of earphones on his head, bent over his set carefully taking a message. Another was leaning over a table in a corner with a bedraggled cigarette hanging from

Pre-war photograph of Gibraltar.

his lips, reading the *News of the World*. The Chief Wireless Telegraphist, down at the far end, was talking quietly and earnestly to another operator. Any urgent messages coming in would have been quite obvious. I caught the Chief's eye but he shook his head and grimaced.

As the minutes dragged by and the waiting time increased, so the tension in the air eased. Our talk became more natural. By now over an hour had passed. As we talked about the encroaching darkness on deck, it began to dawn on us that our chances of action were fast disappearing. In a way, a load had been taken off our shoulders and I sensed a feeling of relief mixed with frustration that we hadn't had our chance to take part in history. Even so, hope persisted that we would make contact. We still had our long-range RDF.

Another hour dragged by and still no word came from the bridge or from the Admiralty or Force H. After a while the hum of the switched-on SRE was heard and a deep stolid voice boomed through the ship. "This is the captain speaking". We all made for the door to hear it more clearly. He said there was no chance we would engage the enemy and we were turning for home immediately. He had just received a visual message from the admiral that the two German battlecruisers had been sighted in the afternoon by Coastal Command a hundred miles off Brest, heading for France. They were right out of reach and would be in port before we could get there. They must have altered course after the aircraft of the *Ark* had first sighted them. He ended by adding that we were not to be downcast, that such disappointments were a daily feature of war. So off we went back to depressing Scapa.

*****

After our sortie to catch the *Scharnhorst* and the *Gneisenau* we returned to Scapa and continued to work up the ship. However, we were not there more than three days before we sailed with an escort of destroyers for Halifax in

31

Canada. Our task was to escort a convoy of fast troop-ships — usually large liners — with reinforcements for the Canadian Army in England. Once again we were told what was happening by our captain and were complimented for having worked so hard to get the ship in fighting trim.

The destroyers had to stay with us for two extra days because of the prevalence of U-boats in the area. We had been receiving many U-boat reports and a number of merchant ships had been sunk quite near us. One message from the destroyer leader *Havelock* stated that *Wolverine* and *Scarborough* had attacked U-73 in position 058 degrees 32 minutes north and 020 15 west (due south of Iceland). The U-boat had been brought to the surface and the corvette *Arbutus* had attempted to take her in tow. This was to no avail, for the U-boat sank at 0950 on 5 April 1941. *Wolverine* had Captain von Hippel, three officers and thirty-six crew aboard while *Scarborough* and *Arbutus* had one survivor each. All this happened just to the north of us. We had also been instructed to look out for German supply ships which were thought to be in the Atlantic to support enemy raiders. However, nothing transpired along this line.

When we were within twenty-four hours steaming time of Halifax we were suddenly diverted back to the French coast. Lieutenant Leppard, the RDF officer, the other Canadian aboard, remarked disappointedly that the air was just beginning to smell good. I, too, was disappointed for I had hoped to be able to ring my parents to whom I hadn't actually spoken for years. Our diversion was prompted by suspicions that our old prey the two German battlecruisers now in Brest, were showing signs that they were about to sail into the Atlantic again. Air reconnaissance reports revealed that one of them had moved out into the roads and had an oiler alongside.

While we headed back at full speed, the RAF carried out a heavy raid on the port, with the result that the ship, at anchor, moved back alongside and could possibly have sustained damaged. We remained on patrol off the coast for three days, but there was no more activity. As we were running low on fuel, we were diverted to Gib, our nearest port. Everyone was ecstatic about this. Anywhere was an improvement on the bleakness of Scapa Flow, especially a place in sunnier climes.

*****

We entered Gib, in early April, in a thundering shower of rain just after a levanter had blown itself out. Each year, with meticulous regularity, these miniature tornadoes descend on the Rock from the mountains of Morocco to the south. This one had struck the area with such ferocity that we had been forced to stay in the straits until it had subsided.

Gibraltar is located on a promontory on the Mediterranean side of the straits, pointing north and south. The huge camel-back rock dominates the rolling, dry hills of southern Spain behind it, with the little town and harbour on the western, protected side. Finally we were able to enter a narrow gate through a mole into the safety of a protected harbour, and secured to a large jetty. This was our first time alongside since we had left Rosyth. Astern was the unhappy sight of a trawler protruding from the water, the only casualty of the half-hearted air attack on Gibraltar by the perplexed French after Britain's violent attack on their fleet at Mers el Kebir in Algeria on 3 July 1940.

The Rock has a long and fascinating history going back to the time of the

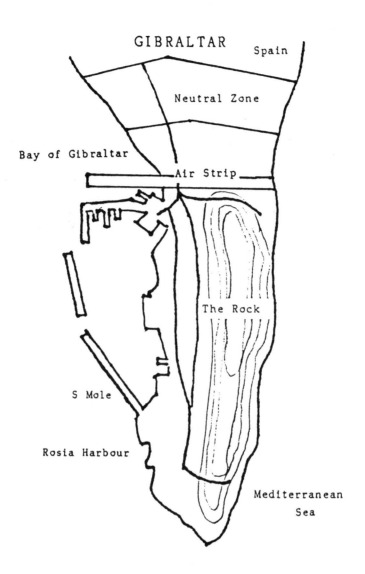

GIBRALTAR

Spain

Neutral Zone

Bay of Gibraltar

Air Strip

The Rock

S Mole

Rosia Harbour

Mediterranean
Sea

Straits of Gibraltar

Phoenicians (1000 BC), the Romans, and the Moors. The British admiral Rooke took it on 24 July 1704 and it has remained a British possession ever since. Among its claims to fame is the fact that Nelson sailed from here for the Battle of Trafalgar of 21 October 1805. It was a day's sailing from Gib to Cape Trafalgar, about twenty miles from Cadiz, the port used by the French and Spanish fleets. After the great victory, the battered British fleet had to face a gale and returned to Gib, entering the little Rosia harbour, which was its only roadstead at the time and lies to the south of the main modern harbour. The dying and wounded were carried uphill to the hospital. Nelson's body was placed ashore in a house. Naval lore has it that his body was preserved in a barrel of rum prior to its return to England, and the tradition lives on in the term "Nelson's Blood" which is given to rum. Fighting at sea in those days was a particularly bloody and terrifying affair, with close contact broadsides at point blank range and finally hand-to-hand combat with ships securing alongside each other.

Gibraltar was as picturesque as one would imagine. The houses and streets of the small town, about the size of a seaside resort, have a touch of Spain to them. The inhabited area lies on the west side of the promontory on a little flat area below the Rock, facing across a bay to the Spanish mainland. The Spanish city of Algeciras compact and low on the seashore below rambling hills, is readily visible. The place was said to bristle with German spies. Certainly they would have had a commanding view of the types and movements of our ships and could immediately relay this information to Berlin. Despite considerable German and Italian assistance to Franco in the Spanish Civil War, he kept his country out of the war and refrained from even putting pressure on Gib. Which was just as well, otherwise our control over the Mediterranean and our supply lines to the Middle East and Malta would have been made very much more difficult.

I got ashore before any other midshipmen in order to purchase wines and spirits for the gun-room. Our stock was very low because of the tight rationing in England. Here we could buy anything we wanted. Tyndall and I, who looked after the mess accounts, had a great time. In glorious weather we set off down the gangway, looking for the wine merchants, Saccone and Speed, whose shop was on the main street. They were awaiting us, knowing full well that we were in port, and treated us royally. What with the beautiful and welcome warm weather after the bleak North Atlantic, and the imbibing of various spirits, it seemed all too good to be true.

In the evening everyone was given leave, except for the duty watch, and we went off for a big run ashore. We had been at sea for three weeks and had barely touched land for three months apart from an afternoon's stroll at Scapa Flow. A large shore patrol was going to be needed to to keep an eye on our sailors, as well as those from *Renown* and *Ark Royal,* which were also in harbour. Once ashore we wandered around absorbing all the scenes and colour of a new place.

Most of us had never been this far south and the white stuccoed buildings with their shutters and their tiny iron-barred balconies were a total novelty to us. The Mediterranean evening sun, the blue sky and the waters of Algeciras Bay, put us in the best of moods after the wet and wartime restrictions of England. The picturesque narrow main street led eventually towards the Span-ish frontier. It was full of bars and a few junky shopping bazaars which were crowded with sailors in their blue and white. Fortunately the commercialism was not overdone so the place still had an attractive air about it. Horse-drawn gharries, drawn up one behind the other beside the road, held drivers who were volubly enticing sailors to take a ride. Up the Rock, to the right, were quaint deserted streets with white stuccoed houses with drawn shutters that somewhat resembled English Victorian mansions. Above them, toward the top, nestled an old Arab castle.

Beyond the town we could see the long landing-strip which extended out to sea so that large aircraft could land. And beyond that were the British lines, a frontier post, an area of neutral ground and then the Spanish frontier post. On the other side of this lay La Linea (The Line) which supplied Gibraltar with most of its labour even in wartime. Each day thousands of Spaniards came across the border to work in the town and dockyard, and I presumed that a very careful check was kept to stop spies getting in.

The airstrip was quiet, so we wandered back into town which was becoming more and more crowded with sailors. We couldn't locate any restaurants or clubs for officers, so made the best of it by persisting with our sightseeing wanderings and doing some shopping.

The ratings, however, were much more exuberant in their pleasures. One very noisy bar was packed with sailors, being entertained by an all female band which included violinists, and seemed quite good. Later I noticed two very drunken dishevelled sailors in the back of a gharry. One of them was swaying so unsteadily that his chum had to attempt to assist him out. Then when the gharry gently moved on again, both were dumped unceremomiously in a submissive heap on the curb. The swarthy shopkeeper with whom I had been haggling raised his hands resignedly and joined me in smiling at the misadventures of this drunken duo. Clearly, this little town seemed to be a friendly and tolerant place, and our sailors probably couldn't get into too much trouble. I had heard the Chief Writer saying that there were good and bad shore leave ports, and Gib was certainly proving to be one of the good ones.

We were only in port for two days before we were ordered back to sea. With barely sufficient time to load our needed supplies, we headed out into the Atlantic with visions of returning to Scapa Flow. But two days later our two escorting destroyers left us and we turned into the South Atlantic. Now that we were out of dangerous waters we could actually start firing our guns live and testing our ammunition supply systems. Any passing ship might have been forgiven for thinking that a sea battle had been joined.

Nothing official was announced about our destination. Perhaps we were heading south after a commerce raider, or being transferred to the Med fleet via the Cape of Good Hope, or even heading for an attack on the Vichy port of Dakar in Senegal? Instead, after five days at sea we steamed into the tropical steaminess of Freetown in Sierra Leone.

The harbour at Freetown was an excellent one with a narrow entrance and a large inner protected anchorage. Ashore was a dilapidated town with a small jetty, certainly not a thriving commercial port. As we anchored in this forgotten African backwater, looking incongruously huge and powerful, we were subjected to a whole new set of images. Long narrow canoes, obviously carved out of a single piece of a tree, like the ones we had seen in African jungle movies, were steered alongside by three or four loin-covered Africans. They were extremely adept at moving around or standing in these very tippy boats. Some were there to dive for coins thrown over the side, whilst other boats were full of exotic African fruits and vegetables.

Once again, everyone was allowed ashore to "stretch the legs." The town itself was something utterly alien to me. There were no proper, paved roads, and about ninety per cent of the houses were definitely substandard, being little more than tin shacks. There were few shops. However, the inhabitants were cleanly, if not what we would call smartly, dressed. They carried themselves extremely well and had the air of being well contented with their lot, happy to be living in a town such as this and not in far worse conditions up country in the heavy jungle.

The only episode of note occurred when most of our Free French sailors, who were not apparently happy aboard, deserted and headed through the jungle for the Vichy French colonies to the north. For a few days we lay at anchor with much speculation about what was going on, when suddenly we sailed north again and arrived back at Gib.

CHAPTER THREE

First Real Action: "Operation Tiger"

Early on the morning of 4 May 1941 we sailed from Gib in excellent weather and steamed to the westward in concert with our destroyer escort. This was D-2 (two days before the start) of "Operation Tiger", a plan to pass a large convoy containing an Armoured Division replete with 238 tanks and men, 43 Hurricane aircraft and ammunition through the Mediterranean to Alexandria in Egypt. The situation in the eastern Mediterranean had deteriorated seriously since General Wavell had routed the Italian army in the Egyptian desert in December 1940.

Since then the German army had entered the Balkans and driven through Yugoslavia into Greece, and Wavell was forced to send British and Commonwealth troops to its aid, because Britain had guaranteed the Greek borders after the recent Italian invasion of Albania. Also the Germans now had an army in Italian Cyrenaica and were attacking Tobruk where they were opposed by elements of a depleted British 8th Army. Our troops were now being evacuated from Greece and there was therefore an urgent need for reinforcements. Originally we were to have been sent around the Cape as a reinforcement battleship for the Mediterranean Fleet. But this was changed and now we were to go directly through to Egypt.

Later in the evening we rendezvoused with the battlecruiser *Repulse* plus a destroyer screen, and a convoy of five large and fast merchant ships. We had steamed out to the west to confuse the German agents in Algeciras.

On the following day Force H met us and *Repulse* left for Gibraltar. As we steamed off Spain waiting to enter the straits, we fuelled several destroyers. This exercise has to be one of most exciting sights at sea. The small destroyer moved slowly up alongside us, maintaining the same speed. Thus you had the dramatic sight and sound of the bows of each ship, close together, crashing into the moving sea. As we looked down at the little ship with her young skipper and his officers, riding up and down, on a small open bridge, we could see him intently looking forward and aft as he carefully conned his ship to make sure that he didn't get too close. A light cord line was fired by a special gun from our ship and fell across his forecastle. When the line had been retrieved, a heavier line was attached to it and then a heavy rope hawser. This was slung between the two ships and the oil pipes were pulled across by an attached pulley. The lines attached to the pulley were hauled by sailors on the upper deck of each ship as in the days of the old sailing ships.

The hosepipe was finally connected to the tanks and the pumps were started and oil was transferred. The procedure was executed very carefully and slowly, with everyone on deck not actually working completely absorbed by the performance. Messages, fresh vegetables, bread and a bottle of scotch for the young skipper were passed over on a second, lighter line. Finally the tanks were filled, the lines were disconnected and withdrawn, and the destroyer with her crew of seasoned veterans pulled away dropping astern with a wave from the bridge.

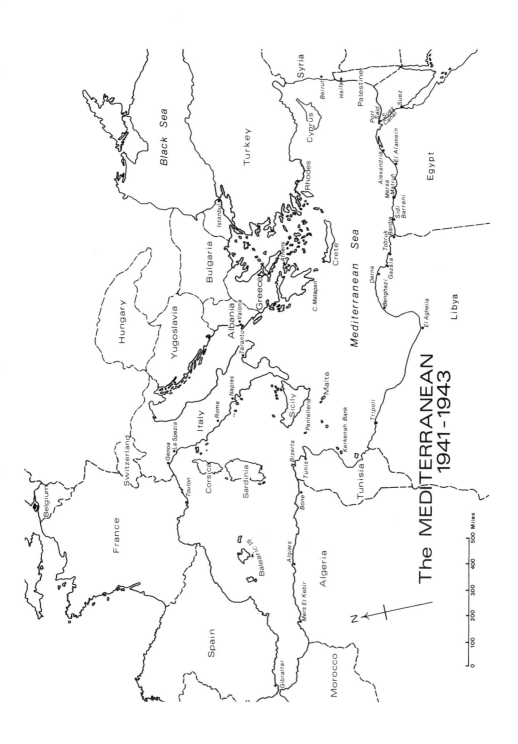

The MEDITERRANEAN 1941-1943

38

During the afternoon after we had taken over the convoy, two corvettes out of Gib were sighted dead ahead. They signalled that they had a submarine contact which they were attacking. With our five extremely valuable merchant ships, this was unwelcome news. The convoy was turned west in an emergency manoeuvre and after an hour or so we had left the corvettes astern still buzzing around their prey.

The force split into two sections for our night passage through the straits. We were ordered to take station astern of *Ark Royal* as part of Force H which went through first, followed by the merchant ships with their destroyer escort and the light cruiser *Naiad.* Our entry was timed to start at 0300. During the night we ran into a fleet of small Spanish fishing boats lying directly across our path and were forced to alter course southwards for a while. After safely negotiating the straits, we had two neutral shores out of sight to the north and south of us, Vichy French Africa and Spain.

We were then ordered to rejoin the convoy which was about twenty minutes sailing time away, while Force H left to carry out a diversionary sweep to the north towards the Balearic Islands.

The second day dawned with a calm sea and a clear blue sky. In the afternoon our RDF picked up what was thought to be an Italian aircraft shadowing us out of visual range. Our cover was now blown and we could expect air attacks off southern Sardinia the next day. At that point we would be within range of the Italian torpedo bombers.

Early on the third day the two forces were reunited and we received word from the admiral in *Renown* that the convoy had probably been sighted and reported by an enemy reconnaissance aircraft, an old-fashioned, single-engined flying boat, a Cant 2501. Our three capital ships *Renown, Ark Royal* and *Queen Elizabeth* were deployed in that order — with plenty of room for the *Ark* to fly off her aircraft. We were two miles astern of the convoy and its escort of a cruiser and destroyers. Fighter aircraft from the carrier were continually in the air, patrolling over us. At about 1000 we went to action stations and awaited the expected onslaught.

The first attack was by three Italian Savoia torpedo bombers. They were three engined, stubby looking aircraft, more like a small airliner than a warplane. The attack was very half-hearted; they dropped their fish a long way off. After it was all over, relief swiftly swept through the ship, with everyone talking about the attack and wondering if this was all we were going to have to go through. After the first fleeting spasm of fear, everyone had been remarkably calm. It was more of an adventure than anything else.

A second torpedo bomber attack soon followed. This time the Italian pilots showed great gallantry. Three of them, part of a much larger group, flying in V formation, came in very low over the destroyer screen, disregarding the heavy ack-ack fire from the convoy escorts. With shellbursts popping all around them, they singled out our most valuable ship, the *Ark Royal.* Flying close to the *Renown* through her fire, they were able to drop their torpedoes directly ahead of the great carrier. Meanwhile the *Ark* had increased to full speed and altered course to put them off their aim. Her deck was ablaze from her light ack-ack armament, shooting at point-blank range.

One minute she was a stately ship moving through the seas in all her glory and the next she was behaving like a cornered stag, using everything she had to escape injury. One of the bombers followed its torpedo into the water, after hovering like a seagull and then plunging headlong into the sea. The other two flew astern of the *Ark,* which had avoided all the torpedoes, and began to approach us. Now was our chance to show our mettle. The two aircraft passed down our port side (left) and then astern; in fact, so close that those on the upper deck said that they could see the pilots' faces. They were flying low, zigzagging just above the water, and our light AA armament failed to bring them down, even though they were so close — we still had a lot to learn. Gradually the aircraft became two black dots disappearing over the horizon.

During the attack there had been several course alterations and the fleet had lost formation. Whilst we were resuming position I had my first close-up view of the enemy when we passed within a few hundred yards of an aircraft which had apparently been shot down by *Renown.* All that remained were two wings floating askew on the water, with two bedraggled looking figures clinging to them. One of them raised his hand and waved slowly. There was a small machine-gun mounted nearby — why it was there no one had been able find out — and I heard a voice beside me say, "Why not put the bastards out of their misery." This we could not do. They were stranded fifty miles from Sardinia without much hope of being picked up. However, there was always the slight chance that they might make it to shore. After this attack our estimation of the enemy went up.

Discussing it later in the gun-room we all agreed that the Italian pilots had shown immense courage in pressing their attack so close to our ships. We were pleased that they had got away.

For the rest of the day after this we remained closed up at action stations.

The next attacks were far more concentrated, and German aircraft — Junkers 87, single engined dive bombers — now joined the assault. The *Ark* was again singled out for attack as were the merchant ships. As we were directly astern of her, we were close to the action. I was below decks at my station so saw nothing but I certainly heard all about it afterwards. The high angle batteries across the passageway from the cypher office were firing on and off for several hours with much banging and shouting. We could hear the empty shell casings clattering to the steel deck after the guns had been fired. The activity inside the turret must have been frantic as it was being moved around and the gun barrels raised and lowered under the guidance of the control positions. What with the the guns going off and the smell and smoke of the cordite from the casings, we were left in no doubt that we were in a battle. We were all wearing our awkward anti-flash headgear and trying to concentrate on our job, while at the same time imagining what was going on up top.

This time the torpedo bombers did not press their attack as closely as they should have. The enormous barrage put up by the battleships, particularly ourselves, no doubt had discouraged them. However, the Germans did press home their efforts and the *Ark* was straddled several times by sticks of bombs. High fountains of water gushed up all around her. It seemed to onlookers as if she had been hit. But no, she steamed calmly out of the cauldron of spray, replying with a firm affirmative to admiral's "Are you all right?" signalled from *Renown.* Several aircraft from this group peeled off and attacked us. We had received a very close call, so close in fact that we all felt the huge ship shake and were sure that she had been hit somewhere. The enemy were obviously making a major effort to stop us by committing seemingly endless squadrons of aircraft. As the attack continued we could feel the old ship listing as we veered back and forth at high speed. All the ships were "snaking" like this to confuse the aim of the enemy bombers. It certainly made for difficult station keeping. In fact at one point in the battle we began to draw far too close to the *Ark*.

An aircraft carrier in company was always fascinating to observe. She was frequently sending up and landing aircraft, whether, as in this action, they were fighters to patrol ahead of the fleet and drive off attacking enemy aircraft or slow recce aircraft to spot submarines or enemy ships beyond the horizon.

The *Ark* had been doing this since we had entered the Mediterranean basin and her Fulmar fighters had been fighting off the increasing number of enemy aircraft, to the point where the job had become too big for them. Several of them had been damaged. One came in over the destroyer escort screen with smoke pouring out of its engine, down back along its tail. It fired a distress rocket and crashlanded in the water. Usually a plane will float for a while if the crashlanding has been successful. This was what happened in this instance and the crew were rescued by one of the destroyers.

Whenever the *Ark* wanted to land her fighters or launch a new replacement flight, she had to turn into the wind and this could be problematical when the fleet was in action. Normally the whole fleet turned with her but in this instance, because of the battle, the carrier had to move out of line away from the ships astern. After she had carried out her flight operations, she would move back into line as quickly as possible for protection.

Toward the end of the day, just as another air attack was beginning, a Fulmar fighter damaged in a dogfight tried to land on the *Ark*. It flew low over the convoy and moved up toward the fleet area. Just then enemy aircraft started to approach and, of course, a heavy barrage of AA fire was put up from the fleet. I'm afraid that our own aircraft was shot down and that we were party to this unfortunate mistake.

At 1900 another torpedo bomber attack started just as Force H was leaving and turning back to the west. *Renown,* the flagship, made a 180 degree wide turn with *Ark Royal* following suit. We proceeded onward. Just at this crucial moment, the Italian torpedo bombers turned into the path of the *Ark* and pressed home their attack, letting go of their torpedoes within 200 yards of their target, despite a vigorous barrage from all ships. It was a miracle that the *Ark* got through unscathed. What saved her was the fact that she had already started to turn into the direction of the attack and could thus "comb" the tracks of the torpedoes, avoiding all of them completely.

Sunset was fast approaching and we were now heading east near the entrance of the Skerki channel, some seventy miles between Sicily and Tunisia. Our plan was to pass north of the island of Pantelleria, which lies almost in the middle of the straits.

As Force H left, its commander, Vice-Admiral James Somerville, sent a message wishing us luck. He had made quite a name for himself and his force. Back in Gib, I had visited the gun-room in *Renown* and was impressed at how the conversation invariably came around to him, usually about something amusing or interesting that he had said or done. He was a great one for visiting his officers and men to keep up morale. Apparently, as often as possible he made a point of getting aboard each ship in his force, including the destroyers, and addressing the crews personally.

We, too, had been visited. Not twenty four hours had passed after our arrival in Gib before he came aboard. It was quite a sight, our ship's company drawn up on the upper deck in whites and the great Rock overshadowing us. His speech was very positive and spirited, delivered in a straightforward manner, so that it appealed to all of us, no matter what our rank. When in harbour, he was sometimes known to pull an oar in a gig with the midshipmen before breakfast. Whether the midshipmen were thrilled about this was another matter. He was not a tall man but somehow had a commanding presence and was undeniably an outstanding leader.

The senior officer of the force was now a Rear-Admiral in the cruiser *Naiad* who remained in command until we met the main Mediterranean fleet east of Malta. We would be facing many problems during the night; mines—the strait was full of minefields, some of which we knew about; Italian motor torpedo boat attacks, or night aircraft attacks not to mention the difficulty of moving a large force through such a narrow channel.

I was not required in the cypher room until four in the morning and was told to get my head down. So before turning in, I went up on deck to look around. The sea was flat calm and an almost full moon shone, and the rippling phosphorescence from the bows and the sterns of the ships around us was all too plainly visible. We could hardly have wished for worse conditions. We brought up the rear of the fleet and the convoy was now disposed in a long line ahead of us with destroyers deployed close in on either side. This formation presumably presented the smallest possible target for the mines.

Our 15 inch guns pointed to starboard (our right) which meant that we were going north of Pantelleria. I learnt later from those on watch on the bridge that the captain had ordered them to be ready to retaliate in case there were long-range coastal guns on the island which might open fire on us.

Feeling very tired from the excitement of the day and with a morning watch in front of me I soon went below. I walked through the heavy double blackout curtains into a deserted after passageway to the gun-room. Two dirty looking stokers were squatting on the deck, part of the after damage-control party. The mess was quite deserted. I thought it safer to sleep there than down below in my usual flat, and composed myself in a comfortable overstuffed chair. My thoughts turned to all my shipmates closed up at action stations; huddled on the open upper bridge, talking in undertones of the day's happenings; high up in the exposed gunnery directors above the bridge; in one of our 15-inch turrets; or far below in the engine rooms or in one of the tiny gunnery transmitting compartments. Possibly because of all the excitement an inexplicable contentment came over me, and to the lazy sound of water lapping the ship's side I fell asleep.

A dull, explosive thud brought me back to semi-consciousness but I turned over and went back to sleep. Not long after I was really and truly awakened. I literally jumped out of my chair to the sound of the continuous rattle of our multiple pom-pom heavy machine-guns directly overhead, and the slow, intervalled crash of our 4.5 inchers. Clearly we were having to use all our anti-aircraft weapons. Suddenly the din ceased as quickly as it had started. But the deck was rising very sharply and I had to steady myself against a table — we were making a very sharp turn. Fortunately we hadn't been hit because the ship soon righted herself. I stood listening but nothing more happened. It seems incredible now, but after deciding that it must have been a false alarm, I inflated my life-jacket, moved to a better chair, and drifted back to sleep.

It was only when I was shaken for my watch at a quarter to four by Tyndall that I learned that the ship had just missed being torpedoed. The first explosion I had heard was when one of the merchant ships, the *Empire Song,* went up after hitting a mine. Realizing that we were right on the edge of a minefield, the captain immediately ordered two destroyers nearby to close up nearer to us to protect us and to narrow the width of the formation. The *Empire Song* was seriously damaged and ablaze and was slowly losing way and drifting back toward the ships astern of her. A destroyer went alongside and took off her crew, and not long after that the raging fire penetrated her hold where ammunition was stowed and she blew up. This must have been the noise that I first heard.

Then, on our RDF we picked up an enemy aircraft coming in ahead of us from our port side to the north east. The moon was still out and we presented a clear target. The aircraft crew, seeing the brilliant explosive flash in the distance, turned in to the attack. The destroyers and *Naiad* opened fire. In the middle of all this, the bridge party suddenly heard an aircraft very close by and it immediately roared into view to port, coming straight astern of us. The captain instantly yelled "hard astarboard" and had the navigator ring down to the engine room to increase speed to twenty two knots. We also sounded a long, ghostly warning blast on our siren for ships close around us to get out of the way. The plane was seen to drop its torpedo within a few hundreds yards. Indeed everyone on the bridge felt sure that we would be hit. It was our RDF which had alerted us, and the captain's quick thinking which saved us. The great ship had swung around, becoming a smaller target to the torpedo, which was actually seen streaming twenty feet away along our starboard side. It had been a very close call indeed. A midshipman friend had heard the old man mutter "that's a damn close one. Reduce speed and straighten up " as he watched it disappear ahead of the ship into the night.

An hour later we steamed by, within four miles of Pantelleria. All hands had been warned to expect trouble, but as we sailed by the place, easily visible from the bridge, it appeared to be fast asleep.

As dawn came up on 9 May 1941 we were expecting the worst day of the operation since we now lay south of Malta and within a hundred miles of Sicily. The Luftwaffe had moved their Junkers 88s, twin-engined fighter-bombers and 87s, called Stukas, onto the island and had been trying to neutralize Malta since the beginning of the year with the most concentrated air attacks yet known in history. In January, the aircraft carrier *Illustrious* had been seriously damaged during a convoy to Malta. She had been able to reach Malta and, after temporary repairs, make it back to Alexandria. During this operation the heavy cruiser *Southampton* had also been sunk by Stukas. We therefore had no illusions about what lay ahead of us.

These Stukas, with bent wings like vultures, attack in large droves. Flying in high over their targets, one after another they peel off and dive directly down at right angles, getting as low as they can before dropping their bombs and angling steeply upwards to get away. Their engines whine, and the fact that they come right down at you makes them extremely intimidating. They and the Italian air force had been pounding Malta for weeks, but once they knew we were in the area they would surely switch their attacks.

One consolation of rendezvousing with the Mediterranean fleet (under

43

Anti-aircraft light cruiser *HMS Carlisle.*

Admiral Sir Andrew Cunningham) is that we would get much increased AA
protection. But there was another consolation as well. This fleet had already
covered itself in glory against the Italian navy, subduing it in no uncertain
terms. Back in November 1940 Swordfish aircraft from *Illustrious* severely
damaged two Italian battleships and damaged another in their Taranto base.
Half their capital ships were thus put out of commission for a long period of
time. On 28 March 1941, just over a month before, the fleet had sunk three
Italian cruisers and several destroyers in a night action off Cape Matapan. As
a result of all this it appeared that the Italian fleet would probably not be out
in force during this operation.

As dawn came up, a flotilla of destroyers from Malta arrived to relieve the
ones from Gib. The weather had now changed to our advantage, with low
clouds and intermittent sea mists. Soon after, three anti-aircraft cruisers the
Coventry, Carlisle and *Calcutta* joined us, having been sent ahead by C-in-C
to provide protection throughout the forenoon until the main fleet arrived. I
had seen the operation orders, so I was on deck to watch the rendezvous. The
cruisers came in ahead of the convoy, dipping and rolling in the heavy morning
swell. They looked very small indeed compared to us, and in fact, as light
cruisers, they were not very much bigger than destroyers. Older ships, they
had been fitted with five twin high-angle 4-inch turrets of a new type, and so
had a very good AA capability. It was both exciting and reassuring to see these
seasoned veterans. That feeling of loneliness which we had felt after leaving
Force H the previous evening left us, and we now knew for sure that somewhere over the horizon lay the Med fleet which we were all so eager to see.

We had Beaufighters from Malta flying overhead, which was also reassuring. They had hardly arrived when enemy air attacks commenced. The
Beaufighters operated well above the clouds out of our range and managed to
keep several flights of German dive-bombers at bay. But suddenly we were the

44

object of a very determined attack. Forewarned by our RDF, the ship had been closed up at action stations the whole morning. A single dive-bomber now managed to get through our fighter cover and skimmed the sea directly towards us, refusing to deviate despite our heavy barrage. Every gun on the port side, including the light machine-guns, fired furiously at it. The plane, having survived the fleet's fire, finally caught a shell from us and dived aflame into the water not far off. A great cheer erupted from everyone on the upper deck — this was a our first hit since we had been commissioned. The old man was on the SRE immediately, imparting the good news to everyone below decks.

Amidst all this drama I had my own battles to fight. I had quite a row with our Petty Officer Steward that morning for not preparing a proper breakfast for the midshipmen. He and the PO Cook were not closed up permanently at action stations, presumably so that they could prepare something hot to eat. When the ship's company briefly came off first degree of readiness that morning, they had been closed up for thirty-six hours and living off canned bully beef, greasy hot cocoa (if available) and hard tack — thick, square biscuits, so hard that you could easily break your teeth on them. Clearly, our action messing would have to be reorganized. The Petty Officer became quite offended and threatened to see the Pay Commander.

Then during the afternoon of 10 May 1941, we finally met the Med fleet. At about 3 o'clock someone burst into the mess with the news that many ships could be seen away over on the horizon on our port bow. By this time we were off first degree of readiness again, and most people not on duty were trying to get some sleep. But on hearing the news, everyone took off for the quarterdeck to join the excited groups of officers gazing to port. Yes, sure enough, there were a host of marks on the horizon — just outlines of masts and high superstructures. People were trying to count them and we were all astonished at the number of ships that were beginning to emerge. From the small dots in the sky above, it was evident that there was an aircraft carrier in company. As time passed one could make out more clearly the various battleships and cruisers and the large destroyer screen ahead of them.

For most of us this was the largest number of ships, particularly capital ships, that we had ever seen at sea together. Maybe the Paymaster Commander, who stood aft with his hands stuck in his uniform sidepockets, a pipe in his mouth, remembered the Grand Fleet in the last war, thirty battleships strong. One of our retired two and a halfs (two and a half stripe Lieutenant Commander) definitely had seen something like this. He was a character and a friendly soul who was always coming into the gun-room bumming drinks and talking about "Jellibags" (Admiral Jellicoe) and his own time as a snottie in the Grand Fleet.

Later we saw the whole fleet at close quarters. There were three battleships — *Warspite*, the flagship, then *Barham* and *Valiant*, our identical sister ship, also the aircraft carrier *Formidable*, one of our latest carriers and numerous cruisers including *Ajax, Orion, Gloucester, Fiji, Perth* (an Australian cruiser) and many others, as well as numerous destroyers. We now took our place in the fleet and left the convoy which, in a way, we were sorry to do; we would have liked to have stayed with it until we reached Alexandria.

These three battleships plus *QE* and *Malaya* made up the five ships of the Queen Elizabeth class. They were said to be the finest class ever built, and were commissioned in 1915 and 1916. All had taken part in the First World

The aircraft carrier _Formidable_ in Alex harbour.

War. _Malaya_ and _Barham_ were never given a major modification like what was done to _QE_.

On swinging in line astern of the battle fleet, the admiral immediately started putting us through our paces. One minute we were steaming along in line astern, when a flutter of flag signals would break from the main yardarm of the flagship and the next minute we would be in line abreast. The sight of these huge, magnificent ships manoeuvring in unison on the blue Mediterranean sea was truly memorable. The sheer size of them, with the seas flaring off their enormous bows, their towering superstructures and their massive menacing gun turrets, presented a picture of enormous power.

That evening we received a visual message from _Valiant_ welcoming us and conveying the surprising information that they had not expected to see us at all; an Italian news bulletin had reported our loss. Later we ourselves picked up the Italian news in English. Sure enough, a very English voice came on and announced that in the studio with him was the very Italian pilot who had sunk the British battleship the previous night. The pilot duly came on and, talking in broken English, related how he had found the ship at about midnight and had been able to get well within range without being sighted before dropping his torpedo. He described in glowing terms how the torpedo had struck home with a terrific explosion. He went off the air with a wild cheer from everyone in the mess. Possibly he may have really thought that he had sunk us, mistaking our gunfire for an explosion. And having got so close, he had perhaps understandably convinced himself that he couldn't have possibly missed.

The next night our first operation came to a great conclusion. The air attacks on us had been relatively light during the day and had been beaten off by our fighters from Malta and our carrier. As dusk approached, we went to

The quarterdeck of *QE* entering Alex harbour with a *Glen* Assault Ship

action stations in earnest. This was a time of maximum danger because the half-light made it difficult for the gun crews to pick out small flying objects in the distance. Not surprisingly, dawn and dusk were the favourite times for low flying torpedo bomber attacks.

When no enemy attacks materialized, we were put on second degree of readiness after darkness fell. Gun crews could relax with a cup of cocoa for a while. As cypher traffic was light I was relieved until 2400 and used the opportunity to visit the signal bridge.

It was a dark night and the vague outlines of the battleships ahead of us could just be seen. As new boy, we brought up the rear. *Formidable,* the carrier, had been moved into line with the battleships to give her added protection.

I had not been up there long before our port 4.5 batteries opened up. For the next three hours or so we kept this up intermittently as wave after wave of aircraft tried to penetrate our barrage.

At several points in the attack the enemy formations attacked from both sides and every ship up the line flashed and glowed on either side. I had a ringside view of the whole spectacle. We might have been fighting it out with another enemy battlefleet; I'm sure the overall effect was exactly the same. The sudden clap of ten, sometimes twenty guns, firing almost in unison, shook the great ship. As each gun fired, there was a flash or series of flashes accompanied by the eerie hiss of departing shells. Add to this the near and distant rumblings of the other ships' guns and you had some idea of the excitement of a battlefleet in action at night.

We fired over 3,000 4.5 inch shells that night. Strangely no one actually saw any enemy aircraft: we were firing strictly from our RDF intercepts. Were there really enemy aircraft out there? Apparently so. It was our concentrated fire and our accurate RDF control that was keeping them out of sight. I heard

Merchant ship *City of Pittsburg* lying in the Alexandria harbour Grand Pass entrance.

later in *Jervis* that enemy bombs were indeed dropped near the outer destroyer screen and our own shells were landing a bit too close to the screen for comfort. In the morning we received a message from C-in-C telling us to conserve ammunition in future as there was a shortage in the Middle East. Perhaps we had been too enthusiastic.

After it was all over, I found the battery deck suffused with a yellow, sulphurous haze and the smell of cordite, and the men, stripped to the waist, glistening with perspiration. It could almost have been the gun deck after a sea battle in Nelson's time. The crews looked completely exhausted and the outside of the barrels of the guns, which had been firing hot, were heavily paint-blistered.

During the action, one of our Polish midshipmen began firing a small Lewis machine-gun mounted on the bridge. The noise and the excitement had got to him and he grabbed it and let loose without any aircraft in sight. Meanwhile *Valiant* had begun to drop back out of station or, maybe we were coming on too fast. Before Glinski noticed, he was spraying tracer at *Valiant* not far from their open bridge. Needless to say, he was quickly stopped and put on the mat.

The last three days of the trip to our new home port proved uneventful. A few air attacks occurred but were not pressed home with much effect, and were driven off by our carrier fighters. Finally, on a clear sunny morning, the fleet lined up and proceeded up the swept channel, "The Grand Pass," into Alexandria. What a stirring spectacle it was to see battleships, cruisers and destroyers moving slowly and quietly in line ahead, with white uniformed figures manning the side. Then we turned in sharply through entrance defence nets into the large, crowded and protected harbour and headed for our anchorage. As we came in, we could see flat low-lying sand which continued off to the west without break, toward the Western Desert.

Modern Alexandria was off to the east out of view. The buildings around the harbour were not very prepossessing being mostly square flat-roofed houses and the usual jetties, wharves and storage sheds. The monotony was only broken by a large imposing palace-like building on the Ras-el-Tin promontory which was linked to a long protective mole. This was one of King Farouk's palaces.

As we inched our way to our harbour berth in a crowded anchorage we sailed past the old French battleship *Lorraine* and were given a bugle salute. Nearby there were several large French cruisers and some destroyers and submarines at buoys. What their status was we were not quite sure. They seemed to be out of the war, but that did not stop them from piping us as we went by.

After all the excitement of the voyage, we ended on a bit of a down note. It took us over half an hour to come to our buoy, long after all the other battleships had finished. All rather embarrassing especially as we received a very uncomplimentary message from our Commander-in-Chief.

A noticeboard memorandum was issued by the captain after the trip as follows:

> To Commander (E) (Engineering)
>
> I would like to inform all your department of my great appreciation of the manner in which, during the middle watch the other night, they went, with extreme rapidity, from 9 to 22 knots.
>
> There is no doubt that in doing this they saved the ship from being torpedoed.
>
> Captain

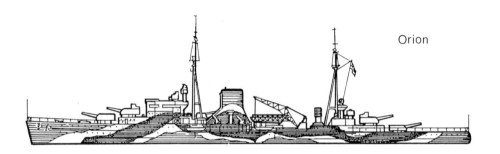

Orion

CHAPTER FOUR

This Sombre Ferocious Battle - Crete

*I do not consider that we should regret the Battle of Crete. I am
sure it will be found that this sombre, ferocious battle, which
was lost, and lost, I think, upon no great margin was well worth
fighting and that it will have an extremely important effect on
the whole defence of the Nile Valley throughout the present year.*

Winston Churchill

We had barely got our bearings of the port when the Battle of Crete
appeared imminent. We immediately sailed in company with *Barham* and a
screen of destroyers to a position off the west coast of Crete to provide
protection for the cruisers which were to sweep to the north of the island in
anticipation of an expected German seaborne attack. Vice-Admiral H.D. Pridham-Wippell had moved aboard with his staff and was in command. The trip
proved uneventful and we were relieved by *Warspite* and *Valiant* and returned
to base. Just as we did so, the Germans launched the airborne invasion of the
island, on 20 May 1941.

I was immediately transferred ashore to join the staff of C-in-C in the
headquarters cypher office. C-in-C had recently decided that his flagship
Warspite was not big enough to accommodate his growing staff so he had
moved ashore to some old buildings at Gabbari dock, which was down the
harbour to the west and near the fleet. Arrangements were made to have the
flagship anchored stern to the shore via a floating catamaran to provide easy
communication between her and the shore staff. The admiral's idea was to run
the fleet from ashore and go to sea only for actual operations. However, in the
case of the Cretan operations he chose to stay ashore and let his second-in-
command and the cruiser admirals conduct the sea battles. One reason for this
was the need for close liaison with the army and air force HQs.

For me, the contrast with my life as a midshipman onboard ship could
hardly have been more marked. My initial billet was none other than the Hotel
Cecil, Alex's finest and the headquarters cypher office was very spacious after
QE's cramped little cubbyhole. The first impression that I had of my new place
of work was the cheerfulness of the busy officers, despite the tragic news of
the sinking of the cruisers *Gloucester* and *Fiji* only hours before.

Apart from the attack on Crete, the war situation in the Middle East was
not good. The army had been depleted by the vain diversion of troops to
Greece, and it was now fighting revitalised German and Italian armies at the
Egyptian border, and Tobruk, having being bypassed by the enemy, was under
siege. The air force was short of planes and those that were available were
being used in support of the army.

But it was the Cretan campaign that chiefly occupied my attention. As an
HQ cypher officer I handled numerous messages, and having access to the
daily signal log, I was able to follow the battle in detail on a day to day basis.

The AEGEAN SEA

Scale of Miles

From the very beginning our prospects in Crete had not looked all that promising. Our troops there were mostly composed of the remnants from Greece and were poorly equipped and lacking motor transport, tanks and artillery. They had been augmented by two fresh battalions, the Leicesters, run across by two cruisers, and the Argyll and Sutherland Highlanders by *Glengyle,* a new type of naval assault transport. In addition the First Mobile Naval Base Defence Force — a Royal Marine unit — was to be sent to defend our main fleet base at Suda Bay on the north coast. However, the despatch of its motor transport and anti-aircraft guns had been delayed. Thus even with these reinforcements our forces on Crete were not strong, but their biggest weakness was their lack of air support; we only had a few Fleet Air Arm aircraft and a few RAF fighters on the island. Yet it was hoped that the island

Cunningham and his Admirals. Left to right, Rawlings, unknown, Pridham-Wippell, Edelston, Cunningham, Dick, unknown.

could be defended with the help of the navy.

C-in-C, probably against his own judgement, had to obey orders and, despite all the negatives, try and get the navy to sway the balance. He had already decided to keep a standing patrol of two battleships off the west coast of Crete to discourage the Italian fleet, and to send a cruiser force further north to strike at enemy convoys. *QE* and *Barham* had carried out the first patrol relieved by *Warspite* and *Valiant* on 18 May 1941, when I was still aboard QE.

The German invasion was preceded by a softening-up air attack of unprecedented ferocity on the Maleme airfield. Then the air drop started, the targets, apart from Maleme airfield, being the Akotiri peninsula, five miles to the west, and the small seaside town of Canae, ten miles east. Suda Bay our naval base nearby was also given a pasting. Gliders came in first followed by paratroops fifteen minutes later. What few fighters we had left had flown out the day before.

Later that day, parachute drops were made at Retimo and Heraklion, both on the north cental coast of the island. German troops met stiff resistance at Akotiri, Retimo, and Heraklion, suffering heavy casualties with survivors being taken prisoner. But at Maleme the Germans attacked in larger numbers and landed right on top of our own troops, who, in the absence of sufficient air protection from our planes, were pinned down by enemy aircraft. By evening, the enemy troops had a foothold to the west of the field. Nonetheless, by the end of of the first day — 20 May, the land situation gave grounds for cautious satisfaction.

Cunningham's initial orders were for ships to stay out of sight of land by day and smaller ships were to stay in company with larger ships, for AA protection, where possible. Later, as losses from air attack increased, particularly after the serious losses on 22 May 1941, the naval strategy changed. Forces were to be to the south of the island by day, to be well away from the German airfields in southern Greece.

Queen Elizabeth seen from a destroyer receiving oil from her at sea.

One force, the 15th Cruiser Squadron under Rear-Admiral E.L.S. King in *Naiad,* including the Australian cruiser Perth and the destroyers *Kandahar, Nubian, Kingston* and *Juno* were to work the east side of the island. The other force, under Rear-Admiral I.G. Glennie, Rear Admiral Destroyers, in the cruiser *Dido,* and comprising the cruisers *Ajax* and *Orion* and the destroyers *Janus, Kimberley, Hasty* and *Hereward* would cover the west. A further cruiser force, consisting of *Gloucester* and *Fiji* plus two destroyers was to back up the western force where necessary, while the battleship force was also in reserve in the west.

On the night of the invasion, 20/21 May, the *Naiad* force had gone through the Kaso strait, between Crete and Skarpanto island and lying less than fifty miles offshore, and attacked and damaged a force of Italian motor torpedo

54

Hotel Cecil, Alexandria.

boats. Meanwhile, Captain D14 (Captain in command of the 14th Destroyer Flotilla) in *Jervis,* with the destroyers *Nizam* (Australian) and *Ilex* bombarded the airfield on Skarpanto which was proving to be a thorn in our side.

At daylight on 21 May, during the retreat south, the Eastern Force was attacked from the air and the destroyer *Juno* took a direct hit from a bomb behind her funnel. Splitting in two she sank within three minutes, her bow portion pointing dramatically upwards before it quickly disappeared. Ninety-one crew members, including the captain, were rescued by the other destroyers, but a large number went down with the ship.

The Western Group had a less eventful night. It went through the Kithera Channel but found nothing. *Ajax* was slightly damaged by a bomb on the way out.

During 21 May — the second day of the battle — the army was still preventing the Germans from getting a firm foothold. However, the Luftwaffe was revealing that it had both the numbers and the expertise to bomb not only land targets in Crete but also deal in a most effective way with the naval opposition.

Our two cruiser forces again ran the gauntlet into the waters north of Crete during the night of 21/22 May, and both located and attacked enemy convoys bringing troops to Crete. The *Dido* force went through the western straits at dusk and around midnight made contact with a straggling convoy of small steamers and caiques (Greek schooners) north of Canea. The action was a terrific shambles. The force went straight into the convoy and sank it all within fifteen minutes. My friend in *Ajax* told me that at one point the ship suddenly came across a small Italian destroyer in the mist and smoke of the melee. She was no more than a few hundred yards away and *Ajax* blew her to bits with one six inch salvo. Thousands of German troops were left in the water.

The convoy that fell prey to the *Naiad* force was smaller and several caiques flying the German ensign were sunk. On this foray the force had been reinforced by the AA cruisers *Calcutta* and *Carlisle,* as it was weaker in AA guns than the western force bringing forces to Crete. *Calcutta* sank a merchant ship and an Italian destroyer was damaged. In the morning of 22 May at around 1100 a large convoy of caiques was sighted, but the admiral decided to call it a day as the force was running low on ammunition and was too spread out to repel air attack which was expected momentarily. The force was now far north of Crete, quite close to Milos, which was somewhat to the west. The shortest way out therefore, was through the western exit.

On this day — 22 May 1941 — all our naval forces off Crete were subjected to an unheard of onslaught by enemy aircraft. They came in droves, one squadron after another, one kind of attack after another, and always the ever-present shadower plane stooging on the edge of the horizon. The bombing was more or less continuous and what was more irritating, extremely accurate and very courageously pressed home. The Germans were undoubtedly using their crack squadrons. As well as the 87s and 88s, medium level bombers — Heinkel 111s — and Messerschmitt fighters were being used. The turn-around to their airfields in Greece was extremely quick.

The enemy's most effective weapon was the Stuka, the JU 87. Very slow, it was vulnerable to fighter opposition but this was lacking in Crete. Consequently, this was probably one of the few occasions in the war when it could be used to its fullest capability.

Heavy AA was useless against them once they were close and our light ack-ack wasn't much better. The Chigaco grand pianos, the multiple 1.5 inch pom-poms, in four- or eight- gun units, were fairly effective but a little unwieldy. Only the very light guns could be shifted quickly from one dangerous aircraft to another. In the heat of battle, this proved impractical, especially when the equipment was poor. I was told that the Swiss Oerlikon gun (.7 inch) which was light, hand-operated, and easily moved about was extremely effective against dive-bombers. These guns also had the penetrating power, but unfortunately, the old story, we hadn't yet received very many in the Med fleet.

My *Ajax* friend said that during the hectic attacks, fifty JU 87s were sighted ahead of the ship in tight formation. After one look at this lot, everyone hurriedly closed up to action stations, inflating their life-jackets thoroughly, and preparing for the worst. The whole ship's company was completely shaken from the Old Man down. A concerted attack on this scale had never been known before. But it happened that the ship was spared, for these machines were on their way to bash the pongos ashore. They flew right past the fleet, every damned one of them.

On the morning of 22 May there was thus a great concentration of our ships in various locations to the west of Crete. The *Naiad* force, which was exiting, after the previous night's foray, from the north of the island to the west was the farthest north and was subject to the heaviest attacks from the air. One hundred and eighty-one bombs were dropped on *Naiad* in the space of two hours and she was even raked with machine-gun fire. She had been near-missed so often her hull had fractured, causing flooding in her forward compartments and a reduction in her speed. Only two of her turrets remained in action. All the ships of the force were now running low on ammunition. *Carlisle* was hit by a bomb but was not too seriously damaged, although her captain, T.C. Hampton, was killed.

The *Warspite* battle group was in the area to the southwest, in company with the *Dido* group. *Gloucester* and *Fiji* were moving south and rejoined the *Warspite* group at 0830. Rear Admiral H.B. Rawlings in *Warspite* then decided to move the combined force into the Kithera Channel to provide AA protection to the *Naiad* group after he had received word of its ordeal.

This placed the main fleet fifty miles from the Greek mainland. At 1330, in the middle of the Kithera Channel, just after the *Naiad* force had been sighted, a heavy air attack took place. *Warspite* took a bomb from a dive-bomber and a twin 4 inch turret was completely destroyed, all the gun crew killed, and a large gash was left in the upper superstructure. Later *Valiant* also was hit by a bomb which went through the quarterdeck and eventually lodged in her bowels without exploding. An unfortunate marine sentry on duty on the Important Keyboard beneath the quarterdeck was the only casualty.

The whole force now retreated as fast as possible for Alex, as most ships were just about out of ammunition and the destroyers would soon need refuelling. Shortly before this incident a caique was sighted to the north of the Kithera Channel, and the destroyer *Greyhound,* one of the *Gloucester* group's escorts was ordered to sink it. This led to a series of tragic repercussions because she had to leave the AA security of the fleet. She was immediately picked out by the German aircraft which attacked her like crows marauding for hatchlings in an undefended nest. Within minutes she was hit by three bombs and sank rapidly, the fleet being treated to the heroic sight of one gun still firing as she went under. By now our forces had spread out with the battleships well to the west. The senior officer present of the cruiser force, Admiral King, then ordered the destroyers *Kandahar* and *Kingston* to pick up survivors. In the course of this operation two rescuing whalers from these ships were brutally machined-gunned from the air as they dragged the floating men out of the sea. Many were killed as they thrashed around in the water. How inhuman and pointless war can get! These German airmen clearly didn't honour the sailor's tradition of picking up survivors, even enemy survivors.

Now *Gloucester* and *Fiji* were ordered to move out and provide more AA support to stop this ruthless German behaviour. Eighty of the crew of *Greyhound* were rescued, including her captain. But by this time *Fiji* had run out of 4 inch shells and only her smaller close-range weapons remained in operation. The boats were ordered back to their ships and rafts and floats were left for the men in the water.

Then, at about 1500, a terrible thing happened. *Gloucester* was suddenly hit by several bombs and was engulfed in smoke and flames. Damage was very serious and she slowly came to a dead stop, later receiving yet more hits; the number of enemy planes seemed to be inexhaustible. *Fiji* signalled C-in-C that she would stand by *Gloucester* until she could make good her damage. But *Gloucester* was settling fast. C-in-C immediately ordered that she be left and that the remainder of the squadron alter course southwards at full speed. Boats, rafts and Carley floats were left for the crew of the stricken ship several of whom, I later heard, managed to reach the Kithera and Antikithera islands. The body of her captain, H.A.Rowley, was washed up ashore at Mersa Matruh a month afterwards.

Later, about twenty-five miles south of Crete, *Fiji* now became the focus of the bombings. The Germans were becoming more sophisticated in their attacks with high-level and dive-bomber raids being simultaneously co-ordinated. *Fiji* had already suffered a number of near misses, some of which were close enough to cause casualties. The gunnery officer, for example, was severely wounded on the open bridge and was carried below. All afternoon she and her destroyers — they had become separated from the main force — fought off the enemy planes. Then a hoped-for lull occurred, allowing the damage control parties to get on with repairs. However, more aircraft arrived and, as her ammunition supply ran out and she became a sitting duck, she was hit and a boiler room was flooded. Finally, as the last rays of the sun disappeared she was finished off by a lone fighter-bomber. Still the aircraft came, forcing the destroyers to leave her. Unfortunately all her Carley floats had been left for *Greyhound* and *Gloucester* and most of the surviving crew had to take to the water with only their life-jackets. As the ship took on an extreme list before she sank, an unfortunate sailor was seen sitting forlornly on one of the propellors, which was sticking out of the water. Transfixed by indecision, he went down with the ship. Later, after dark, the escorting destroyers *Kandahar* and *Kingston,* returned to the spot and somehow picked up 523 of the crew.

After the war, Admiral Cunningham in his fine autobiography, "A Sailor's Odyssey," wrote critically of Admiral King's actions in this engagement. Firstly, he felt that King should have attacked the caique convoy near Milos before he retired south. And secondly, King erred in sending aid to the destroyer *Greyhound.* Where air attacks were so lethally heavy, Cunningham contended, stricken ships should be left to fend for themselves so that the remaining ships were not put in jeopardy.

Be that as it may, on this day reinforcements arrived directly from Malta in the shape of the 5th Destroyer Flotilla comprising *Kelly, Kashmir, Kipling, Jackal* and *Kelvin* under the command of Captain Lord Louis Mountbatten. The flotilla had been ordered to proceed to the area where *Fiji* had sunk and help pick up survivors. But this order was later rescinded, and the flotilla was ordered to proceed directly through the Kithera Channel on the night of 22/23 May 1941 to make another effort to stop further invading convoys. Instead, the Naval Officer in Charge (NOIC) at Suda Bay was asked to send out patrol boats to pick up *Fiji* survivors. However, practically all the local naval vessels there had been sunk.

In the east, Captain D14 in the destroyer *Jervis,* proceeded with *Nizam* and *Ilex* to the north of the island to intercept any enemy convoys that might be coming in from that direction. Thus a continued naval presence on both east and west sides of the island was being maintained. Also on the night of 22/23 May 1941 the destroyers *Decoy* and *Hero* sailed from Alex for Tymbaki, on the south coast of Crete, to take off the King of Greece and his party. The *Decoy* group along with D5 were to rendezvous with the battle fleet to the southwest on the following morning.

Despite over four thousand German troops being killed and around 150 aircraft, mostly transport aircraft, being shot down, the military situation on the island had deteriorated. Since 21 May, the Germans had started to land transport aircraft at Maleme. With great tenacity their soldiers gradually drove ours back so that their aircraft were soon landing unharmed, thereby increasing their numbers of troops. At Retimo and Heraklion, however, our forces still had things well in hand despite further paratroop drops. By now we had captured their operation orders which showed that their main target was

Maleme. It was therefore decided to bombard the airfield, a task that was entrusted to Mountbatten's flotilla.

This was to be a night action, and the flotilla was split, with *Kashmir* and *Kipling* accompanying *Kelly* and the other two destroyers remaining in reserve. *Kipling* soon developed engine troubles and saw none of the subsequent action. With his two remaining ships, Mountbatten sailed directly to the northwest corner of the island and investigated the large Kissamo Bay where a caique, loaded with troops, was despatched. Then they entered the next bay and closed south towards land and bombarded Maleme, sinking another caique on their way out. By dawn they were well through the channel, and moving at full speed to the south. *Kipling* meanwhile had remained to the west to rendezvous later. As to the night bombardment of Maleme airfield, it is always difficult to gauge the success of such operations since it is impossible to know whether targets are being hit. Certainly the area was filled with enemy troops and the bombardment should have been of some benefit to our land forces there.

With two destroyers on their our own close to the island, in broad daylight, it didn't take long before the German air force was on the scene in strength. At 0800 on the morning of 23 May, forty miles south of western Crete, *Kelly* and *Kashmir* were attacked by twenty five Stukas. *Kipling* was still only on the horizon. Both ships were running at full speed, turning and twisting to avoid the hail of bombs. *Kashmir* was hit first under full helm. She was severely damaged amidships and rolled over and sank within minutes. *Kelly* then got it and suffered the same fate, sinking very rapidly. She turned right over and floated on her back upside down for a while with her screws still churning pathetically. Two of my old Conway chums — Mortimer-Booth and Money, both fine shipmates — went down with her.

Luckily *Kipling* was by now at hand and immediately steamed to the scene of the tragedy, heading toward the *Kelly's* survivors. She dropped her whalers and started to pick up survivors. More Stukas appeared and began another fierce attack. However, after four very difficult hours, survivors from both ships were picked up, 120 from *Kelly* and 144 from *Kashmir*, including both captains. A friend of mine in *Kipling*, said that he would never forget Lord Louis's arrival onboard. Although he had been in the water for quite a while and was covered in oil, he shook himself like a wet dog and immediately marched to the bridge to take over.

Kipling also sustained damage from several near misses and literally limped back to Alex. I remember seeing her as she came in. Moving very slowly — she was down heavily by the bows — she took about half an hour to get across the harbour with the help of tugs. She had run out of fuel well out to sea and lay stopped in the water until the Netlayer *Protector* joined her and refueled her. There was an uncomfortable silence from the crews of the other ships as she slowly moved down through the lanes of warships. All she received was the usual piping as she passed each of them although there was some cheering for the tattered survivors who could be seen covering the whole of the upper deck. Finally she berthed alongside. Altogether it was a very depressing sight, rather like a funeral, but a common enough occurrence during this fateful week. Where we wondered was it all going to end?

At the time there was a story going the rounds that Lord Louis was given the option of bombarding Maleme airfield but only on condition that he could be well clear of the Antikithera Channel by dawn. Another story was that he had bombarded it on his own initiative. Both were quite untrue. He had been given clear instructions to carry out the operation. Be that as it may, he had a reputation as a dashing, independent-minded, even headstrong officer. Two ships had already been severely damaged under him, but he had been able to get both back to port. The first one had been *Kelly* which had been torpedoed during the Norwegian campaign. Despite suggestions from a senior officer, he had refused to abandon ship and it was towed back to England. After this he was captain of *Javelin,* whilst *Kelly* was being repaired. He led his flotilla against German Ebling class destroyers in the English Channel and, during a night action, *Javelin* was torpedoed and had both its bow and stern blown off. Yet again he managed to get it towed back to port. In Crete, *Kelly* had been less fortunate, but Mountbatten's personal luck had clearly held.

Our losses to date were two cruisers and four destroyers to say nothing of the battleships, cruisers and destroyers that were damaged and put out of action. In fact, as Cunningham so tartly signalled the Admiralty in a cypher that I saw; "if the Med fleet continued to defend Crete against a seaborne invasion there wouldn't be any fleet left in five days at the rate that we were losing ships." [1]

Without air support we simply could not cope on our own with the seemingly limitless German aircraft. Both the navy and the army were very bitter about this and unfortunately this could take on an ugly form ashore. But these feelings were quite irrational as the air force was already over-committed in the desert war. Our one and only aircraft carrier, *Formidable,* might have been useful if she had carried sufficient numbers of fighters. As it was, she had only a few out-of-date aircraft left.

I saw some pretty caustic signals which Cunningham was sending off at this time to London, harping on the lack of air support. In reply he received nightly signals from both Churchill and the Admiralty, all of them giving advice. C-in-C was none too pleased about this, since neither the Prime Minister nor the Admiralty could possibly be fully aware of the rapidly changing operational conditions.

Cunningham's problems were deeper and wider than air cover. The basic shortcoming was one of supply, and our reliance on insufficient and old equipment in certain areas. This was discussed at great length in the gun-room with some of the blame being laid at the door of the Admiralty. However, this was not altogether true as we had plenty of well designed, modern, or upgraded ships with our amazing new types of RDF and Asdic, much improved gunnery control not to mention the little Oerlikon gun. One of our big weaknesses was that too few of our ships had the effective 4 inch AA gun and more of them should have been retrofitted with RDF gun control. Moreover, while we produced the fine Hurricane and Spitfire fighters, not enough of them plus long-range fighter-bombers were deployed in the Middle East. We needed fighters to provide protection and bombers to attack the enemy airfields in Greece. The root of the problem in a free democracy in peacetime was apathy to the needs of the country's armed forces.

My personal impression of Cunningham was of a battle hardened leader who had seen it all and knew exactly what he was about. He had a very long and distinquished career behind him and was by far the most experienced of any of our senior officers. He had been in command of a destroyer during the

C-in-C in a good mood.

Dardanelles campaign in the First World War and had taken part in the bloody Zeebrugge raid under Admiral Keyes. He had been decorated for bravery early in his career.

He was much admired by the fleet for the way that he had subdued the Italian fleet and for his astuteness in handling delicate political situations such as the Vichy French naval crisis of 1940, of which more later. Although not a flamboyant leader like Admiral Somerville of Force H, he definitely exuded an air of authority and great experience. There was no doubt that he was the boss. His strong suit was his aggressiveness, tempered by judicious caution, in the handling of his ships. He had been forced into the Crete battle and had done everything he could to pull it off. A message that he sent at the height of the campaign to the fleet exhorting them to further efforts typified this attitude. In it he said, "The army is just holding its own against constant reinforcement of airborne troops. We must not let them down. At whatever cost to ourselves, we must land reinforcements and keep the enemy from using the sea. There are indications that enemy resources are stretched to the limit. We can and must outlast them. Stick it out."

By this stage in the battle, ship's companies were beginning to feel the strain. Not only were they at action stations for most of the time at sea, but as soon as they reached port, they were immediately put to work ammunitioning ship and refuelling, and sometimes had to close up at action stations at night during air raids. Then, as soon as the ships were resupplied, many were ordered back to sea again.

On the night of 23/24 May, the day after the *Kelly* sinking, the only ships we had north of the island were the destroyers *Jaguar* and *Defender* which steamed to Suda Bay with more ammunition for the hard-pressed army, keeping an eye out for convoys on the way in and out. From now on we used the eastern passage around Crete rather than the far more dangerous one through the Kithera Channel to the west.

Even though we had been forced to move out of the straits during the day, the situation onshore was still not irredeemable and the seaborne invasion had at least been stopped. Nevertheless, the Germans were ensconced at Maleme airfield and reinforcing their army by air at will, and our army seemed unable to dislodge them. This was the critical land battle.

Our naval base at Suda Bay, not far to the east from Maleme, was gone, having been neutralized by heavy bombing attacks. There were eight sunken merchant ships in the harbour as well as the cruiser *York,* which had been severely damaged by Italian mini-torpedo boats on 26 March 1941 and had been beached beyond repair.

There was no anti-convoy coverage north of Crete by our ships on the night of the 24th, except that *Abdiel,* a fast minelayer dropped off stores and ammunition at Suda Bay. The next night, 25/26 May 1941, *Ajax, Dido, Kimberley* and *Hotspur* entered the Kaso Straits to seek out an invasion convoy apparently heading for the east end of the island. However, nothing was found and they were able to get out unscathed.

On the 25th May, Cunningham decided to make one last effort to help the army, and it proved to be a very costly undertaking. Subsequently there was a lot of criticism of this operation in the fleet. Many felt that it was doomed to failure before it started. Whether it was to let the Germans know that we still had some life left in us, or was due to pressure from England, I didn't know. Certainly it went against the grain of everything that the admiral had been saying in his messages to the Admiralty.

The object of the operation was to carry out a night bombing attack of the German airfield on Skarpanto Island. The Germans had been using a small airfield there for their Stukas and were able to dominate the Kaso Strait, which was now our only entry channel to the north of Crete. The RAF could not spare any bombers, so the navy was left to deal with the problem. None of the German airfields in southern Greece had been attacked, but because this one was so much closer it was considered to be a feasible target.

It was finally decided to bring the aircraft carrier *Formidable* into the battle and use her aircraft to carry out the attack. The problem was that *Formidable* had very few serviceable aircraft left, and it seemed indefensible that this fine carrier should be risked for the sake of an attack by a few old-fashioned torpedo bombers and fighters. What was the point of building these great carriers if they were not provided with the proper aircraft?

By this time the Med fleet had been steadily at sea for over two months prior to the assault on Crete, and ships had been using up aircraft, shells and equipment at an enormous rate, to say nothing of the pressure on the crews. A series of big operations had followed in quick succession. These had included the bombardments of Valona and Tripoli, the action off Cape Matapan, the evacuation of Greece, "Operation Tiger," plus many minor ones. Cruisers such as *Ajax* and *Orion* had not had more than twenty-four hours in harbour for over two months. Most destroyers had had to provide AS escort for all these operations and were in the same situation. Even the battleships, which on average spent a lot of time swinging around the buoy in harbour, had been working hard. It is not an exaggeration to say that the men of the fleet were utterly tired, and this was equally true of the shore maintenance staff who had been working night and day to keep ships operational.

Consequently, the force sent against Skarpanto was exhausted in terms of both men and materiel. *Formidable* would have to sail to a position somewhere south of Crete and fly off her strike force, such as it was, thus placing herself and her escorts within dive bomber range.

On 25 May she sailed with *QE, Barham* and a destroyer escort. The attack was carried out at night and was relatively successful even though only four bombers and four fighters were put into the air. A number of enemy aircraft were destroyed. Next morning the force under Vice-Admiral Pridham-Whippell in *QE* headed south for home. No air attack developed during the morning and it looked like the force would get away unscathed. However, at one o'clock in the afternoon an attack started.

This wave of aircraft was picked up at a long distance and followed by RDF, as it turned twenty miles away and worked its way around the fleet so that it could attack from the west out of the sun. All the aircraft concentrated on *Formidable*. Amid the attacks from all directions, a lone, daredevil aircraft carried out a perfect jump-bombing on the huge carrier. A fire started and smoke oozed from under her flight deck and was swept back down the ship's side by the wind. Soon the whole ship was blotted from view and it looked as if she would be a total loss. Then she was hit again.

Within fifteen minutes, however, the fire had been put out and she began to resume station. Bombs also fell close to the battleships but neither was touched. The destroyer *Nubian* was hit, having been singled out for attack for no apparent reason. Even so, she was able to make port. When the attack began, *Formidable* had just landed two Fulmar fighters and put two reliefs into the air. These two valiantly attacked the Stukas and their supporting Messerschmitt fighters. They fought until they ran out of ammunition and miraculously landed back onboard without damage. The force returned to Alex without further problems, but *Formidable* had received serious damage and was going to be out of the war for a good long time.

The battleship force stayed at sea, to back up the final efforts by the navy to send in further last minute reinforcements. Three destroyers tried to land Special Service troops on the south coast on the night of 24/25 May but were deterred by bad weather. These same troops were embarked on *Abdiel* which sailed for Suda Bay with a two destroyer escort of *Hero* and *Nizam* for a night disembarkation in Suda Bay on 26/27 May, which, as it happened, turned out to be our last seaborne contact with the naval base. *Glenroy* also sailed with troops for Tymbaki on the south coast, but was foiled by very determined Stuka and Italian torpedo bomber attacks on the 26th, and was ordered to return. At this point the Admiralty intervened directly and ordered her to turn back to Crete — no doubt at Churchill's urging. Cunningham, however, instructed her to ignore the order.[2] The *Abdiel* force by contrast, was more successful and, having discharged its troops, embarked excess Suda Bay naval personnel.

A friend, who had been evacuated in *Abdiel*, one of our new fast minelayers, the right type of ship for this type of work, told me the whole story of Suda Bay. Evidently the first parachutists were dropped a few miles inland from the bay. According to him, it was a weird sight as the transport aircraft flew right over the base, disregarding what few AA guns we had, and started to drop large numbers of men in multicoloured chutes which drifted away to the west towards Maleme, some ten miles away. Everyone began to feel very insecure that this should happen, right before their eyes, and that the seas around the island should be completely bypassed.

NOIC and his staff spent a lot of time in slit trenches from then on, as air raids were practically continuous. The twelve small local defence ships (minesweepers, motor launches (MLs), and motorized A lighters, the precursor

Formidable **being hit by bombs off Crete, May 1941.**

of tank landing craft, which could carry six tanks and had a bow drop ramp) were particularly vulnerable. Although they were hard to hit from the air, they had no metal protection plates on their superstructure like other warships.

My friend told an anecdote about Keith, who subsequently worked in the cypher office with me. A sallow faced individual, with heavy horn-rimmed glasses, he was always very friendly. He was born in Malta, and had studied for the priesthood in Rome for a time, and was a mysterious and colourful personality. He had been assistant secretary to NOIC and had the unwelcome job of disposing of secret documents by dropping them in weighted bags in the middle of the harbour from a small boat. Whilst performing this operation, a German plane began to approach. He rapidly jettisoned his load and the boat sped for the shore at full throttle, trying at the same time to avoid tracer rounds which splashed just behind it, as the plane thundered overhead.

By 26 May the situation on the island had suddenly deteriorated, despite the fact that our troops had fought very doggedly. They had put up a tremendous show but enemy air superiority had been our undoing. The Germans had now amassed sufficient land forces to put great pressure on us and showed every indication of breaking out from Maleme airport and advancing on nearby Canea and Suda Bay. In fact this happened the following day. The army's battle had been lost.

Fortunately on 26 May a quick decision by NOIC Suda Bay was made to pack up immediately and move south and the local ships and craft were ordered to make their way back to Alex as best they could. Only three survived; *Lanner*, a minesweeper, the South African KOS 21, and ML 1032. The remainder were sunk en route with heavy loss of life. Those crew members who could swim ashore were able to make their way south, with the help of local Cretans, and were eventually evacuated.

Captain Morse, NOIC, retreated south with the GOC Army, General Freyberg, a New Zealander, to Spakia, the planned evacuation port. Morse's secre-

German paratroops descending on Suda Bay Naval Base, Crete, 20 May 1941.

tary, Pay Lieutenant Dunn, survived the sinking of ML 1011, which was bombed off the south coast while trying to get a wireless transmitter to Spakia, and managed to make it back to Alex.

Meanwhile at sunrise on 27 May the battlefleet was about two-thirds the way from Alex to the Kaso Strait, waiting to give AA protection to the *Abdiel* and *Glenroy* forces that were heading south as fast as possible. Pridham-Whippell, the Admiral in command, had his ships disposed in line abeam (one beside the other), when the attack materialized, an odd disposition to take against an air attack. Normally for this type of attack, the ships were in line astern, ships one behind the other, so that all guns can be brought to bear on either side.

As the attack developed, *QE* again tracked the aircraft on RDF as enemy aircraft worked their way around the fleet. She signalled to *Barham* that *Barham* was about to be attacked. Suddenly three black dots were seen heading directly for *Barham* and were into their dive before they were spotted by their target ship. *QE* was already firing but there was no sign of retaliatory fire from *Barham*, which was missed by a few feet. Her old hull plates were ruptured, leading to heavy leakage in her bilges. Another bomb hit the thick two inch armour plate of her after 15-inch gun turret, actually penetrating it and exploding inside the gun-house killing the gun's crew and starting a fire. As the fire was brought under control, the ships were ordered to return to base, and so the naval battle to save Crete came to its inglorious end.

On the same day, 27 May 1941, General Wavell, the army C-in-C, informed Churchill that the Germans had driven our troops out of the Maleme area and the front had collapsed. The remaining 22,000 troops on the island would therefore have to be evacuated.

The last message we received from Suda Bay stated that the army was retreating to Spakia, on the south coast, where they would form themselves

C-in-C being piped over the side of *Queen Elizabeth* in Alexandria harbour.

into a defensive sector and wait to be picked up. It went on to give estimated troop strengths to be embarked both there and at Heraklion, A further message was promised but was never received. Thankfully, we now had enough information to start organizing the evacuation. NOIC's staff had done a good job.

During the battle, C-in-C, who normally slept at his residence in Alex, moved aboard his flagship *QE*, which had replaced the damaged *Warspite*. A number of times I was on cypher watch from midnight to eight in the morning and had the job of taking the night messages to C-in-C's sleeping cabin and waking him at half past six. It was a memorable experience to have to wake the most powerful man in the fleet at such an hour, especially as the news was always bad and he had had very little sleep the night before. I recall vividly that he slept with only his pyjama bottoms on, with a sheet over him which usually covered only half his body. He was usually difficult to arouse as he was dead tired. Normally two or three good pushes were required before he would awaken and slowly take the sheaf of messages with a peremptory "Thank you boy." He used to address every officer below lieutenant as "boy."

Obviously the first evacuation objective was Heraklion. This small port lay nearly midway on the north side of the island. To reach it, the evacuating ships would have to make a dangerous trip through the eastern Kaso Straits. They would have to be fast enough to get there and be back well south of the island by dawn, and big enough to take large number of troops. Three cruisers *Ajax*, *Orion* and *Dido* and six destroyers *Decoy*, *Jackal*, *Imperial*, *Hotspur*, *Kimberley* and *Hereward* were selected for this dirty job.

On the morning of 28 May, accompanied by everyone's blessings, they sailed once more toward the perilous waters north of Crete — waters which we would never enter again until the end of the war. They left the swept channel outside Alex at full speed, to be in the Kaso Strait by nightfall, twelve hours later. Rear-Admiral Rawlings was in command in *Orion*.

As expected, the force was bombed before it got near the Kaso Strait.

Imperial was near-missed and damaged, while *Ajax*, the old veteran of the River Plate, Matapan, and Greece, was badly shaken by a close miss. Her speed was reduced and Rawlings had to make the difficult decision whether to keep her for her fire power and transport capacity and reduce the speed of the whole force, or let her return home. This was one of many snap decisions, with terrible implications, that had to be made during that fateful twenty-four hour trip.

He decided on the latter course and at nightfall he sent *Ajax* back to Alex. The force pushed on and reached Heraklion safely by 2330 when the evacuation began smoothly. This was hardly surprising, since a similar evacuation had been carried out before in Greece by these very ships. Captain Mcdonald, NOIC Heraklion, a short stout man with a crop of white bushy hair from which he derived the nickname "Snowhite", had everything well arranged. He had been NOIC Suda Bay before the hard-driving Captain Morse had taken over. Mcdonald, in all the confusion, had to leave his wife and daughter behind with a family in Canea. It seemed incredible that an officer would have his wife and dependants on Crete with him in wartime.

The troops were drawn up in the darkness on the jetties in the small harbour, which was sheltered by a concrete mole. They squeezed into the two remaining cruisers and the six destroyers; most in fact were ferried by the destroyers to the cruisers, which couldn't get inside. In two hours, around 3,500 troops were embarked, NOIC and his staff being the last to leave.

The force then headed east at top speed towards the straits. The important factor now was speed so that by dawn it would be well through the straits. The RAF had finally agreed to provide air support with fighters equipped with long-range tanks which were due to be over the fleet at dawn.

Two hours out of Heraklion, still at night, *Imperial* began to give trouble. Her steering gear broke and she narrowly missed colliding with *Orion*. Signals between the flagship and the destroyer failed to elicit whether the gear could be repaired quickly. The Admiral was therefore faced with another difficult decision; whether to gamble on her ability to carry out repairs and catch up, or have the troops and crew transferred to another ship and sink her. He immediately decided on the latter and the force reduced speed whilst *Hotspur* went alongside and took off everybody, and then had the distasteful job of sinking her with torpedoes. All this because the steering gear wouldn't work! The frustration of the captain and crew, particularly the engineering department, must have been indescribable. The force's schedule had now been put back and it was not in the straits by the time dawn came up. The island of Skarpanto was actually in sight as they headed south.

Long before breakfast the attacks started and the sky was filled with Junkers, as one attack followed another. *Hereward* was hit, turned out of line and stopped. To sink or tow her would court disaster. She was therefore left to her own devices and was last seen firing her guns at hovering Stukas. I later heard that she beached herself on the south shore of Crete and that some of her crew and the troops aboard actually made their way to Spakia where they escaped.

The remaining force dashed on at full speed but still the attacks continued. *Decoy* was near-missed and had to reduce speed because of engine room difficulties. The force slowed down to 22 knots to accommodate her. *Dido* was then hit forward, and lost a 5-inch turret and its crew in a split second. Then the flagship *Orion* was holed by a near miss and forced to reduce speed. Shortly afterwards a bomb hit the bridge, mortally wounding the Flag Captain, G.R.B. Back, but miraculously missing the admiral. It didn't explode on contact but crashed through the deck plating, the plot room below, the recreation space, then the supply office, penetrating deck after deck, killing men on its way, until finally it exploded in the main storeroom. Captain Back was carried below and allegedly his last words before he died were, "It's all right men, that one's gone over."

There was a break then between attacks, and all damage control parties tried desperately to make good temporary repairs. The doctors and sick bay staff worked valiantly to tend the wounded and ease the pain of the dying. Then the very worst disaster occurred when a bomb struck *Orion* forward of the bridge. It completely destroyed the foreward 6-inch turret and penetrated into a mess deck which was crowded with soldiers, helplessly waiting and listening to the clamour of the battle above them. The carnage was indescribable. What was perpetrated by that one bomb in a single ghastly moment — 250 soldiers and sailors killed — remained a terrible memory in the minds of everyone in the fleet.

By now the force was on its knees and groggy from all the damage that had been inflicted on it. *Dido* was on fire forward. *Orion* was beginning to list, her forecastle enshrouded in a sickly, flesh-smelling mist and *Decoy* lay far astern on the horizon. Finally the attacks abated. Two Fleet Air Arm Fulmars had appeared on the scene, and the RAF fighters had been operating against the German aircraft far to the north and helping to break up further attacks.

At last the ships entered the safety of Alex, most of them just about out of fuel and ammunition. Several fellows from *Orion* whom I met seemed dazed and refused to talk about the trip. Hundreds of sailors and troops had apparently been killed and many more wounded. After *Orion* had been put alongside, her crew was sent ashore and the gruesome task of cleaning up the carnage was left to Egyptian dockyard workmen supervised by our medical staff.

With the troops from Heraklion now back in Egypt, the next task of the navy was to evacuate the troops now retreating from Maleme through the mountains to Spakia on the south coast. The retreat was proceeding faster than expected and messages from Captain Morse indicated that troops were already waiting to be taken off. Consequently, on the same night that troops were being evacuated from Heraklion, four destroyers of the 7th Flotilla, HMAS *Napier, Kandahar, Kelvin* and HMAS *Nizam* took off about 700 men, mostly wounded, at Spakia and returned to Alex. The flotilla was attacked once on the way back with HMAS *Nizam* receiving slight damage.

Although Spakia wasn't very suitable for evacuating troops, it was the best harbour available on the south coast. It was no more than a small fishing village which had only a small beach for grounding boats. As there was no jetty, our ships lowered their motor boats and whalers and the troops were ferried back from the beach. There was no proper road from the mountains behind it, only a winding track down a steep cliff. Fresh Royal Marines and Special Service troops which had been landed at the last minute, moved to the front and took the brunt of the fighting as the remainder retreated toward the cliff face.

For the night evacuation of 29/30 May 1941, a much larger force was put

Severely damaged HMS *Orion* after Crete trip in Alexandria harbour in May, 1941, during the Battle of Crete. Note missing A turret.

together. It comprised the cruisers *Phoebe,* with Rear-Admiral King aboard, *Perth*, the Australian ship, *Calcutta, Coventry* plus three destroyers and *Glengyle*. Six thousand troops were taken aboard without mishap. The assault ship *Glengyle* used her landing craft to speed up operations to a considerable extent. Air attacks were as strong as ever, but this time the RAF were able to put three Hurricane fighters in the air over the fleet after dawn. They must have got some reinforcements from England. These blunted the effectiveness of enemy air attacks to some extent and the terrible losses suffered by the Heraklion force were not repeated. However *Perth* was hit during the first of three raids and her forward boiler room was put out of action, thus reducing her speed. Nevertheless the force returned in one piece, the only other victim being *Glengyle* which was hit by a small bomb which inflicted only minor damage.

On 30 May, Major-General Freyberg and Captain Morse were flown out by a Sunderland flying boat leaving Major-General Weston RM, to command the rearguard. Also on this night, four destroyers HMAS *Napier*, D7, *Kandahar*, *Kelvin* and HMAS *Nizam* set out for a further evacuation. *Kelvin* was damaged by a near miss and had to return and *Kandahar* developed engine trouble and dropped out, leaving only two ships for the evacuation. However, the two Australian destroyers took off a record number of nearly 1,500 soldiers between them — mostly New Zealanders. Despite RAF and FAA fighter cover, the two ships were attacked by Stukas during the morning and afternoon. Army personnel onboard joined in the air defence with Bren guns mounted all over the ships. Finally *Napier*, the flotilla leader under Captain S. Arliss RN, came to a dead stop from a very close near miss. The engine-room staff got the ship going after an hour and the flotilla reached Alex by 1900 that day.

From the infrequent and disjointed messages that we were receiving it appeared that there was still around 7,000 soldiers patiently waiting in the hills behind Spakia to be taken off. Cunningham made another of his sharp messages to the Admiralty, setting out the situation and declaring that while he was perfectly prepared to lose the entire fleet in helping our gallant army, the time had come to stop the evacuation.

As a result it was decided to make one last trip to Spakia on the night of the 31st May before calling it a day. *Phoebe, Abdiel* and a few destroyers were sent. Not everyone could be accommodated and the scramble for a place on one of those ships must have been a pathetic sight. About 7,000 were brought away, but there were still hundreds left with orders that they should surrender at once. Rumours circulated that they had carried on fighting, poor devils.

Coventry and *Calcutta*, the two old stagers, were despatched to give this evacuation force AA protection the following morning as they headed south from the island for the last time. This day ended like all the others. At about 0900, before they made contact with the main force, they were attacked and *Calcutta* was hit by a stick of bombs fore and aft, and was aflame amidships. Both ships were not much bigger than destroyers and could not take too much punishment. Very quickly *Calcutta* began to sink and *Coventry* was forced to take off her crew before she did so. The rest of the force, however, returned without problems and *Coventry* got back without a scratch. Thus we had suffered our last loss of this sorry, unending operation.

Had it all been worth it? we frequently asked ourselves. Should we have pulled out right at the start and saved all these irreplaceable ships that were sunk and damaged? The Med fleet was now a forlorn shell of its former brilliant self. To carry on we now had two operational battleships, the old *QE* and *Valiant*; only two undamaged cruisers, *Phoebe* and *Coventry;* three more, *Naiad, Perth* and *Carlisle*, which required some repairs, and a few destroyers. In ten days of continuous intensive action we had lost three cruisers and six destroyers sunk and two battleships, one aircraft carrier, two cruisers and two destroyers seriously damaged. In addition to this we lost minesweepers, anti-submarine patrol ships, motor launches, other small craft and merchant ships. All these losses had been sustained with only a single Italian destroyer being sunk.

The two drydocks and all the repair facilities in Alex were crammed with unserviceable ships. Several had already sailed for their repair ports after being patched up. *Warspite* had gone to the west coast of the States, *Barham* had left for Durban and *Dido* for New York. The fleet anchorage was becoming more and more bare and would have been almost deserted if it weren't for the unwelcome presence of the French Vichy ships.

To add to this, we had also heard that the mighty *Hood* had been sunk with all but four hands in the North Atlantic on 24 May. Thank God, we also learned of the sinking of the *Bismarck* two days later. We all thought sadly of our midshipmen term-mates who were lost in *Hood*. Truly, it never seemed to rain but it poured.

Two salient conclusions emerged from this campaign. Firstly, that a purely airborne invasion could work and, secondly, that we had failed to appreciate how effective strong air power could be against naval forces operating in constricted waters without fighter protection. The Italian fleet, in typical style, had made virtually no effort to enter the battle of Crete. But, as it turned out, its presence was not needed. We wondered how long we would be able to maintain the status quo.

The main questions in everyone's mind at the time were: would the Italian fleet go on the offensive? Would Hitler strike out at Turkey, Vichy Syria and then Palestine and the Suez Canal? We could be outflanked from behind. At the time, Cunningham signalled the Admiralty, "The length of time that we hold the island of Cyprus is a matter entirely up to the enemy." It appeared that the battle of Crete was but a trifling prelude to a grim campaign to come.

But perhaps the situation was not as gloomy as we all thought. In his autobiography, Cunningham points out that had we been able to keep Crete, it would have been a great drain on our resources. We would have had to maintain an army and a strong air force on the island. However, he does concede that its possession would have eased our attempts to resupply Malta, which was so important for attacking enemy sea lanes to North Africa.

Moreover, the Germans apparently lost 22,000 troops in the battle for Crete, of which 5,000 were lost at sea, as well as 400 aircraft. Their crack paratroop division was decimated and what was left of it was never used again in an air assault. Because of their experience in Crete the Germans lost their enthusiasm for airborne operations.

The losses that the Germans received in the battle of Crete not only thwarted Hitler's designs on the Nile delta via Syria, but had a profound effect on his catastrophic attack on Russia. The German invasion of Russia was delayed for a month whilst their forces moved into Yugoslavia, Greece, and Crete, so that by the time the Germans reached Moscow in October, they couldn't take it because of the onset of severe winter conditions.[3]

Some experts since the war have also stated that the Germans made a bad mistake in not following up their victory in Crete by moving into Cyprus with new forces, which they could have taken. This they could have used as a springboard for attacks through Syria and Iraq. Others have pointed out that because of the terrible losses that the Germans suffered, Hitler agreed with Mussolini in mid-1942 that an air invasion of Malta should not be carried out.

After the battle, Cunningham offered to resign if the Admiralty and the Prime Minister had lost confidence in him. Soon after this, both the army commander, the great General Wavell, who had earlier driven the Italians to Benghazi but had been forced to divide his forces by sending troops to Greece, and Air Marshal Longmore, the air force commander, were both relieved of their commands. But Cunningham remained with his reputation intact, and all agreed he had done his best in the circumstances. The fighting qualities of his admirals, captains, officers and men throughout the battle had been beyond reproach, and despite everything he still had the confidence of the fleet.

One incident toward the end of the battle showed another side of the admiral which we seldom if ever saw, and this concerned the captain of the ill-fated AA cruiser *Calcutta*, Captain D.M. Lees. The incident took place in the headquarters operations room, the nerve centre of the battle. Captain Lees had just returned to harbour during the night and was summoned to the Ops room where he was ordered to take his ship out once more for the last evacuation. At the end of his tether, after many sleepless night, he threw a fit, berating Commander Power (Staff Officer Operations) in no uncertain terms. His men and his ship could go no further he said. Cunningham was in his offices next door and after hearing the outburst he called Lees in. Lees must have anticipated a dressing down. Instead, C-in-C quietly explained the situation to him so that he left with nothing but respect for his boss, determined to do his best. *Calcutta* went down the next day and Lees was picked up by *Coventry*. Cunningham, as was his habit whenever possible, met the returning ships once they were alongside, and it was with tears in his eyes that he greeted Lees on the quarterdeck.

CHAPTER FIVE

Egypt, Syria, and Cyrenaica

Life ashore in Alex was very different from the life aboard the old *QE*. This had to be one of the most interesting cities that I had ever been in and was certainly a place I had never expected to visit. Initially I was unhappy to leave the ship but as things turned out my move couldn't have been better.

Within hours of joining the HQ staff an RNVR lieutenant took me downtown by car to the Cecil hotel where I was to stay until I could get permanent digs. I was given a large bedroom with a comfortable bed and attached bathroom, certainly the most opulent accommodation that I had ever encountered. The board was no less impressive; a cold beer, potato chips — a new experience — and a four course lunch. The hors d'ouvres, borne to the table on a trolley, were a meal in themselves. I had never had such royal treatment before, and all on expenses I was assured.

The Cecil itself was on the seafront facing the ancient inner harbour, while the headquarters lay about three miles to the west in the newer, larger harbour. This outer harbour was about five miles long and sheltered by a long breakwater, whereas the old inner harbour was too shallow to be used by anything but small fishing boats. Each had separate sea entrances. According to the guidebook, when Caesar fought Cleopatra, he anchored his fleet in the area which later became the outer harbour, and attacked the Egyptian fleet in the inner harbour, across the thin strip of land which separates the two anchorages.

The new part of the city was most attractive, with large lawn-covered squares opening on to the seafront and surrounded by Edwardian stone buildings, all adorned with shutters, balconies and domes; a strange mixture of East and West. A magnificent concrete road, the Corniche, ran along the seafront. Toward the east it led to the European suburbs which had a mixture of good, solid apartment buildings and two- or three-storey houses. Here and there, however, cheap native housing had somehow intruded.

To the west lay the native quarter, large parts of which were out of bounds to service personnel. The famous *Rue des Soeurs,* Sister Street, ran through it and it was along this road we had to pass each day to get to the headquarters. The plastered square buildings on either side were nondescript yet pleasing, seemingly built at random on top of each other. At all angles and higgledy-piggledy, they protruded into the street. A few had interesting domes or balconies. Most had open fronts for various shops, small coffee houses and sordid looking bars. Egyptian men wearing the typical loosefitting cotton smock sat for hours at small coffee tables on the curbside chatting and drinking Turkish coffee, idly watching the world go by. The narrow streets of the district were full of the bustle of people, donkey- and horse-drawn carts, and hand barrows, intermixed with ancient motor cars.

Egyptian women wore black, but not all of them donned the veil. Unmarried women were distinguished by an ornamented string between their headdress and veil. They carried themselves well and were good-looking and had much more poise than the men. The more wealthy men wore natty pyjamas

73

Views of Alexandria in 1941.

instead of the smock. All of them seemed to have a good sense of humour and laughed at the slightest provocation. They did not appear to resent us, even though we had for all intents and purposes taken over their country. The middle and upper class Egyptians wore western dress topped off in many cases by a jaunty fez.

The city was a place of great contrasts; the contrast of great wealth and extreme poverty and the differences of the many nationalities — Egyptian,

English, French, Italian, Greek, Jewish and Armenian. The English and French and some Egyptians were the wealthiest. They frequented the two luxurious sporting clubs which had restaurants, golf courses, polo fields and race tracks. (All officers were automatically members of these clubs.) The Italians and the Greeks were mainly of the lower middle class. Their part of town was colourful, rather like the native quarter. The apartment which three of us subsequently rented was in this area.

The modern part of the city was like most other Western cities except for its Eastern influence. It had good shops, some excellent restaurants, and a

Piping the side on *Queen Elizabeth,* for King Ibn Saud of the Hejaz in Alexandria harbour in 1941.

number of crowded night clubs which we frequented. The Corniche was one of the highlights of the city. It ran eastward for miles past fine beaches, hotels, and seaside cafes. There wasn't the shortage of food that we had experienced in England. Everything was available. So, all in all, one could not have operated out of a better port anywhere in the world, despite the danger once we left the safety of Alexandria harbour.

At the west end of the Corniche, on a spit of land separating the two harbours, a magnificent summer palace had been built for the Egyptian king and was called the Ras el Tin palace — the name of the spit of land. It faced south toward the harbour and next to it was the yacht club. Beyond, to the west, on the remaining part of the point, were more buildings which housed *HMS Nile,* the offices of the admiral in charge of the port — Flag Officer Alexandria. The king's palace remained under Egyptian control. This strip of land had once been the island of Pharos on which the celebrated Pharos 400 foot lighthouse — one of the seven wonders of the world — had stood.

The city of Alexandria had a long history. It was founded by Alexander the Great in 332 BC. After his death one of his generals, Ptolemy, established an Egyptian dynasty which ruled until the Romans came in 80 BC. All the famous Greek buildings have long since disappeared — the famous library and Alexander's mausoleum.

Brought up on naval history, I wanted to see the locale of the Battle of the Nile. Napoleon landed near the city in 1798, but his fleet was bested by Nelson at Aboukir Bay. In the great tradition of the Royal Navy, Nelson wasted no time in attacking the French fleet at night, as it lay at anchor in the bay. I made a point of visiting the site which was at the end of the tramline from downtown Ramleh station. Not much was left on the land that overlooked the bay, where the battle took place, except sand, an old fort, and a small native fishing village.

Right from the start, my impression of the city was very favourable. It was friendly, safe and fascinating. Yet somehow it had a sad aspect which is hard

76

**Battleship HMS *Valiant* firing off her AA guns in Alexandria harbour
during night attack. Royal Fleet Auxillary ship (RFA) in the background.**

to put into words. Perhaps it was the extreme poverty in the native quarter or
the poor white part of the city. These white settlers put on a bold front, but were
really having a tough time making ends meet. Perhaps it was because there was
something odd about a large country having no control over its own affairs.
Britain had been given a mandate over the country in the last century, and had
retained virtual control ever since. For all that, the Egyptians were not our allies
and had displayed some degree of independence by not entering the war.

However, it was not long before the war came to Alexandria. Air raids from
high level German Dorniers started soon after we had cleared out of Crete. The
first were very light, but then they began to get worse. One night, Whiting,
another midshipman who shared my flat, and I were awakened at about four
in the morning by the sound of the fleet's guns to the west, followed by the
whining of bombs. This was indeed a heavy raid. We counted twelve bombs,
one of which landed closeby — we heard a fearful crunch as it landed and
exploded and our apartment building shook. In fact, it had landed in the next
street demolishing four decrepit houses but leaving the surrounding structures
and a small apartment building quite untouched. From what had happened
around us, the city must have suffered a considerable number of casualties.

Next morning, amazingly, it appeared as if the whole of the native quarter
was on the move. Sister street was bursting with streams of swaying carts
overloaded with mattresses, chairs, and all kinds of household effects. Angry
drivers cracked their whips and vied with each other for an opening. The
railway station was completely surrounded by lorries, cars, carts and long
lines of humanity. Open goods cars were being crammed to bursting point with
people. Notwithstanding the crush, there was a certain orderliness to it all.
Where would they be going? Presumably they must have been returning to
their villages in the Nile delta. The police did nothing to deter them. There
was no mistaking that they had had enough of air raids and that nothing would
change their minds, and we couldn't help but be amused by their reaction. The
damage suffered was infinitesimal compared with what we had received in the
English *Blitz*. By evening they were all gone, the main street and the narrow

The Vichy French Cruiser and Flagship *Duquesne* lying in Alexandria harbour with French destroyer alongside.

side alleys were empty. The enemy tried a few more raids, even carrying out a daylight attack, shooting up the Ras el Tin base. But twenty or more planes were shot down and the raids were stopped.

One of the interesting aspects about Alex was the presence of a Vichy French fleet comprising one battleship, *Lorraine,* four cruisers *Duquesne* (flagship), *Suffren, Duquay Trouin* and *Tourville* plus three destroyers and two submarines. They were immobilized and were not taking any part in the war. *Lorraine* lay at buoys near the west end of the harbour near the entrance, while the cruisers lay to the north, near to the outer mole, with the destroyers and submarines alongside.

This state of affairs had developed when France had collapsed and signed an armistice on 25 June 1940.[4] Before this, these ships under their commander, Vice-Admiral R.E. Godfroy, were part of an Allied fleet under Cunningham. The Admiralty was very concerned about their disposition when the armistice was signed. Messages were sent to C-in-C urging him to persuade the French admiral to throw his lot in with us or face the forcible seizure of his ships. C-in-C was also asked to comment on a similar action to be taken by Force H against the much larger French force at Mers el Kebir in Algeria. He replied that he opposed these moves; and pointed out that every effort should be made to work out a compromise without resort to violence. In the case of Alexandria, any forceful action was bound to lead to damage to our own fleet and could cause the French to scuttle their ships haphazardly around an already overcrowded harbour.

After these communications, the Admiralty directed that the French admiral be presented with three options. Firstly, he could continue the fight. Secondly, his ships could remain in harbour with skeleton crews. Or, thirdly, they should be scuttled outside the harbour.

Plans were made immediately to react to the three options and preparations were made to actually fire on the French ships as a last resort. On 3 July 1940 the French admiral was invited aboard *Warspite* and presented with the three alternatives.

Godfroy was quite cordial and commented on each proposal. He would have to obtain the approval of his government for the first (to fight with us) and he knew what the answer would be. The second (ships remain with skeleton crews) he preferred to the third (scuttle). However, he would have to clear the second option with his government. He was given until noon to reply. The negotiations needed to be completed as soon as possible, because Admiral Somerville, with Force H, had started discussions with the French fleet off Mers el Kebir.

Godfroy replied punctually, assenting to the scuttling of his ships. It was agreed by both parties that this should be executed within forty-eight hours. But Cunningham also wrote personally to Godfroy, making a last plea that the problem be resolved without the ships being scuttled. The French admiral had earlier implied that he didn't want to disembark his sailors immediately. It was therefore suggested that the French ships be defuelled, the warheads removed from all torpedoes, and the question of the removal of crews be discussed at a later date.

The French ships duly started to defuel into lighters, and the crisis was beginning to abate. However, the Admiralty, which had been kept abreast of all these developments, sent an urgent order to Cunningham to have all the French crews transferred from their ships immediately. The message ended with the words, DO NOT REPEAT NOT FAIL. C-in-C was none too pleased with this development, not least because it arrived during the night, was interfering and was patently impracticable. So he simply decided to ignore it.

Cunningham had also received a simultaneous note from Godfroy who had by then received news of the negotiations and threats from the British fleet at Mers el Kebir, and had also received orders from the French Admiralty to sail at once. This was not possible but Godfroy had stopped the defuelling operation and stated that he would still go ahead with the scuttling as he had previously agreed.

During the night things changed for the worse, when Godfroy heard of the horrible engagement between the British and French fleets at Mers el Kebir and the great loss of French ships and lives. He then despatched a note stating that, in view of events at Kebir, he was revoking all prior agreements.

When Cunningham went on deck early on 5 July it was obvious that the French ships were raising steam and their guns were cleared for action. Our ships were also ready. The battleships had been re-anchored so that all their guns could be brought to bear. However, no provocative actions, such as removing gun barrel covers were taken.

Cunningham, despite all his efforts at a sensible solution, now faced the prospect of a naval battle right in Alexandria harbour or, at the very least, of the French fleet scuttling itself. Events were unravelling like a Greek tragedy, with both commanders, despite their mutual respect, being subject to constraints beyond their control and helpless to arrive at a proper solution.

Cunningham, however, with his lively mind, would not give up. Either he or someone on his staff dreamed up the bright idea that a captain from a British ship should visit his counterpart on a similar French ship and try to talk him into agreeing to leaving the ships in Alex harbour with skeleton crews. This meant going behind the back of the French admiral, an approach, I am sure, that C-in-C probably found distasteful. Nevertheless in such an emergency something new had to be tried. The French were to be told that they were not betraying their country if they agreed to such a solution.

At times during that day it must have seemed that Caesar's battle with Cleopatra nearly 2,000 years before was about to be re-enacted. The atmosphere must have been tense on that hot clear Egyptian day, with the crews of all ships on alert, and no movement in the harbour except for the motor boats scuttling between the two fleets. Great meetings took place on the forecastles of the French ships as the matelots were informed and harangued by their officers and in turn put their own ideas across.

After lunch, the launches of French captains converged on the French flagship *Duquesne*. Finally, in the late afternoon, Godfroy visited Cunningham and after a very short meeting an agreement was signed. The French ships would discharge their fuel, their armament would be de-activated, and their ships' companies would return to France except for a skeleton crew. To the relief of all, the crisis was suddenly past and these ships remained put.

Godfroy remained with his ships until the bitter end. His was the classic story of an officer implicitly obeying the orders of his superiors to the letter no matter what he may have thought himself. Even after North Africa fell to the Allies in 1942, and Admiral Darlan, his naval superior, had thrown his lot in with us, Godfroy still refused to commit his fleet to the war. Presumably this was because the Vichy goverment still retained some semblance of authority in France, even though Germany had taken over the whole of the country in contravention of the original armistice.

Only after the fall of Paris on 25 August 1944, did he finally agree to recognize the authority of the new French government under General de Gaulle. By then he and his men had been in purdah for four long years. Crazy as all this appeared to us, he was, in his own estimation, only carrying out his orders as an officer and a gentleman. And in the same gentlemanly spirit, he would periodically despatch letters to Cunningham commiserating with his reverses and congratulating him on his victories.

The French officers and men of the skeleton crews kept to themselves. At one point, a Free French Commandant class sloop came into port and the shore patrol had more trouble dealing with fights between the Free French and Vichy French sailors than ever it did between Vichy and British sailors. The sloop was quickly transferred to another port.

There was very little respite for the fleet after the Cretan campaign, as it was thrust almost immediately into operations off Syria and to the supply of Cyprus, which was now open to German airborne attack. Whilst the operations in Greece and Crete had still been in progress, the Germans had been sending agents into Syria and Iraq to increase their influence there.

Iraq was under British control in much the same way as Egypt was but there was considerable nationalistic resentment and the local British garrison was very weak. The regent, ruling on behalf of the young king, was pro-British but was removed by the Iraqi army which installed the pro-German Rashid Ali as premier. By early June 1941, the Germans were flying supplies to the Iraqis and the hard-pressed British army in the Middle East was landed with the additional unwelcome undertaking of having to take firm control of the country. A makeshift air force of old planes from a training base near Baghdad, plus an army formation from Palestine and an Indian brigade, which landed at

Basra, very quickly subdued the Iraqis and the German designs were thwarted. The regent was restored and the country ceased to be a problem.

During the Iraqi episode, German aircraft were known to be using airfields in Vichy Syria. Before this, the British commanders had held that Syria posed no real threat and, in any event, the army had enough on its plate without further commitments. However, they were now being bombarded with messages from the Prime Minister and, something new, from General de Gaulle, who was urging that Free French troops be used to attack the colony. This didn't go down too well with the service staffs. However, after the Iraqi affair it was decided to mount an invasion. A Free French brigade, an Australian division, a cavalry brigade, and a Palestinian Jewish brigade attacked Syria on 7 June 1941. Orders were given to all forces not to open fire until the Vichy forces did so.

Rear-Admiral King once again returned to sea to go into action. He sailed on 9 June 1941 in his flagship, the cruiser *Phoebe* along with the cruiser *Ajax* and the destroyers *Kandahar, Kimberley, Janus* and *Jackal*. They were to provide support to another force, composed of the *Coventry,* the AA cruiser, and the destroyers *Isis* and *Hotspur,* which was escorting the landing ship *Glengyle.* The latter was to land Special Service troops north of Tyre in Lebanon. The landing was successful but the situation onshore was too confused for the cruisers to provide supporting fire. Consequently, they withdrew to the west leaving the destroyers on the scene.

Two French heavy destroyers now appeared and *Janus* closed immediately for the attack. The French destroyers were almost the size of cruisers, and were more heavily armed and faster than our destroyers. Thus *Janus* was quickly hit and severely damaged. Everyone on the bridge except the captain was killed. *Jackal* then laid a smokescreen to shield *Janus,* which was later towed away by *Kimberley* to Haifa. *Isis* and *Hotspur* now entered the fray with *Isis* cheekily flying Nelson's famous message, "Engage the enemy more closely." The cruisers now returned but the French destroyers retreated northward with their superior speed. This was not an auspicious beginning to the operation.

The French were determined to make a fight of it on both land and sea. Their determination prompted much bitterness, especially as their Alexandria fleet was well treated and they had no chance of winning. They also had submarines operating in the area as torpedoes had been sighted.

Fighting on land proved quite fierce and our troops did not make the progress that had been hoped for. Operations on the coast road to Beirut were particularly tough. Further troops were brought in from Iraq to strengthen the original forces and our units slowly began to close in on the capital, Damascus. On 15 June our destroyers bombarded French troops with the help of naval liaison officers attached to our army. By now we were also being attacked by German Stukas operating from Syrian airfields.

In further bombardment operations both *Isis* and *Ilex* were damaged. The cruisers *Naiad* and *Leander* — a newcomer — relieved *Phoebe* and *Ajax.* RAF fighter cover was much better than over Crete because operating distances were much shorter. Many of the German and Vichy air attacks were broken up and their airfields were being bombed, which was an improvement over Crete.

Moreover, a relief French destroyer sent from the south of France was sunk by Fleet Air Arm torpedo bombers operating from Palestine and our submarine *Parthian* sank a French submarine. There was also a brief eleven-minute action between our force and French destroyers early on 23 June during which two

French destroyers were hit, and retreated to Beirut behind a smokescreen. With the situation in the air now improving, we could have attacked the French ships in Beirut harbour, but refrained in order to avoid hitting civilian targets.

The Stukas were suddenly nowhere to be seen, having apparently been withdrawn. A momentous event had occurred on 22 June 1941 when the Germans invaded Russia. It made little sense to us that the Germans would do such a thing, but it was bound to take a lot of pressure off us. Indeed this became immediately evident in the closing days of the Syrian campaign. There were no further major naval actions except for the bombardment of French troops on the coast in support of our attack on Beirut. It was now only a matter of time before the French would surrender and on 9 July they sought a ceasefire and an armistice was signed on 15 July.

It had been an odd affair from start to finish with a number of our ships being severely damaged and many of our sailors being killed by our ex-ally. Certainly, we were unhappy with the actions of the Syrian French and there was much bitterness in the fleet. To add insult to injury, General de Gaulle at times had acted in an obstinate and unhelpful manner during the affair. Every day a message arrived from him about some issue that he wasn't happy with.

Matters came to a head after the armistice when he complained that our troops had ignored the Free French forces when they occupied a certain building. I suppose he was worried that we were going to take over Syria on a permanent basis.

What really upset him was that the Vichy commander didn't want the Free French to have anything to do with his men. Presumably the Vichy commander wanted to avoid a vindictive and vicious family quarrel. De Gaulle, however, wanted his officers to have a chance to talk to the French Syrian troops to get them to join his Free French forces. To make his point he suddenly withdrew his troops from British command, but this was ignored. In the end, all was sorted out, about a third of the Syrians came in with him and the country was taken over by a Free French administration. The area came firmly under Allied control and our rear was properly protected.[5]

As has been previously mentioned the army operations in the desert during this period had not being going well. When Italy declared war in June 1940 it had about 200,000 men plus tanks and aircraft in Tripolitania and Cyrenaica, considerably more than the British armed forces in Egypt, which amounted to three divisions of about 50,000 men.

After a stalemate at the Cyrenaican border, the Italian army moved into Egypt and took Sidi Barrani on 13 September 1940. General Wavell responded three months later by launching an exploratory counter-offensive on 9 December 1940, which turned into a rout for the Italians. Egypt was cleared by 15 December and 40,000 prisoners taken; Bardia fell on 5 January 1941 helped by a naval bombardment, and Tobruk on 31 January. By 5 February Benghazi had been cut off and the 10th Italian Army of 130,000 had been either killed or taken prisoner, with its commanding general and most of its divisional and corps commanders captured.

In February 1941 the German *Africa Korps* with its attendant tanks, motor transport and aircraft had moved into Tripolitania by air and sea to help the Italians. Its commander General Rommel took El Agheila on 24 March and a weakened British 8th Army, which had had to transfer troops, guns and aircraft to Greece, was again in retreat. The Germans bypassed Tobruk on 11 April

Old Italian cruiser *San Georgio* sunk by aircraft in Tobruk harbour in January 1941.

1941 and it came under siege. During the Crete campaign, Rommel had driven our army back to the Egyptian border. On 15 April, the Germans occupied the port of Sollum just inside the border and also a commanding point on the high escarpment south of it called Halfaya.

Here a stand was made by the 8th Army and the desert war now came to a standstill, with opposing armies reorganising after bitter fighting and heavy losses of men and material on both sides. Later Wavell conducted an unsuccessful three day battle called "Operation Battleaxe", using the tanks that we had brought out in "Tiger," in an attempt to relieve Tobruk. The situation remained the same all through the summer and autumn. After this action, General Wavell was replaced by General Auckinleck.

Throughout these events, a most interesting group of ships left and arrived in Alex. They were the ships of the Inshore Squadron which had been formed to support the army in the western desert. Its job was to bombard coastal towns and enemy concentrations, bring up and evacuate troops, supplies and armaments, provide AA protection for forward ports and take out prisoners of war.

They were an odd collection of ships, mostly of First World War vintage. The largest was the 8,000-ton monitor *Terror* designed to carry out lightning bombardments and get away fast. It was armed with two 15-inch and eight 4-inch guns as well as lighter armament. There were also four river gunboats, *Ladybird, Aphis, Gnat* and *Cricket*. They were queer looking ships, rather like barges with a small superstructure amidships and two thin funnels aligned beside each other. Quite small, being under 1,000 tons, they drew only a few feet of water and thus had very poor sea-keeping qualities. They had worked

San Georgio **later as a derelict after repeated bombings.**

in their earlier careers on most of the great rivers of the world, primarily in China. They bristled with an odd assortment of guns, two 6-inch and two 12-pounders plus several machine-guns. Also old V and W destroyers, built in 1916, and some fleet destroyers assisted as required.

In addition, there were a netlayer, the South African Southern class whalers, and four small Indian coastal passenger ships, commissioned as naval ships. Also sloops, corvettes, minesweepers and powered A lighters. Last and most interesting were the captured Italian steamer *Tiberio* and the more famous, ex-Italian three masted schooner *Maria Giovanni.*

Apart from these commissioned naval vessels, there were many small merchant ships — tankers, water carriers, coastal merchantmen and small coastal passenger ships, all of which played a big part in the operations. The planning and organization of this squadron bespoke close inter-service co-operation and imaginative staff work. Once again the inspired hand of Cunningham was discernable.

Long before I had arrived, the Inshore Squadron had already made a name for itself carrying out its duties in the see-saw desert warfare.

It had taken part in the capture of Bardia, Tobruk, Derna and Benghazi and the evacuation of most of them. It was during these operations that the Italian naval schooner *Maria G* was captured by the destroyer *Dainty,* on 1 January 1941, off Tobruk. She was pressed into service and had an active career ferrying prisoners and supplies between Sollum, Tobruk, Derna and Alex. Partially rearmed with Italian guns which had been scrounged from various ports, she was commanded by Lieutenant "Peddler" Palmer of the Royal Australian Naval Reserve (Merchant Navy Reserve). Subsequently she was officially commissioned into the Royal Navy.

Small though she was (200 tons and 180 feet long), she was immediately noticeable because of her appearance when she made one of her few visits at her berth near the main Alex landing pier.

Initially, the Inshore Squadron was immune from aerial attack, since the

Gunboat HMS *Gnat* leaving Bardia harbour.

RAF had caught the Italian air force napping and most of their aircraft had been destroyed. But the arrival of Rommel and his *Africa Korps* in the theatre in March 1941 changed all that for the army as well as the squadron. German air attacks on the desert ports were continuous and on a relatively large scale, particularly on Tobruk after it was besieged and our own fighter squadrons were moved east. The toll of ships then began to mount.

The minesweeper *Huntley* was the first to fall victim on 31 January 1941 as a result of an aircraft attack off Derna. The whaler *Southern Floe* was fatally mined off Tobruk on 11 February 1941 and *Terror* suffered damage from an air-dropped magnetic mine in Benghazi harbour on 22 February 1941 and sank after being bombed off Derna the following day (Benghazi was never used as a forward supply port because of enemy air attacks). The minesweeper *Ouse* was sunk off Tobruk on 20 February and four days later *Dainty* sank after a determined air attack near the entrance to Tobruk harbour, some of her survivors being rescued by the very ship she had captured some eight weeks before, *Maria G.*

The Italian schooner was the last ship to leave Derna, where she embarked the Indian troops who were the last of the rearguard. Later on 12 May, she played a gallant role in rescuing the survivors of *Ladybird,* the Tobruk AA guardship, a role she shared with other small craft including the army scow *Eskimo Nell.* During her career up until she was lost, eight out of her twelve man crew were killed. But the little ship was too small to be hit and she apparently accounted for several attacking Stukas. During the retreat the small Indian naval troopers, the *Fiona* and *Chakla* were added to the squadron's casualty list.

By the time I arrived in Alex the naval situation up the coast was very difficult, especially at Tobruk which was now surrounded and had to be supplied by sea. In addition to handling the messages for the Crete actions,

South African armed whaler HMSAS *Southern Floe*.

there were many that I saw concerning the Inshore Squadron.

At Tobruk the Germans had set up shore batteries which commanded the harbour entrance and made conditions even worse and meant that ships could only enter and leave the harbour during the silent hours. On 24 May a small convoy consisting of the 3,000-ton coastal freighter *SS Helka* escorted by the sloop *Grimsby* and the whaler *Southern Maid* could not enter the harbour because of a very bad sand storm which reduced visibility to heavy fog-like conditions. They were therefore ordered to move out to sea and come in the following night. This was not a pleasant option, given the closeness of the German airfields.

The next afternoon they were attacked by two large sorties of Stukas with supporting fighters. In the second attack *Helka* was sunk and *Grimsby* was hit and also sank. *Southern Maid* picked up and became overloaded with survivors from both ships. Fortunately she then received RAF fighter protection and was able to get into Tobruk.

A week later *Southern Maid* with the sloop *Auckland* (Royal New Zealand Navy) were able to get a coastal tanker, the *SS Pass of Balmaha,* into Tobruk despite heavy air attacks on the day preceding the night arrival.

Three weeks later on 22 June, *Auckland* was sunk in company with the Australian sloop *Parramatta* while once again escorting the *Pass of Balmaha* to Tobruk. The tanker was stopped in the water by a near miss and had to be abandoned off Bardia. The Australian destroyers *Waterhen* and *Vendetta* then came to the rescue, *Parramatta* returning to Alex with the survivors while *Waterhen* towed the *Pass of Balmaha* to Tobruk to offload another 750 tons of petrol. Nearly 100 enemy bombers and fighters took part in this attack. It was a miracle that all our ships were not lost. Our light AA guns were having some effect as a number of the enemy aircraft were shot down or damaged.

There was now a bomb alley from Sollum to Tobruk, a distance of seventy-

Sloop HMS *Grimsby*, her back broken and stern blown off, sinking off Tobruk.

Old destroyer HMAS *Waterhen* alongside naval dockyard in Malta.

five miles or five hours sailing at fifteen knots. Nevertheless, a good sized convoy was able to get through unscathed at the end of June. The sloop *Flamingo* and the whaler *Southern Isle,* with the gunboat *Cricket,* escorted two Greek coasters, *Miranda* and *Antiklia* to Tobruk despite numerous and determined enemy air attacks. Ships lowered their shell fuse settings to 1,000 feet and waited until the planes were well within this range before opening fire, to good effect. *Cricket* suffered damage to her engine room and her speed was reduced to five knots, but she made it to harbour. Amazingly, she was towed back to Alex by *Flamingo* without further damage. *Waterhen* was sunk off Bardia on 29 June.

As a result of these losses, it was decided to cut out daylight convoys and use tiny ships such as powered lighters or small motor ships, which were difficult to hit from the air. Fast fleet destroyers were to be used at night for the bulk of the work. Sailings for these ships were planned so they were not off the enemy coast in daylight. The distance between Alex and Tobruk is 300 miles and, proceeding at full speed most of the way, ships could leave Alex in the morning, be alongside at Tobruk by midnight for a quick one hour unload, and be back in Alex by noon the next day. Fleet destroyers could carry 60 tons of stores and 200 soldiers.

Petrol tankers were to be sent up on moonless nights. The very little ships were to work their way up the coast as best they could. Using this system, our losses were reduced considerably. But the situation around Tobruk remained hazardous. The destroyer *Defender* was sunk on 11 July 1941. The Luftwaffe had started a new tactic, attacking at night. They would pick up the phosphorescent wake of our destroyers and come in low from astern for their approach. This was how *Defender* was sunk. She was hit at 0300 on her return from Tobruk. *HMAS Vendetta* took off 275 troops and eventually her crew. She tried a tow but was ordered to sink *Defender,* which was in bad shape, after dawn came up off the enemy coast.

From then on the fleet destroyers played the biggest part in the movement of army personnel and stores. In August, September and October 1941 the 9th Australian Division and other Tobruk troops were relieved by the 70th British Division and a Polish brigade using the 14th, 10th and 2nd Destroyer Flotillas backed up by 7th and 15th Cruiser Squadrons and, in October the fast minelayers *Abdiel* and *Latona*. These operations were all of the fast overnight type. Thousands of troops, supplies and even tanks were transported in and out of the beleaguered fortress.

The cruiser *Phoebe,* at the end of August, was badly damaged by an aircraft torpedo but got back to Alex. On 21 October the gunboat *Gnat* had her bows blown off by a submarine torpedo off Bardia, but was towed back to Alex stern first by the Destroyer *Griffin,* luckily without mishap. She made quite a sight coming into Alex harbour. On 26 October *Latona* was bombed during a troop movement and seriously damaged. Her deck cargo of ammunition caught fire and began to explode and, after several hours, she sank. The destroyers *Hero* and *Encounter* were, however, able to take off her crew and the troops being transported. *Hero* was damaged by a near miss while alongside. On 23 November the assault ship *Glenroy* was torpedoed by a U-boat while transporting small lighters to Tobruk. She was beached near Mersa Matruh, repaired temporarily and towed back to Alex. Four days later *Parramatta* was sunk at night off Tobruk by a submarine while escorting the small cargo ship *SS Hanne.* Only twenty of her crew were saved — a tragic loss — but the *Hanne* got through.

Other ships lost or damaged were the other two little Indian packet ships *Chakdana* and *Chantala,* both sunk, the former by aircraft torpedo and the latter mined in Tobruk. *Maria G's* luck finally deserted her when she ran ashore in rough weather in enemy territory and her crew was taken prisoner on 22 November 1941. The sloop *Flamingo* was damaged by aircraft in December 1941. In this month also *Tiberio* capsized in rough weather off Mersa Matruh after her cargo shifted. The trawlers *KOS 21,* the whaler *Thorbryn* and the little minesweeper *SKUD III,* manned by Newfoundlanders, were all sunk in Tobruk harbour or nearby.

However, a great many of the other little ships, both warships and merchantmen survived the 242 day siege until it was lifted on 9 December 1941. General Auchinleck, who had relieved Wavell had launched "Operation Crusader" and had driven Rommel and his army back from the Egyptian border in a series of brilliant thrusts, starting on 18 November 1941. After this, Tobruk was supplied by rail to Mersa Matruh and thence by road.

Sometime after this, I met a young Canadian sub-lieutenant, Don McGill at the Monseigneur night club. He told me that he had some cartons of Canadian *Sweet Caporel* cigarettes and I went back to his rooms and he gave me one.

McGill had been sent to England in 1940 with 149 other Canadian officer candidate sailors, to be trained by the RN and serve in their fleets. He had travelled around the Cape of Good Hope in the cruiser *Galatea*, arriving in Alex in March 1941.

He was immediately transferred to the South African whaler *Thorgrim*, operating out of Mersa Matruh, to replace an officer who had been killed on her in an air attack in Tobruk. He joined her in early April 1941 and stayed in her until the end of the year. Tobruk had just then come under siege by the Germans, so his ship was soon escorting small convoys to the beleaguered fortress.

He had been well treated in *Galatea* and loved the ship and its crew. *Thorgrim* was another story. He travelled by rail from Alex to Matruh in an open touring carriage filled with Arabs. There was no-one at the railway station to tell him where the ship was moored. He finally found out that the little port was half a mile away on the coast. After lugging his baggage across the hot desert, he finally arrived onboard.

The captain and first lieutenant were asleep and couldn't be roused. The coxswain told him, as they weren't available, he would have to take the ship out for a harbour night patrol. This he did reluctantly with the help of the coxswain.

It wasn't an auspicious start and for some reason that he didn't understand, for the rest of his time aboard, neither the captain nor the first lieutenant were very friendly to him. Neither of them would talk to him. So what with the hazardous trips and the inhospitable atmosphere onboard, it was not a happy time for him.

The engineer officer, a Norwegian, fortunately was friendly and he met some congenial South African Naval Division types serving in the *Southern* whalers. *Thorgrim* was manned by Lowestoft trawlermen. She was armed with a 4-inch gun and two old Lewis machine guns on either side of the bridge. She had a maximum speed of 10 knots.

Mersa Matruh was a small narrow harbour protected by a half mile long sandbar. It was located on a sandy flat desert area with the craggy dry hills of

Sub-Lieutenant Don McGill, RCNVR.

the Libyan Plateau visible twenty miles inland. About six or seven small vessels were alongside small jetties with the usual white flat roofed buildings ashore.

He took part in a number of dangerous trips to Tobruk. The small convoys going there usually consisted of one or two self-powered A-lighters with the *Thorgrim* herself sometimes towing a flat bottomed barge. On some occasions, other small ships were in company, such as the *Maria Giovanni*. The ships would be heavily loaded with personnel, ammunition, food, water, military stores and drums of fuel.

The distance between Matruh and Tobruk is 200 miles, so, at four to five knots, the one way trip took about two days. A course would be laid to keep close to the coast during the early part of the voyage to cut down on the range of the air cover fighter aircraft. Once they got near the army front line near the Egyptian border, the convoy would turn northwest. Bardia, which was near the direct course across the Bay of Sollum, was given a wide berth.

They were almost always attacked by Stukas and other types of German bombers during the daylight hours. Air protection was provided by RAF Hurricane fighters for most of the voyage. Usually the Stukas were escorted by ME 109 fighters, which were faster than the Hurricanes. However, our aircraft put up a good fight and great air battles were fought over them. Once they rescued a downed German pilot. The captain had to be restrained from kicking him, as he was dragged aboard. On one occasion they picked up two Canadian pilots, serving with RAF 33 Fighter Squadron. One of whom McGill knew from London, Ontario.

Whilst these air attacks were terrifying — once a bomb missed the ship by twenty feet — *Thorgrim* lived a charmed life, surviving while other ships were being damaged or sunk.

The conditions on arrival in Tobruk were worse. Sailings were timed so that the ships arrived at night. This was because the Germans had a long range gun, which was dubbed "Bardia Bill" which commanded the port area during the daylight hours.

Trips were planned so that arrival was around midnight, to avoid air attack and shelling. A careful night landfall had to be made to pick up the small green entrance light.

There was also the possibility of running onto moored, magnetic or acoustic mines laid by German or Italian submarines or aircraft. Although the little minesweepers of Tobruk nightly cleared the channel. Ships couldn't move during the day because of Bardia Bill.

Once inside *Thorgrim* would proceed alongside a wrecked Italian troopship, the *Liguria*, sunk during the Wavell push, which lay near the shore nearly a mile up-harbour, not far from the port shore facilities. Navigation in the harbour at night was difficult because there were 65 wrecked ships strewn around it.

Then army harbour boats would come alongside to start the unloading. Once unloaded, the ship would take on the wounded, personnel and equipment needing repair, for passage back to Matruh.

The army 35 foot *Eskimo Nell*, an old fish boat without a mast, usually looked after the ship. Unloading and loading took time and the ships were forced to stay over during the next day whilst it was completed. The larger more valuable destroyers were given higher priority. There were no usable jetties so everything had to be transferred ashore by barge.

The first job of the army crew was to cover the ship with camouflage nets. These were moved as the unloading and loading progressed.

When daylight came, the shelling and air attacks would start and the *Liguria* was always one of the enemy targets. Like stories from World War One, the Germans fired Bardia Bill at certain set times during the day.

On one trip, a shell hit the other side of the *Liguria* from where *Thorgrim* was tied up. Miraculously nobody on *Thorgrim* was killed or wounded. Another time, when McGill was on deck, the ship was attacked by dive bombers. The army types made a head first dive for the small forward hatchway of *Eskimo Nell*, and two of them got stuck. The legs and bottom of one was sticking upwards out of the deck, adding a humorous note to a difficult situation.

They never heard the whine of approaching shells if they caused a near miss, but would hear them if they landed far away. Thus confirming the theory that if you heard a shell coming it wouldn't hit you.

There were several Canadians serving in the little ships of Tobruk. They got together from time to time. Lieutenant Mac Ruttan, in the Norwegian whaler minesweeper *Skud V*, painted "Tobruk Division, RCNVR" on the side of *Liguria*.

By midsummer 1941, the harbour AA defences at Tobruk were beefed up to the point where enemy air attacks, particularly from the Stukas, were not quite so bad, but the shelling continued.

McGill says that war correspondents Ronnie Noble of the BBC and the American Larry Allen of Associated Press, came aboard to do a story. It happened that this was the one time that they weren't attacked. On the return leg, the newspapermen were getting so frustrated that they prevailed upon the captain to cooperate so that they could take some phoney photographs. It was explained that they would be used with true stories picked up from the crew.

Depth charges were dropped and some oil thrown into the water to indicate that a submarine might have been sunk. Also the little German aircraft models

Downed German Stuka aircraft.

which were kept onboard for aircraft recognition training were hung by thin wire above the bridge so that they looked as if they were attacking the ship.

As well as air attacks there was also the risk of being attacked by a U-boat. *Thorgrim* carried no asdic. Several barges enroute to Tobruk were sunk by gunfire from a surfaced submarine.

One of the first operations McGill took part in, was a Commando raid on Bardia on the night of the 19/20 April 1941. *Glengyle* accompanied by cruisers and destroyers landed the attackers. The purpose of the raid was to blow up bridges and supply dumps and beat a hasty retreat. It was hoped that this would put a scare into Rommel, who was then attacking at the Egyptian border, and force him to divert frontline troops to defend his rear.

It probably did achieve this to some extent. However, it was not much of a success as the landing craft went to the wrong beaches, no garrison was found there and there were no major supply dumps to blow up. The force withdrew with no troop casualties or ship damage, although, through a mix-up, a few men were left behind.

Our total losses from the time that Tobruk was taken on 22 January 1941 to the time that it was relieved in December 1941, were two destroyers, one monitor, one minelayer, three sloops, one gunboat, seven small anti-submarine vessels and minesweepers and seven small supply and transport craft. In addition many other vessels were damaged.

HMAS Vendetta put in the greatest number of runs to Tobruk- thirty-nine. One sailor Able Seaman Brien RAN did forty-six runs — thirty-nine in *HMAS Vendetta* and seven in *HMAS Napier,* probably the greatest number by anyone.

Most books published since the war agree, in retrospect, that the defence of Tobruk was a worthwhile undertaking. The garrison from Tobruk was able to play a part in "Operation Crusader" by moving out from their fortified perimeter to help the main forces in driving back the Germans and Italians. Rommel must have been concerned about the threat posed by Tobruk to his lines of communications, and this must have been a constraint on his plans. In fact the Germans were planning an attack on Tobruk when Auchinleck started "Crusader," and were caught completely off guard.

From the point of view of the navy, one wonders whether it was worth it. But in the end, at Churchill's urging, Tobruk had become a psychological rallying point in the dark days of 1941 when we needed any kind of achievement to cheer us up.

CHAPTER SIX

Desert Trip

After the whirlwind naval operations from January to June 1941 focusing on Greece, Crete, Malta, and the Syrian campaign, things began to settle down a little. Both sides had run out of steam and needed a well-earned rest. The desert front had now stabilized at the Egyptian border so that our only major job was to ensure the supply of Tobruk.

With the build up of the German air forces in Sicily, Tripolitania, Cyrenaica and Crete, our ships were kept out of the central Mediterranean and convoys to Malta were run only from the west. This was a much safer route because the whole of North Africa in that area came under Vichy control, whereas in the east we faced enemy air attacks from north and south within twenty-four hours of leaving Alex.

In July, a successful convoy was run from Gibraltar to Malta and our contribution was to create a diversion by sending the battle fleet, comprising *QE* and *Valiant* plus cruisers and destroyers, to sea. They were out for three days but had no contact with the enemy. A similar diversionary exercise was carried out in September, when nine merchant ships were passed from Gibraltar to the island. This time *Barham* was added to the fleet, having recently returned from South Africa where she had undergone repairs.

C-in-C was now flying his flag in *QE* with the staff still using the Gabbari dock buildings. After three enjoyable months on staff ashore, I was transferred back to *QE* at the end of August.

In September I had the good fortune to run into a friend of mine, a midshipman with whom I had taken the course at Dartmouth. We called him Frankie, short for Frankenstein, because of his thin professorial face and his heavy glasses. When the class broke up we had gone our separate ways and I hadn't seen or heard of him until the day I bumped into him on Rue Cherif Pasha. He was gazing at a bookstore window, looking very serious and totally absorbed, a major achievement in the hustle and bustle of Alex. I had to jog his arm before he looked up in utter amazement. After suitable felicitations, we repaired to the nearest cafe and exchanged news. He had just come around the Cape from England and was awaiting appointment to a ship. After some further talk he produced a yellow guidebook, and declared his intention of journeying into the desert to visit some amazing ancient ruins one Sunday afternoon.

Some weeks later I bumped into him again. Over the finest pastries in Alex at Pastroudis tea shop, he regaled me with the story of his desert trip. At Burg el Arab, on the Mersa Matruh road, he had met a lonely professor who led a hermit's life in a tiny village completely unconcerned about the war. Frankie had found him most engaging, especially as he had told him about the various ruins that were located all over the area. A visit to them would be much more fun, Frankie said, than the usual run ashore. Here I disagreed with him. How could the desert, with its dust and heat, surpass Alex? It had everything for a break from work. An afternoon game of golf could be had at the French club or a swim on the seafront, followed by an excellent, inexpensive dinner at one of many first-class restaurants. Then to round off the evening a couple of drinks could be ordered at the Monseigneur Club while watching the floor show.

But attitudes change and the next time I met Frankie I was ready for something new. The lull in the fighting was still on and the battlers only went to sea every month or so on diversionary forays. The first romantic impressions of Alex were beginning to pall. In this state of mind I was easy prey for Frankie and his fertile plans. He was charged up for a new venture and had decided on a bumper mummy hunt, to break the monotony. I countered, rather half-heartedly that while I was willing to try anything, an extended desert drive in a suspect second-hand car was a peculiar form of relaxation. But Frankie finally prevailed.

We would set off the following Sunday, providing both our ships were in harbour. He already had a stalwart recruit from his ship, and I was to enlist another friend. One important point was left unresolved. Could I drive? I murmured vaguely about having had a little experience, but preferring that someone else do it. Then I remembered the perfect candidate. Edery, a fellow Paymaster Midshipman, who had boasted to me once or twice about his driving prowess.

The following morning I approached Edery whose real name was Henry Tyndall. He got his nickname when, as a small boy afflicted with a heavy cold, he had been asked by the schoolmistress to state his name. Edery he replied. Funnily enough, the nickname stuck. He was a bit of a workaholic who hardly ever went ashore. From nine in the morning until evening he could be found in the captain's office wading through paperwork. He liked to give the impression of being overworked and a martyr to the war effort, but a lot of the time he was really having a yarn with someone. He gave me the old line that he was far too busy, but I countered that he needed relaxation to restimulate his efficiency and that he could do all the driving. That night he informed me he would come.

Finally the great day dawned. The weather was beautiful, as is always the case in Egypt. In Alex, for example, it was never too warm, rain fell about once every three years and it never froze in winter. At Divisions that morning I was happy in anticipation of the trip despite a slightly sarcastic comment by the captain about the meagre attendance by the Accountant Division, most of whose members were on weekend leave.

I hadn't seen Edery all morning and finally located him in the captain's office. He assured me that he would be ready. Knowing him and seeing the number of people waiting to speak to him, I had my doubts.

At 1115 I was waiting patiently on the quarterdeck. No sign of the redoubtable Edery, of course. The junior officers were already moving down the gangway into the picket boat. I continued to wait but soon the senior officers were moving down, so in a state of some agitation I had to follow them down quickly and without creating a stir. Then with its usual roar and vibration the picket boat moved away from the great ship. Then, and only then, did Edery come rushing across the quarterdeck and watch us depart. What a fine start I thought, leaving without the most important member of the party.

Frankie was undisturbed at the news when I finally got aboard his ship, a Dido class cruiser, after having visited practically every other ship in the fleet.

Sunday forenoon is officers' visiting day in the navy and juniors must wait upon the needs of their superiors. I was introduced to the other member of the expedition and we repaired to the wardroom for a beer and to wait for Edery. Sure enough, it wasn't long before his beaming visage appeared around the door and we could proceed. Frankie produced some bulky sandwiches and we boarded a motor boat which was waiting for us at the quarterdeck gangway. Clearly a midshipman got much better treatment on small cruisers than on a flagship.

This favourable impression soon proved illusory, since we were soon being gassed by the engine as we sat in the after cabin. Smoke seeped through from the floorboards and oozed from underneath the leather seat cushions. Frankie and his shipmate appeared unconcerned, saying that this was quite normal. Once ashore, we cleared our lungs, chose the least dilapidated looking taxi and sped downtown. With many directions from Frankie in broken Arabic (he was the supposed interpreter of the party), we arrived at a dirty garage up a narrow sidestreet.

The scene before us was far from promising. Lying in the dimness of the garage lay an ancient Ford V8 along with some other derelict cars. A wizened old man with one eye came out and immediately went into a huddle with Frankie. Edery, looking, I thought, a trifle nervous, got into the driver's seat and began to tinker with the controls. Frankie seemed to be making no headway with the proprietor so we all moved into the office to give him moral support. The old boy apparently was asking for more money than had been originally bargained for. Then he quickly reverted to his original offer—two pounds to hire the car for the day and a three pound deposit. It was all just a case of honouring the ancient Egyptian practice of bargaining, with all the teasing and argumentation that went with it. That settled, we all squashed into the car and prepared for take off.

Edery, still looking anxious, gingerly tried the starter, but to no effect. Only now were we informed that there was no petrol in the tank. Out we piled while the tank was filled, and Frankie forked out the necessary additional shekels. Back we climbed into the car and the engine roared into life, with the car rattling ominously and the old proprietor shaking his head. Edery then confessed that he had had only fifteen minutes experience' driving a car. That gave rise to gales of laughter as none of us had had much more ourselves. Continue, we cheerfully told him.

Edery then let out the clutch and the car began to back into the garage. In desperation he switched the engine off. This didn't seem to bother the old man one bit as he kindly came over to the car and showed Edery the various gearshifts. Evidently the American gearshifts differed from their English equivalents. Edery's nervousness mounted and with despair in his voice he began to express doubts about his ability to drive, particularly in the crowded Alex streets. The engine again burst into life. This time Edery released the clutch too quickly and we shot out into the street, watched by two wide-eyed Egyptian children dressed in their best with their little fezzes and pressed white shorts. Anticipating the worst, they had stood back well out of the path of these mad foreigners.

And so it went. Edery was learning to drive in the hardest possible way, in the crowded, bustling streets of Alex. For the first fifteen minutes the occupants of the car were unnaturally silent. In breathless apprehension we sat as Edery almost pinned an unfortunate local against a wall, narrowly escaped being squashed between two streetcars and held up a MT convoy of army vehicles in Mohamet Ali square whilst he extricated himself from a wrong turning. He kept stalling the engine until a kind Egyptian came over and showed him how the gears worked. This advice, which had not been solicited, seemed to give Edery renewed confidence and he gradually started to get the hang of things as we drove past C-in-C headquarters at Gabarri Dock and headed for the desert to the west. Leaving the fleet at anchor behind us, we passed Lake Maryat, the inland lake behind Alex, and came to a fork in the road at Mex, a small seaside suburb in front of the airport.

Past Mex, the road was deserted except for the occasional army truck or snail-like MT convoy. Soon we came to large fenced-off enclosures which contained line upon line of old lorries. There were English lorries, South African lorries, American trucks and even Italian and German lorries. These enclosures stretched for several miles along the road. More interesting was the enclosure full of about 200 enemy tanks. Among them were a few Churchills and Honeys, battered but proud guardians of a vanquished enemy.

Edery pressed on the accelerator and we began to make good speed down the highway. Someone remembered the sandwiches and, after some debate, we ate them because Frankie insisted that there wasn't time to stop for a picnic. Then we came to a split in the road where there was a small tent, from which a dusty South African MP came out and waved us to a stop. Weatherbeaten and with a leathery face he asked us where we were going. We laughed nervously as we told him. He smiled and pointed down the coast road—the other one which turned inland went to Cairo.

We hadn't got much farther when we hit another checkpoint. This time a turbaned bearded Sikh accosted us. "Identification cards, please," he said. We were all in tropical white uniform with shoulder rank badges, but he was not to be deterred from carrying out his orders by the book. "Where you go?" he added. Edery grandly replied "Tobruk." Unimpressed, the Sikh unsmilingly allowed us to proceed.

The landscape now began to pan out into flat, unending, hot desert, with the coast road clinging to the Mediterranean Sea which sparkled in the sun in a blue strip to our right, its colour contrasting strikingly with the sand and the washy tinge of the sky. Sand dunes covered the coastal fringe and Frankie explained to us how they shifted constantly with the wind. You could see where the wind had blasted lines and symmetrical indentations into them. The scene was very much as we had expected. A few palm trees dotted the roadside and, except for some unhealthy looking brush, were the only sign of vegetation.

Every so often remains of stone buildings partially buried by sand would appear. These had once been part of a chain of lighthouses built at the time of the great Pharos lighthouse. They were used for lookouts and ship navigation. Warning towers for invasion were not so original after all! There were few signs of human life apart from the occasional Bedouin encampments with their tents and motley collection of goats tethered nearby. The tents were astonishingly small, being only about two or three feet above ground. This was undoubtedly the lowest standard of living that I had ever seen.

A large hill appeared now to our left, capped by a substantial structure; the ruins of the temple of Osiris, Frankie informed us, hurriedly thumbing through the guidebook. We learned that these were the oldest ruins that we were ever likely to see in our lives, 600 BC. The place was called Abusir and had once been an important town. According to the ancient census of the Libyan Nome, the region was noted for the quality of absinthium marinum, which had been much employed in the worship of Isis.

Not being much the wiser, we parked the car and got out to inspect the ruins. There were a few remaining foundations, some battlements that must have been built at a later date, and a winding staircase which led nowhere. Except for the antiquity of the place, it hardly warranted a stop. I remembered being much more impressed by a Norman church in southern England which dated to 1080 AD. At least there you could see the complete church, but here very little was left.

Some native boys mysteriously appeared with a collection of Roman coins which they wanted to sell. Frankie was in his seventh heaven as he pointed out the images of various Roman emperors and the other interesting markings. The price seemed reasonable — probably a bargain for such ancient treasures — and after some haggling we each bought one. An old man with a black skullcap and yellow bloomers invited Edery into his house, which was about five feet square and patched together out of old, flattened army petrol cans. Initially keen, Edery was about to enter when the man put out his hand, and not quite certain what the gesture was for he decided to withdraw.

We pressed on and soon reached a sideroad which turned south into the desert. This, Frankie assured us, led to the village of Burg el Arab. It wasn't long before we came to the village. But this was no native village. Instead we found a stuccoed, two storeyed house surrounded by a wall. It was quite large, with Tudor beams built into the stucco and French doors opening out on to a courtyard. It reminded me of the attractive old high street alms houses in southern England, and looked like nothing so much as a misplaced prop on a Hollywood set. Perhaps it was the proverbial mirage?

Nothing so romantic. This was the house of the professor and had been built after the last war by some of the many Arab soldiers who were unable to get jobs. Keen as we were to visit the professor, Frankie insisted that we must press on to the ruins of St. Menas, the ancient site that he wanted to visit.

A few miles farther we encountered an army petrol dump, which could not have been more convenient as our petrol gauge was wandering between half-full and empty. Encouraged by a big sign which read "Army Petrol Store - Check your supply", Edery politely asked the sentry if we could fill up. A sergeant then appeared from a tent sunk deep in the sand. He seemed overjoyed to see us and could not have been more obliging.

"You want some petrol, sir?" he said. "You've come to the right place. If there's anything that I can do for the navy, it shall be done." In between rousing his subordinates to action, he went on to tell us that he had been evacuated from Dunkirk in a destroyer.

This particular dump was large and well camouflaged against enemy air attack. The cans of petrol were stored in long, wide six feet deep ditches which were covered with a corrugated iron roof piled high with sand. Each storage area was spaced well apart from the next, to minimize bomb damage. The place was extremely isolated and the sergeant complained that no one ever called there because it was too far behind the front line. It was presumably built in case of a retreat, which was a disturbing thought.

He was obviously overjoyed at the prospect of company, and pressed us to come to his mess for cigarettes and chocolate. We could hardly turn him down. So we drove off in a cloud of dust, leaving the sentry to continue his watch in the broiling sun. The enemy had bombed the railway not far up the line that morning, we were told but so far, they had not discovered the dump.

The mess was located past a few flat roofed huts near the small railway station of Bahig. Here we were on the famous Alex — Mersa Matruh railway which had saved us so many headaches in supplying the desert army.

We accompanied the sergeant into a small stone building, which was cool and scrubbed white inside. Our attention was immediately engaged by a strange moaning noise coming through a tiny barred window at the back. These, it transpired were the sounds of mourning of the family of the village headman, whose wife had died three days earlier. We looked through the tiny window and saw him and his daughter squatting on the dusty ground with their heads between their arms."Depressing, isn't it?" the sergeant said. "They've been at it ever since she died. Why they have to keep doing it right outside here I'm buggered if I know."

"He's not a bad old boy," he added with some concern, "and his daughter, well." He raised his eyebrows and grinned. They seemed to be rather overdoing it and I am afraid to say we all laughed.

The sergeant then presented each of us with a carton of Victory cigarettes. After thanking him, we were off on our travels again.

"What a hell of a spot to be based," said Edery, summing up the thoughts of all of us. Yet by Western Desert army standards they were probably fairly well off.

Bumping across the railway tracks we pushed on south into the open desert. From now on there was no road, just level firm sand as far as the eye could see. Where the hell was Frankie taking us? We all wanted to know if he really knew how to get to this ruined site miles off in the desert. Stories of how even experienced 8th Army men had got lost passed through all our minds.

However, Edery, bless his heart, now came into his element, thinking he was a rally ace. Without roads to cramp his style he pressed his foot down hard and pushed the old car to its limit. Bahig was soon no more than a dot on the horizon astern of us. With gay abandon he zigzagged and drove around in circles. Frankie was quite unconcerned, and pointing to the map at the end of the guidebook — not the most accurate chart to be using in the desert — assured us that we had only about ten miles to go.

Then a real live camel caravan hove into sight over the horizon and we closed to inspect and prepared to give broadsides. On closer inspection, it wasn't quite as impressive as we had first thought; just two mangy camels and a donkey. The Arabs on these animals seemed unimpressed and, without even a nod, bumped on uncomfortably by. Not a proper caravan, true, but something that we could boast about in the mess.

By now there was nothing but desert all around us, relieved only by a few hardy bushes dotted here and there. We were a little unsettled by this development, especially as we didn't have a compass. Then Edery, who had been scanning the horizon for the ruins, cried out that he could see a V formation of aircraft flying low towards us. We turned and looked and, sure enough, they were flying straight for us.

"Christ, they could be German. I think I can see the German markings on them," Edery cried, turning away from them and increasing speed. What should we do? Carry on regardless, or stop the car and start digging slit trenches? While this debate was still raging the planes turned north and headed for the sea.

Hugely relieved, Frankie next explained to us the background of the ruins that we were going to see — if we ever found them. They were the remnants of an ancient Christian shrine commemorating a Roman soldier, St. Menas, who had been born in Egypt. Whilst serving in Phrygia in what is now part of Turkey, he had openly declared himself a Christian. He was tortured and beheaded in 296 AD and his body was returned to Egypt. According to the guidebook, a legend existed that the camel that was carrying his body refused to budge at an oasis en route and the body had to be buried there. Later, when Rome became Christian under Constantine, the place became a shrine to the martyr. A large church was built as well as a small town, and pilgrims came to take the waters from the oasis well. They would purchase ampullae — small, beautifully designed pottery bottles — which contained the holy water. These ampullae, inscribed with a head or figure of the saint dressed as a soldier have been found all over the Mediterranean. Later the shrine was despoiled by the Ottoman Turks and was abandoned. It was rediscovered and excavated by a German archaeologist, Kaufman, in 1905.

At long last we sighted the ruins in the distance to the south. As we approached them there seemed to be some signs of life there. We could see an old man pushing a medieval wooden plough which was being drawn by an equally ancient ox. Why on earth anyone would try farming in this inhospitable desert was beyond us. But our thoughts were cut short, for the old man had, upon seeing us, hurriedly left his plough and grabbed, of all things, a gun. We were game for most things, but this was too much. Edery quickly stopped the car so that we were not too close and we did the by now routine "looking at one another" act again. Frankie, our leader, gingerly got out of the car on the opposite side from the old man. Happily, he wasn't too truculent and approached the car with his gun pointing down in the traditional manner, and a big smile on his face. On closer inspection he proved to be not quite so old, but he seemed friendly enough, so we got out to greet him. I suppose this gun-toting act was standard practice among desert fellahin, just to be on the safe side. The gun itself turned out to be practically useless. It was an old double-barrel shotgun with the barrels tied together dangerously with wire.

We were endeavouring to exchange courtesies in sign language when another character appeared. He had a blue towel around his head and his frame was swathed in a rather shabby blanket. Very unoriginally we named our two new friends Joe and George and followed them as they proceeded to show us around the site.

It stretched for about a quarter of a mile in each direction, and was much bigger than we had imagined. Most of the ruins were down to the level of the ground foundations, although the walls of some buildings were as high as six feet in places. The streets were clearly evident and were laid out in parallel lines in the Roman fashion. The remains of the room walls in each house were still there and one could make out the function of some of the rooms, the entrance hall, the built-in bath in one room, empty rooms that could have been bedrooms or living rooms, the rectangular courtyard at the back surrounded by room wings. It was indeed exciting to think that Romans had walked around and lived in these houses some 1,500 years ago.

A wider road led to what once must have been an open square, behind which were the foundations of a large church. Inside the church ruins was a raised area at the back, up two levels of wide stone steps, and this must have been the site of the ancient altar. There were also two circular wells about nine feet in diameter. Their depth was enormous for when Joe dropped a pebble into one of them, it seemed an eternity before we heard it strike water. Edery estimated the depth was 300 feet. One could imagine how the domes and roofs of the many churches, baths, and larger buildings of this mysterious sacred city had dominated the empty desert for miles around.

The beauty of these ruins was that they were completely unspoiled by visitors or trippers. Many of the Roman carvings on the heavy masonry that was lying around were intact. However, all the valuable statuary and other moveable pieces had been removed during the excavations and lodged in the Alexandria or other museums. With the help of Joe and George we took a couple of small stone souvenirs which had floral designs inscribed on them and in one case the Roman mason's initials.

As a final lark, we asked George to fire his gun before we left. He seemed so embarrassed that we dropped the matter. We gave them each fifty ackers as a token of our friendship and for their help in showing us around. They were overcome with gratitude as if we had given them an enormous tip.

The trip back proved blessedly uneventful. We found Bahig station just as dusk was falling, and finally dragged our weary selves into the garage at about 1030 at night. Edery was now an experienced driver, Frankie had achieved his life's ambition, and the rest of us had had a good time. The last I remember of this happy trip was arguing with the car proprietor. The usual Egyptian bargaining routine was in progress for the return of our deposit.

CHAPTER SEVEN

Tragedy

*Be pleased to receive into thy almighty and most gracious
protection the persons of us thy servants, and the fleet
in which we serve. Preserve us from the dangers of the sea,
and the violence of the enemy.*

Naval Prayer

It had been a warm day, with a slight wind and a chop to the sea. The sky
was a serene blue as only a Mediterranean sky can be. Clusters of clouds
moved overhead blocking out the sun for short periods; a fine day for late
November.

On the quarterdeck most of the off-duty officers were gathered, smoking their
cigarettes and pipes, enjoying the warmth and tranquillity of the scene before
them. The low, continuous rumble of the propellers echoed from below, and if
you walked right aft to the stern to watch the bubbling and frothing wake of the
great ship, the rumble grew to a pulsating roar. Now and then the occasional cloud
blocked the satisfying sensation of heat, but in a few moments it would have
passed and once again the sea was bathed in late afternoon sunshine.

**Paymaster Midshipmen on quarterdeck of *Queen Elizabeth*, with battleship *Barham*
in background, on the day *Barham* was sunk.**

True, the admiral had earlier been putting us through our paces. But in essence we were enjoying what people paid good money for — a Mediterranean cruise. And although we were steaming in a villainously hazardous stretch of water north of the Cyrenaican coast, where our army was fighting; if you let your imagination run, you could easily be at peace again.

We had sailed to intercept an enemy convoy bound for Benghazi from Greece, but our chances of catching it seemed thin by this time according to the latest reports.

The background for our foray was that the Italian navy had been getting convoys through to Africa to build up their Axis desert armies. It was therefore imperative that something be done by our naval forces to try to put a stop to this.

The use of surface warships based at Malta during the summer and early fall had not been practicable because of the heavy bombing of the island during this period. Malta was being supplied from Gibraltar by the odd convoy but was still in a parlous state. Unfortunately we had suffered a serious setback just two weeks before this operation. Force H had moved into the western basin so that *Ark Royal* could fly off thirty-seven Hurricane fighters to Malta but was torpedoed on the way back to Gib and sank just twenty-five miles from there after being towed successfully overnight.

Despite the air activity over Malta, it had recently been decided to put surface ships back there to stop the flow of enemy convoys, and a new cruiser squadron, fresh from the Home Fleet had accordingly been sent to the island again. This force, designated Force K, consisted of the light cruisers *Aurora* commanded by Captain W.G.Agnew, Senior Officer, and *Penelope* and the destroyers *Lance* and *Lively*.

They had arrived at Malta on 21 October and in a relatively short space of time had achieved a great victory. In response to aircraft sightings, they were

N Code   9th November 1941.

To:-General.   From:-C-in-C Med.

        A light force attacked escorted Italian
convoy of ten ships 220 miles ENE of Malta about
0100 this morning 9th.   Nine merchant ships sunk.
One tanker left ablaze still burning at 1100.
Two destroyers sunk four escaped one of which
damaged.   No damage or casualties in our force.

                              2012 B/9/11

Operational RAA S QE 3 FAYO A80 COTS R

C-in-C Med's signal to the fleet reporting the sinking of the Italian *Duisburg* convoy of actually seven merchant ships on 9 November 1941 by Force K from Malta. Named for the largest ship in the convoy.

directed on 9 November to a large convoy southeast of Sicily. A night action ensued, during which they sank all ten ships of the convoy as well as one destroyer.

On 23 November 1941, we in Alex received reports from Malta that two further convoys were sailing from Italy for North Africa. Later, word came of a third one from Greece. This was obviously an uncommonly large movement of Italian ships, and implied the possible use of their battleships. As a result, our force, designated A, composed of the battleships *Queen Elizabeth,* the flagship, *Barham* and *Valiant* and eight destroyers of the 14th and 10th destroyer flotillas sailed as support for Force B comprising the cruisers *Ajax,* the flagship of Rear-Admiral Rawlings, *Neptune, Naiad, Euryalus* and *Galatea* plus four destroyers. The plan was that we would work in conjunction with Force K from Malta to sink all the convoys and, hopefully, make contact with the main Italian fleet.

Noon reports from Malta on 25 November 1941, indicated that there was no sign of the convoys and it was assumed that they had turned back. Nevertheless, we continued to steam westward on the off chance that they might be spotted.

Everyone was in the best of spirits, not least because getting to sea always put the big ships' crews in a better frame of mind. This was especially true of the admiral, who had spent the day putting us through our paces. Most of the forenoon we went through complicated station-keeping gyrations. We had steamed north, south, east and west in line ahead, in line abreast, and in quarter line. Every which way, in fact, to get the cobwebs out of these huge battlers. It had been a stirring sight to see them moving again at sea. If we were to be in action against the Italian fleet C-in-C wanted to be quite sure that our ships could hold their formation no matter what the circumstance.

So the day passed until the admiral retired from the bridge to his sea cabin for a cup of tea, and the fleet headed west in line ahead. Enemy air attack had been non-existent throughout the day, probably because the luftwaffe was heavily involved in the nearby land battle. And so a few off duty officers were able to enjoy the Mediterranean weather.

Nothing happened until around half past four in the afternoon. At this time I was working in the forward cypher office situated on the flag deck, high up in the forward superstructure under the admiral's bridge. Two of us, being close to the main plot and the admiral's sea cabin, were decyphering the more important messages. If anything urgent cropped up, there would be no delay in passing these messages to him. I was just in the middle of a short message from the NOIC Tobruk, when shouting erupted and there seemed to be some kind of commotion going on among the signalmen on the flagdeck outside.

Now we were under severe helm and the great ship began to list. I glanced across to my watch partner, a dour Scot, who was looking out of the port to see what was going on. Suddenly he dropped his pencil, closed his books and exclaimed in a controlled but earnest voice, *"Barham's* been hit."

With thumping hearts we both moved to the flagdeck to get a better view. There was no doubt about it, she had indeed been hit. We both could clearly see her pulling out of line and rapidly taking on a list. *Valiant* pounding up behind her at full port helm, her siren wailing plaintively, was desperately trying to avoid a collision. Several destroyers had turned out of the screen and were running at full speed towards the stricken ship.

The whole fleet, the battleships and the screening destroyers, was in complete chaos. *Barham* soon stopped dead in the water and was lying almost a right angles to her original course. All the time she listed ever more alarmingly and with each second assumed an increasingly dramatic position. It was all happening so fast; she was tipping over like a canoe. Soon the port side of her upperdeck was awash and the gaping barnacle-covered starboard side was slowly and weirdly rising out of the water. We knew then, each one of us, that she was going to go, and very quickly. It seemed incredible. Only five minutes before she had looked so damned powerful, completely secure as only a capital ship could look.

Now she was utterly helpless. What had done this to her? Soon she was even further over and hundreds of white-clad figures could be seen trying to scramble down her huge barnacle-crusted starboard bottom. As I watched, I saw a figure running determinedly up the forecastle to the bow and diving resolutely over the port side. What coolness in extreme stress. Other figures seemed undecided, riveted to the spot, waiting to see what other people would do. I felt for them and could well understand their fateful indecision. Mesmerized, not one of us said a word. But why was she going so quickly? She had hundreds of watertight compartments, and even though she was old, a veteran of the Battle of Jutland, she shouldn't be sinking as fast as this. Half her ship's company would probably lose their lives, a harrowing thought. Oddly enough, what shocked us sailors most was the sight of this great ship itself so suddenly rendered hapless. A sight like this lingers in your mind forever.

By now she was lying right over on her side. The smoke had stopped churning from her funnel, her aftermast dangled absurdly just above the water, and her normally submerged starboard rubbingstrake was beginning to appear from the sea. A pool of dark, heavy oil was forming in her wake as she lay quite helpless, almost stopped and almost stationary. It was all a frightful nightmare.

We were steaming away very fast. *Valiant* had made a complete circle

Penetration of Destroyer Screen by U-331
in Sinking of BARHAM

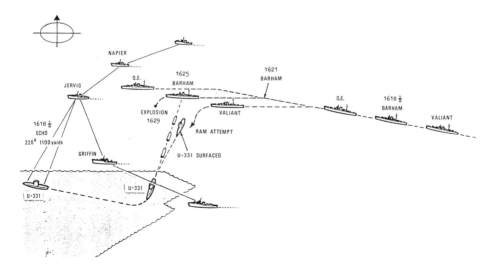

106

Barham **taking on a severe list. View from** *Queen Elizabeth.*

before coming up behind us to get back into line. The tragic ship meanwhile was left farther and farther astern. The white figures could be seen clustered along the starboard side, which was now lying parallel to the water, making it more difficult for the survivors to jump off. We could hardly make them out, but each one of them represented a human being struggling for life itself. Every head was glued to the horrible scene. From where I was, high up in the forward superstructure, I looked aft over our gun positions and the various decks, more in an attempt to take my eyes off what was going on.

Then she blew up with a resounding roar. Where the sinking ship had been, all I saw was smoke, acres of it, billowing out and spreading upwards in huge spirals and puffs. The ship herself had gone.

I could bear no more and my watchmate and I trudged silently back into the office, profoundly shaken. I returned to my message and forced myself to concentrate but I kept reading the same words over again. I wondered what had happened to the crew and the admiral, our Second-in-Command, Vice-Admiral Pridham-Wippell and his staff? He was a veteran of many actions in the Med, right from the start. He and his staff had been in *QE* during the summer and had only recently transferred to *Barham*. I knew all of them well, particularly the Pay types.

Pridham-Wippell himself was particularly well liked, always exuding benign gentlemanliness and taking most things with a smile. Maybe it was his gaunt face which gave him an air of distinction. He certainly was a good sport,

Sinking of H.M.S. Barham
25th. November 1941

862 Lives lost - 495 Survivors

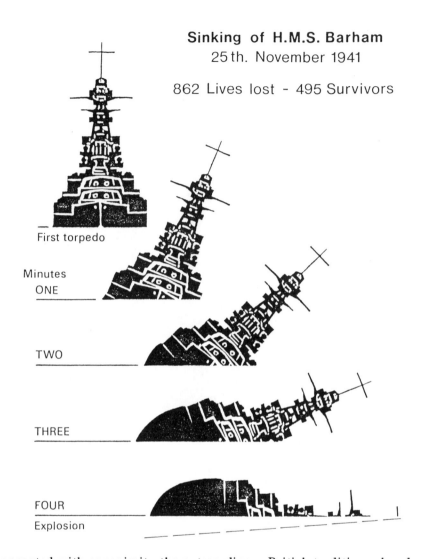

First torpedo

Minutes
ONE

TWO

THREE

FOUR

Explosion

and accepted with equanimity the extraordinary British tradition whereby he was debagged by midshipmen when he attended a mess dinner in the gun-room. His secretary Paymaster Commander H. Prevett was also very amiable. One wondered what had happened to them. I finally finished my watch and went below to the mess for my supper.

Apparently *Barham* had been hit by three torpedoes from a U-boat at point blank range. Nowson, our VR (Volunteer Reserve) sub-lieutenant had seen it all from the after director. Three distinct explosive pillars of water had shot up from the port side of the ship, and immediately afterwards, to his surprise, the German U-boat surfaced just off the stricken ship. She must, we thought, have been blown to the surface by the force of the explosions, indicating that she was practically under *Barham* when she had fired her torpedoes. Her conning tower nosed out of the water for about two minutes, drifting down towards *Valiant* and then disappearing. Meanwhile, some destroyers from the screen went after the sub and hunted her for hours, without success.

Barham **exploding. Photo taken from** *Queen Elizabeth.*

Valiant, when she saw the conning tower breaking surface to her port immmediately turned in an attempt to ram and to avoid hitting *Barham.* She tried to shoot at the submarine, but her 4.5 guns could not deflect far enough, and by the time her pom-poms were firing, the submarine had dived below the surface.

The German U-boat commander was Lieutenant Hans Diedrich von Tiesenhausen, who by an extraordinary coincidence later became a Canadian citizen and lives in Canada. I have compared notes with him about the sinking and have thus been able to piece together a full picture of the events of that fateful day.

Tiesenhausen was a regular officer who had served in the light cruiser *Karlsruhe* off Spain during the Spanish Civil War. Ironically, his ship was acting in co-operation with the Royal Navy. He had transferred to the submarine command and at the beginning of the war had served in U 23 with Kapitan-Leutnant Otto Kretchmer, one of the most famous of all the U-boat captains.

He obtained command of his own submarine, U 331, in early 1941. After one patrol in the Atlantic, his submarine was the first to be sent into the Mediterranean, in September 1941. He operated initially in the eastern basin from the island of Salamis, near Piraeus, the site of the great naval battle between the Athenians and the Persians in 480 BC. He took part in several actions before the *Barham* sinking, damaging a powered lighter off Bardia in October 1941; later laying mines off Famagusta in Cyprus in April 1942 and also sinking three small sailing ships.

Later still, in November 1942, his boat was sunk off Algiers during the American and British landings in North Africa. He was caught on the surface and bombed by aircraft from the carrier *Formidable.* At the time he was on the deck of the conning tower and was able to escape with seventeen other survivors. He was subsequently imprisoned in Canada, which led to his later

Oberleutnant Hans von Tiesenhausen, captain *U331*, which sank *Barham*.

decision to emigrate.

His attack on *Barham,* which by his own admission contained an element of luck, began when he sailed from Salamis on a special operation to land commandos sixty miles west of Alex to blowup the Mersa Matruh railroad. He successfully discharged this duty but was unable to recover the troops the following night. His orders after this were to head west to attack small British convoys headed for Tobruk.

It was during this patrol, on the morning of 25 November 1941, that his asdic located a surface target in the far distance to the northeast. He headed east towards it, running on the surface, but was forced to submerge twice during the day because of aircraft. Presumably he was not spotted, because no submarine warning was passed to the fleet. In the early afternoon he spotted the masts of ships just over the horizon and then lost them in a cloud, probably as we turned away on a zigzag.

Then late in the afternoon he picked up the fleet again and closed for action. He steered east directly towards the fleet which was then steering northwest at 290 degrees. At 1615, before he realized it, he was passing under the outer destroyer screen, slipping between *Jervis* to the north and *Griffin* to the south. He continued at periscope depth and shortly thereafter raised his periscope, despite the risk of being sighted. Somewhat surprised, he found that he was almost on top of the battleships, for we had turned south 22 degrees towards him on our next zigzag leg.

It was subsequently revealed that *Jervis* had indeed made asdic contact, but the sound was raspy and loud, quite unlike a true submarine noise. It was also being received on a 20 degree arc and not on a narrow angle which was usual in the case of a good contact. The Mediterranean is a tricky sea for sub contacts because the water layers are at different temperatures at certain times. The officer of the watch incorrectly decided that this was not a proper contact and so did not inform either the A/S officer or the captain. Ironically, the ship, being the senior destroyer flotilla leader, had one of the top anti-submarine specialists in the fleet onboard. It was a truly fatal error.

The escorting destroyers were spread out two miles ahead of the battle-ships. As the closing speed between our force and the submarine was 24 knots — the fleet was doing 17 knots and the submarine 7 knots — Tiesenhausen had only five minutes before he would be right up with his targets.

When he raised his periscope, he was only 1,000 feet away from the leading battleship, about the length of long city block. He was now in a perilous position. If he didn't decide at once, he would be under us before he could fire his torpedoes. So in a moment of quick decision, he immediately ordered hard a port and stopped the port engine, which rotated the boat 90 degrees directly towards the battle fleet. With his periscope still up, he took one last glance, adjusted his course, and fired four bow torpedoes at *Barham*.

His strongest recollection was the sight of three huge ships charging down on him. He was already past the first one, *QE*, at the moment of decision, so decided on the second, *Barham*. Then he checked out the destroyers astern of him.

Having retracted his periscope, he ordered a deep dive and prayed that he could get under *Barham* without being hit. However, he experienced a lot of turbulence as he tried to get his ship down. It was then that his conning tower broke surface from the upward thrust of the boiling water. At first, he didn't realize this had happened until he was informed by one of the crew. He thought that the surfacing was due to the wake of *QE* and *Barham,* which had the effect similar to a bed of roadside flowers being blown back by the air turbulence of a huge passing truck. Then he heard and felt the three explosions as his torpedoes hit *Barham.*

After being told that the conning tower was exposed, he ordered the men in the upper compartment to retire to the control room and close the hatch.

His next problem was that his submarine was diving too deep, because of a mistake on the depth control setting by one of his crew. He ended up at 265 metres (900 feet) below the surface, the deepest that any German submarine had ever dived to at that time. Indeed this craft was only designed for a depth of 500 feet. Finally he rectified the problem and brought her to a safe depth without any ill effect.

So engrossed was he throughout this whole period of a half hour or so that he neglected to keep his crew informed of developments. Only when a seaman asked if he had sunk a destroyer did he reply "No, a battleship."

In fact he was unable to confirm that he had sunk *Barham* because he did not resume periscope depth until long after the fleet had passed. However, the probability was great that he had succeeded. On return to port he became an instant hero in Germany, but the sinking was only confirmed much later.

After the ship had exploded, two destroyers left the screen and headed for the spot where she had sunk and began to pick up survivors. It was amazing that there were any. After seeing what had occurred, you wondered how any human being could possibly live through it all. In fact, about 495 men were saved, about a third of the ship's company.

Cunningham had signalled the three assisting destroyers *Jervis, Hotspur* and *HMAS Nizam*, asking whether they had rescued the admiral. The answer was in the negative, but the rescue was still continuing and there was always hope. However, one of the few redeeming features in the whole melancholy business was that Admiral Pridham-Wippell and his secretary were ultimately saved.

After our return to port, a story was circulating that the admiral told men around him to abandon ship and gave his life-jacket to a young sailor who didn't have one. He then made his way over the side at the insistence of his faithful secretary. Hearsay had it that he was picked up unconscious and covered with oil. On reaching *Hotspur,* he was put up foward with the other seamen survivors in the forecastle. The oil had obscured his gold braid and no one had recognised him. Ultimately when they got around to cleaning him up, a leading seaman rubbed the oil off his uniform and exclaimed, "Blimey a ruddy admiral." As it turned out, and as I will explain later, this was partly untrue. Only then, two hours after the sinking, could *Hotspur* signal Cunningham that the admiral was alive and well.

There were many stories going around about the event, as one can imagine. Like any large organization the navy was always full of gossip, most of it untrue, and highly imaginative stories always cropped up after a major fleet action or sinking. To give you an example, another baseless story going the rounds was that Captain Cook, of the *Barham,* who went down with his ship, ordered the duty marine boy bugler on the bridge — they were always mere boys and the youngest onboard; they were the only ones who could join up at fourteen — to stand beside him and play "The Last Post" as the ship sank.

Several true stories were told to me by my messmates. A midshipman who was on the bridge of *QE* said that our captain was actually in tears, but Cunningham remained unmoved. He took one look at *Barham,* then went up to the bridge where he coolly began giving orders and cursing the navigator. Another midshipman, backed up by other members of the mess, claimed that when he scanned *Barham's* bridge through powerful bridge binoculars, he saw Captain Cook, standing at attention, steadying himself with onehand and formally saluting with the other.

Twenty year old Engine Room Artificer 4th Class Ken Gibson (RN), now living in West Vancouver, British Columbia, was having a cup of tea in *Barham's* ERA's mess when she was hit. This mess was located one deck below the forecastle deck forward of A turret, so was well placed for abandoning ship. He said that the ship suddenly shook from a terrific bang somewhere aft. After this, it quickly started to list to port, and it became obvious to those present that something serious had happened; that there had been an explosion or that the ship had been hit and that it was not just making a sharp, emergency alteration of course.

Everyone made for the door to get to the nearest hatchway to the upper deck. This was very close but they found that there was already a queue waiting to go up the ladder and more men were coming up the hatchway from below. The problem was that the large hatch to the upper deck had only a small man-sized manhole cover exit hatch that was open. These large hatches were very heavy and difficult to raise, and only used for loading stores. Normal pedestrian traffic used other hatchways to the superstructure, where exit to the upper deck was through doors. Thus only one man at a time could escape to the upper deck.

The ship continued to list at an alarming degree so Gibson, with considerable coolness, made a quick decision that would save his life. Having decided that matters were getting desperate, he rushed down the passageway aft to another hatch which he often used. He wondered whether he had made the right decision because the heavy steel lockers in the passageway — on the higher side — were starting to fall across his path, almost hitting him.

Arriving at the hatch he found it empty and made his way up with much difficulty because the ship was going over even more. He struggled up the angled stairs two decks to B turret deck and came out into the open.

The massive bridge superstructure hung over him. In desperation, he looked around for a spot to jump from, but decided to climb around the back of B turret away from the sea. He couldn't jump to that side because of the decks sticking out below. He had to get up higher.

Scrambling around the turret grasping and jumping from spot to spot — the ship was now almost at 45 degrees over on its side — he found a ladder which went up the starboard side of the large 15-inch twin gun turret. What he did from the time he got to the upper deck until he got to the turret is the only thing that day that he is unclear about. However, he found himself climbing up the turret side ladder almost on his knees as the ship was now right over on its side and the turret dangled over the water. When he got to the top of the side of the turret he stood up and dived as far out as he could, to avoid the deck stanchions, about six to eight feet above the water.

He had no problems getting to the surface. But when he came up, he could see nothing around him but darknesss and heavy black smoke. He could breathe, yet he had the terrifying sensation that he was trapped underneath the ship. There was no one near him and he couldn't understand why everything was so dark and forbidding. The ship had exploded whilst he was underwater but he had no idea that this had happened.

He was wearing serge trousers, a shirt and a zippered sweater but had forgotten his life-jacket. As he swam, the smoke began to clear and he began to get his bearings and slowly came to realize that he had indeed escaped, had been able to clear away from the ship and had, by quick thinking and a miracle, saved himself. He could make out a destroyer in the distance and, as he was a good swimmer and had played for navy water polo teams before the war — he was a regular — he felt that he had a chance to be saved.

Finally, he was able to make out small black heads in the water ahead of him and he noticed that the sea, which was relatively calm, was covered with thousands of globules of sooty, sticky bunker oil which stuck to his face, his hands and his clothing. The black-faced men swimming around him were making for a large mess cushion, about seven feet by five feet in size, which they were able to cling to once they had got to it.

Nearby an older man, probably an officer, seemed to be trying to take charge, giving orders and encouraging and assisting men to swim to the cushion. Then this man, with a crazy dramatic flourish and summoning up some unexpected reserve of energy, started singing, of all things, in a fairly strong voice which could be heard for some distance over the water, "There'll always be an England."

Gibson found out later that this was the renowned Pridham-Wippell whom he had never seen in person before. Later when he was on the upper deck on *Hotspur,* after he had clambered aboard, he saw the admiral being helped on to the deck. There was no official piping of the side! Later, he and his shipmates were mustered on the stern of the little destroyer to hear the admiral give a situation report of the sinking and praise them for their conduct. Gibson remembers him as a lean, athletic-looking older man with a distinctive head of whitish hair.

Gibson actually swam to the *Hotspur* which had slowly and carefully

Lieutenant T. Herrick, captain of HMS *Hotspur*.

worked its way into the groups who were swimming or were clinging to floating debris and rafts. The destroyer had lowered a whaler, commanded by a midshipman which was picking up stragglers, and scramble nets had been lowered over the side with sailors positioned on them to help up the injured. Gibson got up the scramble nets on his own steam after about an hour in the water.

He was led to the ERA mess which he found crowded with some of his mess mates. He has a poignant memory of a friend asking him if he had seen an electrical artificer, a very close chum of his friend. The EA (Electrical Artificer) mess had been one deck below the ERA mess and most of its members had been lost including the chum.

After being given a couple of tots of rum he was helped to the bathroom, to the showers where he tried to scrub off all the sticky hard fuel oil. He had already taken off his clothes on the upper deck and had wiped a lot of it off with cotton waste, after which he was given a blanket to cover himself. By this time the destroyer's supply department had run out of clothing and the ship's officers and men had given all their spare kit to the survivors. The only items left that could serve the purpose were towels and blankets. Gibson was stark naked except for a blanket until he was put aboard the repair ship *Resource* in Alex twenty-four hours later.

Gibson said that the man whom I had seen diving off *Barham's* bow, was a Stoker Petty Officer; a cheery friendly soul. He was the only survivor who had not been touched by oil and who was able to wear his own clothing — his overalls — after they were dried.

A friend of mine, a VR Pay Lieutenant, G.M. Peake, with whom I had worked when Pridham-Wippell had been aboard *QE,* had managed to survive through great presence of mind. He had been in the wardroom when the ship was hit. This was located aft, on the upperdeck, very close to the exit to the quarterdeck. Everybody rushed out on to the quarterdeck, and when they saw what had happened, many rushed back to the wardroom lobby just inside the quarterdeck door to get their life-jackets. These were usually left hanging on hooks by their owners before they went into the mess. The distance was only about seventy-five feet.

Peake, recognising that the ship was settling fast, decided, although he didn't have his life-jacket, not to return but to take to the water before the ship listed any more. He was on the port side of the quarterdeck which was soon awash. All he had to do was walk right into the water. Just as he getting away from the ship and into his swimming stroke, she blew up. Down he was sucked, holding his breath as best he could and fighting with all his strength to get back to the surface. He was under a very long time, but when he finally surfaced he found that he was in complete darkness. Exhausted, frightened and almost unconscious, he looked about him and thought, "My God, I'm in hell." None of those who went back for their life-jackets survived.

The captain of *Hotspur* was Lieutenant T. Herrick,

Engine Room Artificer 4th class Ken Gibson, *Barham* **survivor.**

the youngest commanding officer in all the destroyers, and says *Hotspur* was the "boots" of the fleet! Being the junior ship, she was given jobs no-one wanted. He is a four generation New Zealander and joined the Royal Navy at age thirteen in 1925 and went to Dartmouth Naval College. He says he still gets letters about, as he says, "that disastrous afternoon."

He says that, after the Crete evacuation, some destroyer captains were replaced due to exhaustion. He was then First Lieutenant of the destroyer *Decoy* and, because there were no reliefs on the station, he was luckily picked to become the CO of *Hotspur*.

He says the *QE* midshipman who commanded the whaler which picked up the survivors got into trouble when he returned to his battleship after his tour in *Hotspur*. One night during a particularly amusing run ashore in Alex a small Egyptian rat was purloined from a Gulli-Gulli man. These men, who were always characters, made their living doing conjuring tricks for tips for people sitting at streetside cafes having a drink.

They had an extraordinary slight of hand. They would get you to put your hand out and open your palm, and before you knew it, you would be holding a small snake, even a chick or a small rat. This rat was made the wardroom pet and the shipwright made a fancy cage for it. The "Middy" being the junior

Barnham survivors leaving Hotspur in towels and blankets in Alexandria.

officer aboard was appointed as its keeper.

Unfortunately he became too fond of it, and, instead of leaving it in *Hotspur* when he went back to *QE,* he took it with him for the gunroom. Big ship routine was much stricter. The PMO, Surgeon Commander Kirker, when he heard about the new pet in the gunroom, made him drown it; as he was harbouring a rodent in one of His Majestry's ships which was contrary to Naval Orders.

Barham was sunk about 55 miles northwest of Sidi Barrani in position 32.34 N 26.24 E. An interesting aspect to the sinking was that the explosion was seen ashore by the 8th Army, who within a week knew that the great battleship had been sunk.

Vern Harrington, now living in North Vancouver, was serving with 1st Royal Natal Carbineers, which was part of the 1st South African Brigade of the 1st South African Division. His unit was then on top of the 300 foot high escarpment which runs from Mersa Matruh westward to Sollum. They were on the west side of the rocky ridge, probably about 65 miles away from the sinking. At that height they could see well out to this distance. He says that he and his chum happened to be actually looking out to sea when they saw a cloud of a huge explosion. They realized that some kind of ship, and probably a big one, was in trouble.

After the tragedy, a Board of Inquiry was assembled in *Woolwich* under the presidency of Rear-Admiral Glennie, RA Destroyers, on 4 December 1941. From the evidence given, *Jervis* had indeed received a loud, rasping echo bearing red 70 (to the south) at 1,100 yards. No HE (hydrophone effect) was heard and the bearing had been over a wide angle — too wide for a submarine. *Griffin,* the destroyer 2,000 yards directly to the south of *Jervis,* did not pick up anything. The A/S rating in *Jervis* had two years' experience, where as the one in *Griffin* was new to the job. An A/S expert at the inquiry confirmed that a contact with such a wide angle was usually due to a heat layer and not a submarine.

Pridham Wippell testified that he got stuck on a bridge superstructure deck while trying to abandon ship because the ship had heeled over so badly. He had no recollection of what happened after this until he regained conscious-

J class destroyer alongside maintenance ship HMS *Woolwich*.
Inver tanker in background.

QE backing into Gabbari dock, Alexandria. Note J class destroyer in
dock in background.

HMS *Jervis*.

ness in the water about 15 yards clear of the port side of the ship.

There were no major recommendations in the report — which was very-short, only twenty pages — except that more A/S exercises with one of our own submarines should be undertaken by the destroyers, but this was difficult to arrange because they were all being used constantly for operations.

There were no recriminations. The facts, as testified, were reported and the unhappy incident was closed.

CHAPTER EIGHT

A Treacherous Night

All of us thought that the Italian navy was hopeless, inefficient, and even cowardly. Certainly, every time they had been in contact with our fleet they had tended to withdraw, even when they outnumbered us. However, we soon revised our opinions about their heroism and ingenuity. Perhaps we should have been less complacent all along, since there had been press reports that their army had shown gallantry in the desert and that their real trouble was not in heroism but in logistics.

On the evening of 18 December 1941, the Commander on *QE* cleared lower decks and had everyone onboard muster on the quarterdeck. He then told us that Intelligence believed that the Italian navy was planning an attack on Alex harbour. Exactly what sort of attack, and how it would be conducted, was unclear. He informed us that they had already carried out several earlier attacks using one-man surface mini-torpedo boats. One such example had been at Suda Bay, where they had finished off the cruiser *York*. Moreover, a few months earlier they had tried a similar attack on Valetta harbour in Malta but had been unsuccessful. Their latest venture had been at Gib where they had used some kind of small submarine to blow up one of the protective nets. He pointed out that we were still not quite sure how these small craft operated and that we would all have to be on our toes. The ship's company would not be closed up at action stations during the night, but extra guards would be set, and all ship's boats would patrol around the ship dropping small charges if necessary. Anyone who saw anything suspicious was to report it immediately.

The reaction in the mess was one of unconcern. How the devil did they think that they could penetrate a harbour as well protected and defended as this one was, with its very substantial entrance boom? We further consoled ourselves with thoughts of proverbial Italian inefficiency, and by ten o'clock had forgotten all about the matter.

The next thing was that we were all rudely awakened at 0400 by the alarm rattlers buzzing us to action stations and a bugler blowing the alarm over the SRE. Clearly something urgent was afoot.

I hurriedly dressed and went up to the quarterdeck. The harbour was in complete darkness except for a large arc light over a dock about a quarter of a mile to the east. Cunningham had hastened up from his cabin in a raincoat over his pyjamas. I heard him give a brisk order to have the arc light extinguished, after which he ordered the 14th Destroyer Flotilla to sea.

I enquired of the officer of the watch, Sub-lieutenant Nowson, what was going on. His reply was that *Valiant,* lying just ahead of us, had just signalled C-in-C that she had discovered two Italians swimming around the anti-torpedo nets ahead of the ship. One was a Lieutenant-Commander and the other a Petty Officer. They had refused to divulge anything, but it was suspected that they were the crew of a two-man submarine and had been attempting an attack on *Valiant*. The Italians had been placed under guard and further instructions were now awaited. At this point, Nowson was relieved and called forward to the bridge.

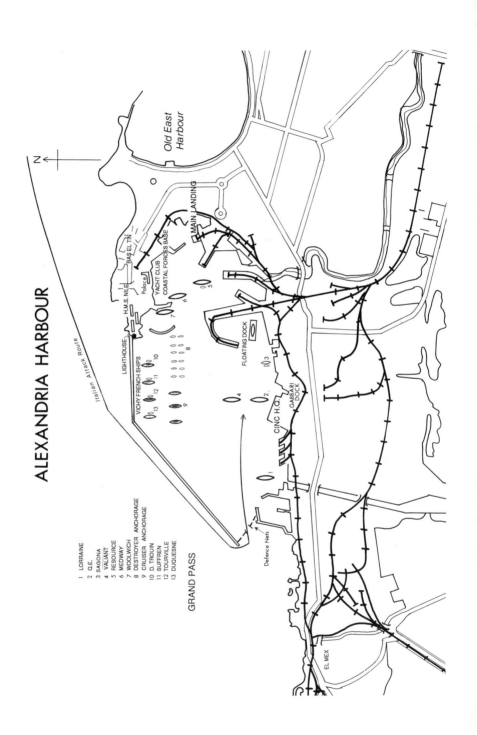

ALEXANDRIA HARBOUR

N

Old East Harbour

Italian Attack Route

LIGHTHOUSE

H.M.S. NILE

BASE EL TIN

Police

YACHT CLUB

COASTAL FORCES BASE

MAIN LANDING

VICHY FRENCH SHIPS

GRAND PASS

Defence Nets

CINC H.Q.

GABBARI DOCK

FLOATING DOCK

EL MEX

1 LORRAINE
2 Q.E.
3 SAGONA
4 VALIANT
5 RESOURCE
6 MEDWAY
7 WOOLWICH
8 DESTROYER ANCHORAGE
9 CRUISER ANCHORAGE
10 D. TROUIN
11 SUFFREN
12 TOURVILLE
13 DUQUESNE

Queen Elizabeth moored stern to Gabbari dock with anti-torpedo nets around her.

It seemed incredible that the Italians had actually penetrated the boom, despite all our precautions. At the time, however, I like everyone else, didn't think that they had actually achieved anything. About twenty minutes later the ship went off action stations and I went to the gun-room and the rest of the mess came in. Nobody knew any more than I did and we all assumed that nothing was amiss. Nonetheless, most of us decided to play it safe and spend the rest of the night sleeping in the gun-room, where we would be much safer in the event of an explosion than in the tiller flat, two decks below. We all curled up as best we could, on settees, chairs, and the gun-room table and struggled back to sleep.

At about quarter to six I woke up with an uncomfortable crick in my neck and decided to return to my camp-bed. As I got out on to the quarterdeck the light was just beginning to creep over the harbour. I immediately noticed that C-in-C, now in his uniform, was still standing at the after end of the deck with Captain Dick (the Assistant Chief of Staff for Operations). Once again I approached Nowson, who was back on duty, for further information. He told me that he had been sent over to *Valiant* to interpret (he spoke fluent Italian) during the interrogation of the two Italians.

On the instructions of the captain of the *Valiant* he was told to speak to them by himself and adopt a friendly manner, in the hopes of winning their confidence and lulling them into divulging what they had been up to.

He found them unexpectedly relaxed and calm after their ordeal.

The Lieutenant-Commander looked typically Italian; slight, tanned, with dark eyes and Roman nose. The Petty Officer was chunky with black, wavy hair. Both had expected to be shot or roughly treated. As instructed, he offered them a cigarette and started talking to them in a friendly way.

121

After a few minutes they warmed to him, and had quite a conversation. Nothing too substantive was elicited. However, when Nowson had casually observed that the training for their mission must have been tough, they both enthusiastically agreed, even admitting that they had shaken hands with the Duce before leaving and had been promised the highest Italian award for gallantry if they were successful. During the conversation the Lieutenant-Commander remarked what fine ships the battleships were and what a shame it was that they had to go. From this remark Nowson deduced that they had placed an explosive under *Valiant*.

After this exchange they were taken ashore to Ras el Tin to the Intelligence offices which had by this time come to life. Nowson and the captain of *Valiant* went with them. The Italians were put through a mild form of third degree, with the Intelligence Lieutenant Commander taking a hard line. They immediately clammed up and only gave their names and rank. It was obviously pointless acting tough with these men. After this abortive interview, the intelligence officer concluded that there was no evidence that they had been successful and he dismissed Nowson's suggestion that they had been able to achieve their objective. On the orders of C-in-C, the prisoners were returned aboard *Valiant* and, to intimidate them, they were to be put down in the bowels of the ship. If it were going to blow up, they would surely warn us to save their skins.

As Nowson was continuing with his account there was a low, rumbling sound like a tympani roll, which then climaxed in an explosive roar. Nowson immediately pointed to *Valiant* which was already beginning to take on a slight list. Figures were scuttling around her quarterdeck, and the ship's picket boat was hurriedly leaving her starboard after-gangway. There was now no doubt about it; she had indeed been tampered with. But apart from the list there was no sign of damage. All the while C-in-C stood silently watching *Valiant*.

The early morning glow was by now much brighter, highlighting the buildings at Ras el Tin on the breakwater and the French cruisers. There was a terrible sense of helplessness. All we could do was wait and establish the extent of the damage to *Valiant*. No one stirred in our ship; most had not heard the underwater explosion. *Valiant's* list had stabilized, presumably the damaged compartments had been closed off. Then a small Morse light began to wink from her signal deck, probably informing C-in-C what was happening. The admiral continued to look on impassively without a word.

Then we blew up. Again there was the low, rumbling underwater explosion and the quarterdeck was thrown upwards about six inches, maybe more. I bent my legs and threw out my arms to keep my balance as the huge ship lurched beneath me. A blast of thick smoke and flame shot out the funnel. Then the ship seemed to settle rapidly. Calmly, Nowson, his telescope under his arm in the prescribed manner, walked out on to the port gangway platform to inspect what had happened forward. I walked to the ship's side, just in case of the worst eventuality, and grabbed the rail as the ship started very imperceptibly to list to starboard. The admiral remained there, as silent and imperturbable as always, steadying himself against the starboard guardrail for balance.

What must he have been thinking as he witnessed his last two battleships being blown up under him? And it was only a month since he had lost *Barham*. On top of that, there was the litany of recent naval losses elsewhere: the *Ark Royal* in November, the U.S. fleet in Pearl harbour, *Prince of Wales* and

Above: Valiant ahead, floating but down at the bow.

Left: Queen Elizabeth resting on the harbour bottom, with submarine alongside for power.

Italian two-man submersible used in Alexandria night attack on 19 December 1941.

Repulse in the Far East, and so on. The sight of him standing there with Captain Dick, still not saying anything, not giving an angry order or cursing, is something that I will never forget.

QE continued to list. Someone said that the ship's bow had been blown off, and everyone was now pouring up the after-hatch from the cabins below, the chief of staff in only a pair of trousers and Edery in his pyjamas. Bemused, they blinked in the light, cursed, and fired off rapid questions.

Then suddenly there was another explosion, this time to starboard. It was from *Sagona*, a fleet oiler lying not more than 200 yards away from us with a destroyer alongside. Everyone stood still waiting for the next man to make the first move. We waited for a few more minutes but nothing further happened.

Finally word came from the bridge that the ship had been blown up forward, that three boiler rooms had been hit and completely flooded, and another one partially so. Damage control parties had the situation in hand, and the flooded compartments had been isolated and sealed off. The ship was now resting with her bows on the bottom.

After lingering for a further period, doing nothing more useful on deck than gawking and chattering, we began to drift down below to shave and wash up.

Fleet oiler, *Sagona* with damaged rudder post, and stern out of water.

During the morning after the attack a number of flaming flares popped to the surface. At first we were mystified, but upon further reflection we realized their purpose. They had been distributed on the bottom around the battleship anchorage, and were to rise and ignite the oil which was expected to spill from the damaged *Sagona*. However, the bomb had been attached to the rudder post of the oiler, so the explosion only blew a hole in the stern of the ship, flooding the engine room but not touching the oil tanks forward.

Captain Morgan of *Valiant,* knowing that his ship had probably been tampered with, was able to clear lower decks and get all his men on deck in good time before the explosions occurred. Consequently *Valiant* suffered no casualties. This was not the case in *QE.* Ignorant of the explosives beneath us we took no special precautions with the result that we lost fifty engine room personnel in the boiler rooms. Our damage was more severe than *Valiant's* because we were lying in much shallower water so that the explosive reverberation from the bottom was much greater. Also, our bomb had been attached directly to the ship.

Later the crews that carried out the attacks on our ship and *Sagona* were apprehended. The two who attacked us were at large for forty-eight hours, finally being arrested at Rosetta. The other two were able to swim ashore and were only picked up after several hours, when they were caught by the Egyptian police as they were trying to get out of the dockyard.

Don McGill was then working ashore in HMS *Nile* at Ras El Tin and remembers there was quite a flap when it was learned from intelligence that there might be an attack on Alex.

Officers and men ashore were organised into boat crews and arrangements were made to get light charges for dropping in the harbour. The explosives were delivered to the *Nile* boat jetty and his crew and other crews waited throughout the night for small boats to arrive. Some boats came but quite a few crews, including his, never got a boat to patrol the harbour.

Since the war, the full story of this treacherous night has become known. It was undoubtedly one of the most successful wartime operations of the Italian navy, and was part of an attempt on their part to move a large convoy full of reinforcements to their hard-pressed army in the desert. While the convoy was sailing from Italy with the full support of the Italian fleet, a number of submarines were positioned off Alex to wait for us to put to sea. They had further plans in the event of our not coming out. A specially fitted submarine which carried three small satellite submarines strapped to its hull formed part of this force, and these small submarines were to attempt to attack our battleships in Alex harbour.

These two-man submarines were nothing more than torpedoes fitted with two seats, in tandem on top of them. Two crew members controlled the craft like a submarine, submerging it or bringing it to the surface as necessary. It was equipped with a propeller, small hydroplanes, and air tanks, and the crew wore something like our Davis submarine escape-gear which supplied them with oxygen when underwater.

On 15 December we had sailed the 15th Cruiser Squadron to escort the fast fleet supply ship *HMS Breconshire,* which carried both oil and supplies, to Malta. The plan was for this force to pass her on to Force K steaming out from Malta. Thus it happened that our operation coincided with the Italian operation.

When the battlers didn't put to sea, the specially modified Italian submarine *Scire,* which had transported the craft from Leros, proceeded to a point about a mile off the old harbour, and at 2030 dropped off its small charges. The Italian craft were led by Lieutenant-Commander Luigi de la Penne. They moved westward toward the land, close outside the outer breakwater, with the craft trimmed so that the heads of the riders remained above water. After they arrived at the entrance at about 0140 they moved to one side and rested for a while, still in a semi-submerged position.[6]

Almost immediately the cruisers of CS 15 and destroyers under Admiral Vian arrived, and the mini-submarines followed them in. The three of them moved in line abeam as they passed through the defence boom. They were buffeted about in the turbulent wake of the surface force and one of them was almost rammed by a destroyer. Once inside the harbour, they then separated and each craft proceeded independently to its target, with only the forward man keeping his head above water. In this position he could remove his oxygen facepiece and move his head more easily. De la Penne has stated that he went near the *Lorraine.* One lower deck story going the rounds at the time was that he went alongside *Lorraine* and a French sentry pointed out *QE.* Perhaps one of our ratings had seen something suspicious around the French ship. Thus it is conceivable that someone did see him but no one had paid attention to the report of the sighting.

The crews had been well briefed as to the location of our battleships in the harbour from recent aircraft reconnaissance photographs, and each was given a ship to attack.

Unbelievably, de la Penne took his craft over the anti-torpedo nets surrounding *Valiant.* He had his Petty Officer leave the craft and push down the top wire of the net. Despite this, no one saw them. Then they submerged and, in darkness, endeavoured to place themselves directly under the funnel of the battleship. However, their propeller caught a wire which upset the controls and the craft sank to the bottom, fifty-five feet down. After inspecting the damage, de la Penne swam to the surface for a further look and once again should have been seen by someone on *Valiant.*

When he got back down again his assistant had gone, so he was left to manoeuvre the craft and attach the bomb himself. After great exertion lasting for forty minutes, he finally managed to position the craft so that it was just about under the great ship. He was able to do this because physical objects weigh so much less underwater. Without the help of his assistant, there was now no possibility of attaching the explosive section to the ship, which was the planned procedure. These manoeuvres were all done, incredibly so, in the pitch blackness of the water. There was no underwater illumination equipment on the craft, and even if there had been it couldn't have been used because it might have been seen.

By this time de la Penne was utterly worn out, so he set the timer on the bomb and swam to the surface. He was finally detected as he swam to the mooring buoy and was sprayed with machine gun fire under the glare of a searchlight. There he found Bianca, his assistant, who had been forced to the surface because his air supply had stopped and had decided to hide behind the buoy to avoid detection. De la Penne said that he was taken prisoner at 0330 and the bomb was set to go off at 0620.

In retrospect if *Valiant* had been moved immediately after this, she would not have been damaged, as the unattached charges would have exploded harmlessly.

The crew that carried out the attack on *QE* were Lieutenant Marceglia and Diver Schergat, and they had a much easier time. They apparently moved around the harbour protection nets semi-submerged, got their bearings and moved easily beneath our nets. The bomb support wires were attached to the port and starboard stabilizer fins and the bomb hung close below the ship.

The sequel to this action is one of the most bizarre twists of war imaginable, and occurred three years later. After the fall of Mussolini in September 1943 and the armistice which followed, many units of the Italian armed forces joined the Allies. De la Penne helped our frogmen in an attack on the German submarine base at La Spezia in 1944. In March 1945, just before the end of the war, the former captain of *Valiant,* now Rear Admiral Morgan commanding our naval forces in the Adriatic, was accompanying Crown Prince Umberto on an inspection of the Italian naval base at Taranto. On this occasion de la Penne was to be awarded the Italian *Valore Militare,* Italy's highest decoration for bravery, for his work at Alex. And who should present it to him? None other than his old adversary, Admiral Morgan.

At the same time that we were losing our battleships, our Malta forces were also suffering setbacks. In late November and December the Germans started to intensify their air attacks on Malta again, making it very dangerous for our ships there. Nevertheless, we hung on and kept up our attacks on enemy convoys. After the decimation of their seven ship convoy on 9 November, the Italians started to send only small one or two ship convoys each escorted by a single destroyer. This made it harder for us to intercept them all.

On 27 November 1941, Rear-Admiral Rawlings in *Ajax* with *Neptune* and the destroyers *Kimberley* and *Kingston,* sailed from Alex to Malta to reinforce Force K to give us more flexibility in attacking greater numbers of convoys simultaneously. He was accompanied by our Alex force, under Rear-Admiral Philip Vian, comprising *Naiad,* the flagship, and *Euryalus* with the destroyers *Griffin* and *Hotspur.* Vian, the famous commander of *Cossack* and hero of the *Altmark* episode, had recently arrived to relieve Admiral King. This, his first operation in the Med was successful and suffered no losses. On its return trip, the force did a sweep off the desert coast to intercept any small enemy convoys that might be trying to get into Derna or Benghazi. Fierce land fighting was now going on east of Tobruk. However, nothing was found and the force returned uneventfully to Alex.

At the time we were receiving a barrage of cyphers from the Prime Minister urging Cunningham to do more to stop supplies getting to North Africa. The invariably polite reply was that we were already doing as much as was possible with the ships that were available.

Then on 30 November the Italians sailed four small convoys, the outcome of which was that a small freighter and a small trooper, a tanker and a destroyer (which fought back courageously) were sunk by our aircraft and Force K.

In the first week of December, *Breconshire* was passed to Malta under escort from our Alex force and met by Force K. On 8 December the 14th Destroyer Flotilla supported by the cruisers *Naiad, Euryalus* and *Galatea* did another sweep off the desert and bombarded Derna and returned, after heavy air attacks, to Alex. On this outing the destroyer *Jackal* was hit and damaged by a submarine torpedo. German and Italian submarines, especially German, were now becoming a real hazard.

Tobruk was relieved on 9 December and shortly thereafter the Gazala line, fifty miles to the west, was established. This meant that our air forces, including Fleet Air Arm fighter squadrons, were diverted to airfields in the vicinity. We now enjoyed air coverage well to the west of Tobruk.

On 13 December both our Alex and Malta groups sailed because the Italians were mounting another major effort to pass several small convoys to Africa. After our submarine *Urge* torpedoed the Italian battleship *Vittorio Veneto* in the straits of Messina, all these convoys were turned around and our forces were recalled. On the way back to Alex, our light cruiser *Galatea* was sunk by a submarine with the loss of her captain E.W.B. Sim, and many of her crew. These light cruisers only had a tonnage of about 6,000 and, although they were more than twice the size of our fleet destroyers, didn't seem to be able to take any more punishment.

On 15 December, three days before the loss of our battleships, our very busy fleet again sailed on another *Breconshire* run to Malta. The cruisers *Naiad, Euryalus and Carlisle* and the fleet destroyers *Jervis, Kimberley, Kingston, Kipling, HMAS Nizam, Hasty, Havoc,* and *Decoy* took part in this operation.

Why our battleships did not sail with this force was the subject of much speculation. If they had done so, they would have never been severely damaged in harbour. The gossip was that Cunningham had been ordered to keep them in harbour because of the rash of naval losses that we had recently been suffering. Actually, the reason was that we did not have sufficient fleet destroyers to provide anti-submarine protection. A minimum of six was needed for the battleships. We only had eight destroyers at this time at Alex, leaving insufficient destroyers for the Vian force should the battlefleet have to split up. Thus the battleships, much against the wishes of Cunningham, had to remain in harbour and miss the ensuing sea battle.

At 0900 on 17 December, due north of Benghazi, the Vian force rendez-voused with part of Force K, comprising the cruisers *Aurora* and *Penelope* and the destroyers *Lance* and *Lively* plus four new reinforcement fleet destroyers *Sikh, Maori, Legion* and the Dutch *Isaac Sweers. Carlisle* and *Kingston,* escorted for a while by *Havoc,* had already been sent back to Alex; *Carlisle* was too slow and *Kingston* had engine troubles.

Air cover was initially provided by our desert air force. However, enemy air attacks were continuous throughout the day, with no losses to our ships.

Then at 1000 a report was received that the Italian fleet, including battle-ships, was again at sea about 100 miles or four hours' sailing to the north. Apparently they had turned right around and remounted their convoy operation unbeknownst to us. Luckily, by this time the remainder of Force K had arrived in the shape of *Neptune, Kandahar* and *Jaguar* to reinforce our fleet.

The Italian fleet came in contact with ours at 1700 and as dusk settled the two forces exchanged fire. *Breconshire* was turned south at full speed away from the action. Once again, the Italian fleet, which far outnumbered our ships, failed to press the advantage and turned away. During the night the Vian force headed home, since its mission was to get *Breconshire* to Malta and not engage the Italian fleet. En route it searched for the Benghazi portion of the Italian convoys but to no avail. Force K meanwhile took *Breconshire* on to Malta, arriving at 1550 on 18 December 1941.

Air recce from Malta later reported that the Tripoli convoy—a different convoy from the Benghazi one—was still at sea, so Force K once again sailed on the 18th and headed south to intercept it at around one in the morning of 19 December off Tripoli. This force consisted of the cruisers *Neptune* whose Captain Rory O'Conor was in overall command plus *Aurora* and *Penelope* escorted by destroyers *Lance, Lively, Kandahar* and *Havoc.*

O'Conor had quite a reputation in the fleet for his training methods. One story going around was that he decided to make directly for Tripoli so as to ensure that the convoy had no way of escaping. Be that as it may, at about 0100, *Neptune* caught a mine in her paravane in a hitherto unknown minefield about twenty miles off the coast. The weather conditions were terrible with heavy seas and a full gale blowing. She had reduced speed after crossing the 100 fathom mark, just as the squadron was about to turn to sweep along the coast. After this, *Aurora* was hit while trying to get out of the field at slow speed. *Penelope* also caught a mine in her paravane but incurred little damage. *Aurora* could make way, whereas *Neptune* had stopped and was in real distress. She detonated a second mine trying to turn to get out of the field and had her propellers and steering gear blown off. Too dangerous to have a destroyer take her in tow, it was decided to have one take off survivors. *Kandahar* was then hit and the idea had to be abandoned. Rory O'Conor had already signalled all ships to keep away from him.

Havoc and *Lance* left with *Aurora* to try to get her back to Malta (200 miles away to the north) before dawn. *Neptune* hit more mines and capsized and sank and we had no message about survivors. It was a dark night with tremendous seas, making it extremely difficult to manoeuvre ships alongside each other. One could imagine all too vividly the predicament of *Neptune's* crew as they struggled to launch their boats and floats in the raging waters while the ship was sinking fast. Terrible conditions and an awful catastrophe. Nor was *Neptune* the only ship in dire straits. Captain Nichol of *Penelope* made one of the most heartrending messages of the Mediterranean naval war to the stricken *Kandahar,* "I clearly cannot help you. God be with you." Then he and *Lively* left at full speed for Malta leaving *Kandahar* in the stormy darkness to fend for herself as best she could.

It was only after the war that the full story of the terrible end to *Neptune* was found out. We had no word of any survivors at the time. In the frightful weather conditions that existed that night only two carley floats were released from *Neptune* and only a few men were able to reach them. Captain O'Conor was one of them. Some men tried to swim to *Kandahar* but drowned in the attempt. Presumably the floats were washed out to sea and drifted for days. Weather conditions in the Med are good except in the winter months, and this proved to be one of the few times when we could not pick up our own survivors.

Indeed, there was only one survivor from *Neptune*, Leading Seaman J. Walters, a Newfoundlander. He has stated that Rory O'Conor had been in the float with him but died of exposure. Walters himself was picked up by the Italians when the storm had abated, after five days at sea.

Next morning *Jaguar* was sent from Malta to see if *Kandahar* was still afloat. Weather conditions were still poor, but she had been finally located by a Wellington aircraft. *Jaguar* reached her in the afternoon of 19 December — the very day that we were blown up. She had drifted from the minefield out to sea and was submerged aft of her funnel. Her stern had been blown off but her bulkheads had held. As it was too rough to go alongside, the crew were rescued by an extraordinary bit of seamanship. *Jaguar*, lying to the leeward of the stricken vessel, had the men float down towards her — a very nerve-wracking way to be picked up. When all the survivors had been saved, *Kandahar* was despatched by a torpedo.

By this time Vian's force from Alex, along with the new relief destroyers, had returned and during the night of 18/19 December had been let into harbour along with the Italian two-men underwater craft. All in all, it had been a tragic twenty-four hours for our side.

A Board of Inquiry was conducted in Malta afterwards to investigate whether a serious error had been made by the senior officer in taking his force so close to the coast, twenty miles in about ninety fathoms of water (500 feet). The conclusion was that as the location of this minefield was unknown, and as O'Conor had just ordered a reduction in speed before the force encountered the field (which indicated that he would be turning to patrol) he was not responsible for the disaster. It was held that the unfortunate results of this action were simply due to the uncertainties of war.[7]

Both Italian convoys to Tripoli and Benghazi reached their intended ports. So all our efforts to stop them were to no avail.

However, there was one plus for us, in addition to getting *Breconshire* into Malta, and this happened partly out of sheer luck and partly because of the very quick and efficient measures on the part of four of our destroyers.

They were being sent as much needed reinforcements from Gibraltar via Malta to Alex. The *Sikh, Maori, Legion* and the Dutch *Isaac Sweers*, were to replace the Australian fleet destroyers *Napier, D7, Nestor* and *Nizam* that had been recalled to the Pacific after the attack on Pearl Harbour (7 December 1941) — the old Australian V & Ws *Vampire, Vendetta* and *Voyager*, plus *Stuart*, had worn themselves out and had returned to Australia for major repairs six months previously. On the night of 13 December, when they were to pass through the Straits of Pantelleria, they planned to head south and hug the Vichy French coast of north Africa, remaining within the three mile territorial water limit to avoid Italian mines.

At 0320 in the early morning as they began to turn south around Cape Bon, in northernmost Tunisia, they encountered three Italian warships — two cruisers and a corvette — just starting to turn north. Our ships lay between the enemy and the coast and were fortunately hidden by the cliffs of the Cape. They had been warned previously by Malta that they might come upon an Italian squadron, and were consequently well prepared and at action stations. The two forces were on a rapidly closing course, with the Italians quite unaware of the situation. Our ships opened up with torpedoes and gunfire at

1,000 yards and the two cruisers were sunk within five minutes. Only the smaller Italian warship was able to escape.

We had all learned of this brilliant action and had expected to give the victors a rousing reception when they arrived at Alex. But that was not be, after all the havoc that had been wreaked during the night of the 19th.

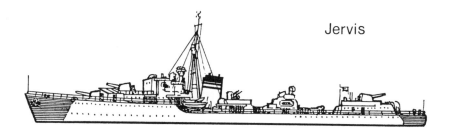

Jervis

CHAPTER NINE

Malta Convoy

"The story of the Merchant Navy throughout the war in the Mediterranean is one of unostentatious gallantry and hardihood."

From East of Malta, West of Suez
Admiralty Account of Naval Mediterranean War.
1939 - 1941

At the end of December 1941 *Valiant* was placed in our large floating dock at Alex. She was less damaged than *QE* and therefore could be patched up quickly and sent on her way for major repairs. But *QE* herself lay pathetically on the bottom with her stern to Gabbari dock. C-in-C stayed aboard in an effort to confuse any enemy agents in Alex that she was not damaged.

It was almost like being posted to a shore establishment as the ship was clearly going nowhere. Some of the crew were transferred to other ships or shore establishments or sent home. The great Med fleet had been reduced to four light cruisers, *Naiad, Dido, Euryalus* and *Carlisle* plus three small destroyer flotillas backed up by the cruisers *Penelope* and *Ajax* and some destroyers at Malta.

We were back into the "work during the day and enjoy the delights of Alex at night" lifestyle which was not too hard to take. It was even better after we went on tropical routine when the weather got hot in May, for then we worked early in the morning and got ashore in the afternoon.

Plenty of sports and recreation activities were organized. Rugger, soccer and cricket matches were arranged as well as golf for the officers at the Sporting and Smouha clubs. And then there were always the excellent restaurants, nightclubs and bathing beaches in the city and there was no shortage of food or drink.

They say that wherever there is an Englishman you will find a theatre. This was not true of Alex, so we organized our own shows. We were lucky to have on *QE* a V.R. Lieutenant, Kim Peacock, a London West End theatre director. He put on three shows, each one much better than the last. They were respectively dubbed "*QE* Blues," "Up Spirits" (after the pipe for the daily rum issue) and, at the end January 1942, "Cinderella afloat," our most lavish production and an original pantomime. We had an excellent Royal Marine band under the direction of Bandmaster E.H. Weller to back up our talented cast of players and singers. Two popular senior officers were great theatre types and played star roles. The Surgeon Commander, who was quite fat, was Fairy Godmother, and Commander (E) (Engineering) who was Duchess Stokes, a reference to the stokers under him. Our padre, Reverend Fleming was cast as George, an Egyptian. Several of the ratings who participated were practically professionals. It was an indication of the good spirit and morale in our ship

Valiant in floating dock — side view.

Captain Barry addressing the ship's company of *Queen Elizabeth,* on the quarter-deck, in Alexandria harbour, May 1941. Yours truly to his right.

Accountant Branch on quarterdeck of HMS *Queen Elizabeth*, summer 1941.

that everyone took a great interest in these shows and thoroughly enjoyed them.

Most of us were in two minds about not being able to go to sea but there was no doubt that we were enjoying the chance to get ashore in such agreeable surroundings. The usual shipboard activities continued despite the serious damage; training exercises, ship upkeep and maintenance work. We could still fire our AA guns during air raids, and these resumed when the enemy tried to bomb *Valiant* in the floating dock.

We also had the usual incidents which help to break the monotony of shipboard life. *QE* boasted several cats which lived on the messdecks with the sailors. One of them had kittens in the commander's cabin, to the extreme chagrin of his Marine servant, who hastily tried to remove the proud mother and family but was caught in the act by none other than the commander himself. He was jokingly berated for being so inhumane. Anyone passing by after this — the commander always kept his cabin door open — would frequently see him and No. 1 down on their knees playing with the kittens. No 1 and the commander were inseparable and could be found, with a few sailors around them, morning, noon or night, somewhere in the great ship checking on some kind of problem. After I left *QE* there was a frightful row about who should have the kittens.

There were also childish antics beloved of the young and not so young alike. *Valiant,* having been patched up, was due to sail for Durban for major repairs on 3 April 1942. The midshipmen of *QE* had their eyes on a framed colour picture of Ginger Rogers which their counterparts in *Valiant* had purloined from the Mohammed Ali cinema and which hung in a position of honour in their gunroom. Several unsuccessful attempts had been made by us to appropriate it. However, with the ship due to leave, a really serious effort was called for. Orders were drawn up for "Operation Ginger." One of our motor boats was to go alongside *Valiant* on the night before she left, under the guise of a despatch boat. Midshipman Bray was then to go aboard and, if necessary, draw the keys of the gunroom from the keyboard sentry just off the quarter-

Left: Surgeon Commander Kirker, Fairy Godmother. Centre: Commander (E)
W. Davey as Duchess Stokes with A. N. Other and Right: Chaplain W. Fleming RN
as George, an Egyptian in *Queen Elizabeth* show "Cinderella Afloat", March 1942.

deck. He was then to "liberate" the picture. Everything went according to plan
and the picture was safely brought back to *QE*.

Next morning, quite early, a counter raid was mounted by the *Valiant*
midshipmen to retrieve it but we had hidden it safely. Then semaphore messages began to pass back and forth between the two battleships as the matter
was put on a more official basis. Clearly the whole episode had got out of hand
and was now to be settled by the two captains, with threats that it would go to
C-in-C if necessary. *Valiant* maintained that the picture had been taken on
charge on the stores ledger as a trophy in accordance with King's Regulations
and Admiralty Instructions and could not be struck off. Much to our dismay,
we were made to give it back and *Valiant* sailed with her accounts in proper
order.

Bray had been transferred to the famous submarine *Torbay* under the
command of Commander Tony Miers, in August 1941, for one patrol. The
submarine had proceeded to a small coastal village in South-western Crete to
take off Allied soldiers. It took three nights to get them off. The boat would
lay off the land submerged during the day.

On the third night, the village was alive with Commonwealth troops and
Cretans, with consequent noise and activity. The submariners worried about
the Germans arriving on the scene but the narrow approach road had been
firmly blocked by the Cretans.

131 troops were taken aboard plus some Greeks. Many more Greeks
wanted to come. Bray said that several tried to climb down the conning tower
into the submarine and had to be forcibly ejected. Miers visited the gunroom
and met us all. He was a jolly man with a forceful personality, and you could
see that he was a leader. He was awarded the Victoria Cross for sinking three
merchant ships in a defended anchorage off Corfu and other exploits.

After *Valiant* left, *QE* was immediately put into drydock. It proved to be an unusual experience living in a ship, a huge one at that, lying high out of the water. All you could see through the port was the bare metal sides of the dock. To get ashore one had to walk down high, narrow stairs to a platform at water level. The ship and the dock looked uncomfortably top-heavy — a truth that was brought home to us very forcibly when we began to receive more air raids.

One night we were called to action stations at around midnight. There was nothing much we could do as we couldn't fire our guns for fear of dislodging the ship. That night the attack was aggressively pressed home and there were two near misses within fifty feet of the dock. For a few terrifying moments the great ship rattled on her blocks and the floating dock jerked from side to side, and we could all imagine, too vividly for comfort, what would happen to us if it keeled over. But the old veteran came though again, settling back in an upright position, secure in her dock. After this, everyone was advised to stay ashore at night unless they were on duty. I might say that there was no reluctance on the part of anyone to take up this suggestion.

On 27 May 1942 I joined a new ship, a J class destroyer, *HMS Jervis*. I had joined at an inappropriate time as the ship's company was still suffering the after-effects of a dreadful trip which they had undertaken two weeks before. Most aboard were still in a state of shock and were uncommonly quiet, reserved and somewhat reluctant to talk about their recent experience.

Jervis had sailed on 11 May in company with *Kipling, Jackal* and *Lively,* all ships of the 14th Destroyer Flotilla, to intercept a small Italian convoy en route to Benghazi via Greek waters. Only *Jervis* returned. All the other ships were sunk, the heaviest loss of destroyers in a single action since the war began. During four murderous hours on 12 May, the flotilla had been attacked repeatedly by large formations of Stukas operating from Crete. *Kipling* and *Lively* sank in short order. The severely damaged *Jackal* had been taken in tow by *Jervis* but had to be sunk later.

Jervis had managed to rescue survivors from all three ships but many of them died later from injuries sustained in the water from machine-gunning and bombing during the attack. Men had clambered up over the side looking quite fit, but died within the hour from internal injuries. Six hundred and thirty survivors were picked up by a ship that normally carried 240. Men were all over the upper deck — standing, crouching, lying, groaning, mumbling, and dying. There just wasn't enough room below to handle them all. As the Gunner (T) (Torpedoes), who was a pretty hard-nosed character, said, "They died right under the torpedo tubes."

All agreed that *Jervis's* escape was a miracle, adding to her reputation as a lucky ship. With three extra crews on board and sundown fast approaching, she was subject to one last attack by twelve JU88s coming in from all directions.

The old man, Captain A.L. Poland, had just joined the ship, and this was his first outing. He immediately turned the ship over to the navigator. He had been ashore for eighteen months defending Tobruk as Senior Officer Inshore Squadron and his ship handling against dive bombers was a little rusty. As the attack developed he turned to the navigator and told him, "Take her over, you've had more experience dodging these things than I have." It was the smartest thing that he could have done. Pilot (Navigating Officer) had a reputation for being able to take a bearing on a falling bomb and then alter course in a split second to avoid it. He was treated with special respect by the

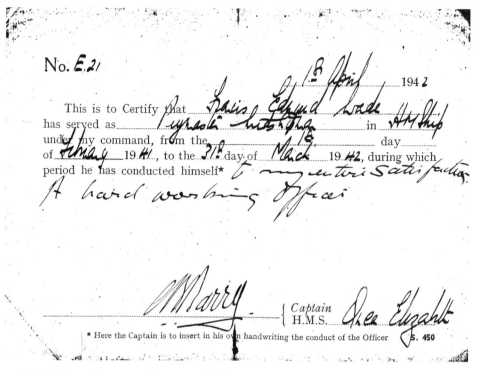

No. *E.21*

This is to Certify that *Francis Edward Wade* has served as *Paymaster Midshipman* in *H.M. Ship* under my command, from the *6* day of *February* 19 *41*, to the *31st* day of *March* 19 *42*, during which period he has conducted himself* *to my entire satisfaction. A hard working Officer*

{ Captain H.M.S. *Queen Elizabeth*

* Here the Captain is to insert in his own handwriting the conduct of the Officer   S. 450

The "Flimsey" report given to each officer on leaving a ship. Signed by Captain Claud Barry, RN of *Queen Elizabeth.*

crew who were forever in his debt for saving them on more than one occasion. Whether by luck or pilot's skill the ship was surrounded by an almost symmetrical circle of bombs, and although everyone on deck was soaked to the skin from the spray of the explosions, they suffered no injuries.

Finally night fell and the ship struggled back to Alex with each of the doctors from each of the original ships tending the sick and dying, and three extra engineering officers adding their advice on how to repair the damage incurred during the attacks.

When I came aboard, the wardroom was still haunted by the smell of antiseptic, a smell that constantly brought back memories of that terrible trip. The Gunnery Officer referred to the fact that it must have been a little disconcerting for me to join the ship just at this time. However, everyone was very friendly and helpful despite the fact I was the only midshipman aboard and very much the youngest of all the officers in the wardroom. All this was an entirely new experience for me. I was given much more responsibility in my new job as the captain's secretary — looking after the ship's correspondence—in addition to being the cypher officer. I also had my own cabin, a great improvement on my accomodation on *QE*.

Jervis had been commissioned in mid-1939, just before the war started and was the first of a revolutionary new class of fleet destroyers. She was larger than previous destroyers and therefore had more room and better accommodation for the crew and more armaments — three twin 4.7-inch gun mountings, a four gun AA pom-pom mounting, two Oerlikon guns, and ten torpedo tubes.

14th Destroyer Flotilla leader HMS *Jervis*

This class of destroyer was the first to have twin mountings, thereby increasing the number of guns for a destroyer from the usual four to six and the torpedo tubes from eight to ten.

Eight ships made up the class — *Jervis, Janus, Javelin, Jackal, Jaguar, Juno, Jupiter* and *Jersey*. Of these, only three had survived — *Jervis, Javelin and Janus* — and even these had not remained unscathed. *Javelin* had had her bows blown off under Louis Mountbatten in the Channel but got back to port, and *Janus* was badly damaged in the Syrian naval operations. Both were repaired and put back into service. *Jackal* and *Jaguar* had been sunk off Cyrenaica, *Juno* off Crete, *Jupiter* in the Java Seas, and *Jersey* off Malta. It just went to show how dangerous life in destroyers was.

The one big disadvantage of the class was that the 4.7 guns could not elevate over 60 degrees and were thus not very effective as anti-aircraft weapons. They could throw up an AA barrage at a distance but were not much use when aircraft came in low over the ship. Moreover, there was no ranging RDF onboard; guns were controlled manually.

Jervis, being the first of her class, was built to carry a flotilla commander, and was immediately commissioned as such. The first duties of the flotilla were escorting convoys up and down the east coast of England. Then, during the Norwegian campaign, it was transferred to the Home Fleet for escort work — the job these ships were designed for. Her first skipper was Captain Philip Mack who had only just been relieved by Captain Poland when I came aboard. Captain Mack became very famous as a typically dashing destroyer commander. He was a particular favourite of Cunningham, himself a former destroyer man. This was especially true after the flotilla was transferred to the Mediterranean in mid 1940.

Survivors being brought aboard the destroyer leader *Jervis* when she picked up men from the destroyers *Kipling*, *Lively*, and *Jackal*, all sunk on 12 May 1942.

Just prior to this, *Jervis* had been in refit, following a collision with a Swedish freighter in the Humber River during the evacuation from Dunkirk. She became the most senior destroyer in the Med fleet and had taken a prominent part in most of the major sea battles with the Italian Navy since the sea war had started in June 1940. She was known as a ship with a charmed life.

One of her great claims to fame occurred during the Battle of Matapan on 28 March 1941. This action happened when the Med fleet was escorting convoys to Greece, and Cunningham in *Warspite*, with *Barham*, *Valiant* and *Formidable*, plus destroyers attacked two Italian cruisers *Fiume* and *Zara* with their escorts at night and sank the two cruisers and two destroyers at point blank range.

The Italian ships had been sent to the assistance of another cruiser *Pola*, which had been damaged by torpedo aircraft from *Formidable* the previous afternoon.

Pridham-Wippell, with a cruiser squadron and destroyers, had found *Pola*, using RDF, but had pressed on to make contact with the main body of the Italian fleet. *Jervis* came upon *Pola* at 2330 lying dead in the water with many of her crew swimming around her. Captain Mack ordered *Havoc* and *Griffin* to pick up survivors and then, with considerable aplomb, took *Jervis* alongside the stricken Italian ship. Two hundred and fifty prisoners were embarked and *Nubian* was ordered to finish her off with torpedoes.

Apparently *Pola's* captain had decided to scuttle his ship and abandon her because his guns were inoperable due to a major electrical breakdown. However, some of the men in the water decided to come back aboard and were given blankets and a drink. It was at this point that *Jervis* came upon the scene and was treated to the bizarre spectacle in her searchlight of Italian sailors drinking from bottles on the upper deck of *Pola*. It rather looked as if there had been a complete breakdown of discipline in the Italian ship! Certainly *Jervis* had been involved in some extraordinary seaborne happenings before I joined her.[8]

After this, for a brief period, *14 DF* and *Jervis* operated out of Malta attacking Italian convoys sailing to Tripoli. On 15 April 1941, the flotilla went into action against three Italian destroyers and five merchant ships off the coast of southern Tunisia. All the enemy ships were either sunk or forced aground on the Kerkenah Bank, about twenty miles off the coast. *Mohawk* the Tribal class destroyer in the flotilla, was sunk by a torpedo during this action but all her survivors were rescued.

The ship also made a number of trips on the "spud run" to Tobruk during the period January to December 1941. I was told many stories about these mad nightly dashes in and out of the beleaguered port.

The ship, of course, took part in all the remaining operations of 1941 — the evacuation of Greece, "Operation Tiger", Crete, Syria and the *Barham* sinking. During early 1942, after the sinking of the battleships in Alex harbour, *Jervis* and *14 DF* were in several notable Malta convoys.

In January 1942, *Breconshire* and *Glengyle* plus a few merchant ships were passed back and forth between Alex and Malta by the fleet without incident, except for the loss of the destroyer *Gurkha*.

On 12 February 1942, another exchange of merchant ships from Malta and Alex was made by Force K and the Alex force. *Breconshire,* and three merchantmen from Malta were returned safely, but unfortunately the merchant ships *Clan Chattan* and *Rowallan Castle* from Alex were sunk by aircraft, and the third, *Clan Campbell* was damaged and had to be diverted to Tobruk. Thus, on this occasion, none of our supplies got through. Enemy air pressure on Malta was increasing again at this time, making operations in the central basin very dangerous.

Naiad, Vian's flagship, was sunk by a German submarine off Tobruk on 11 March, after a sweep by the Alex force to intercept an Italian convoy. The tough old admiral was one of the last to leave the stricken ship and was, thankfully, saved.

On 20 March 1942, another attempt was made to run a convoy through to Malta where food and fuel supplies were desperately low. The island had been under continuous air attack for weeks and few supplies were getting through. We were even sending them in by submarine. The Alex force sailed with *Breconshire* and three merchant ships, *Clan Campbell, Pampas* and *Talabot,* and rendezvoused with Force K early in the morning of 22 March 1942, midway between Benghazi and Malta. The Hunt class destroyer *Heythrop* (a new, small class of destroyer with high-angle 4-inch AA guns, newly arrived from England around the Cape of Good Hope) was sunk by a U-boat en route.

A gale was blowing up at this point when enemy cruisers were sighted in the afternoon. After a short gunnery exchange at ten miles—the extreme range of our guns—the enemy retreated northwest and the action ceased. During much of this period the fleet was also subjected to heavy air attack from both southern Sicily and Benghazi.

At 1837 the enemy reappeared, this time accompanied by the battleship *Littorio* and more destroyers. Our force turned southwest and the enemy followed suit, attempting to block our passage to Malta. Afterwards, during a two and a half hour battle, we laid a thick smoke screen between the enemy and the convoy and carried out sporadic attacks through it. Luckily the wind direction was favourable for us. We were heavily outgunned but received only light damage.

What caused the enemy to back off was a determined torpedo attack by the 14th Flotilla. I heard many accounts about this great action. *Jervis,* leading *Kipling, Kelvin, Kingston* and *Legion,* the latter ship from the Malta force, left the protection of the smokescreen in line ahead (to present a smaller target), and headed at full speed straight for the Italian battleship. They had to close the intervening distance of four miles between the smokescreen and the point where they could discharge their torpedoes, at a range of three miles, as quickly as possible. At 28 knots they would be vulnerable to heavy enemy fire for about twenty minutes from the time they left the smokescreen until they returned into it.

The ships crashed through the heavy seas with the spume and spray drenching the open forward gun positions and the open bridge. At the same time, great explosions of water burst nearby as shells from the Italian battleship and cruisers fell around them. As each ship reached the torpedo range, they followed their leader, *Jervis,* by turning north and south to fan out and discharge their torpedoes. Having completed this, they swung back to the west for the protection of the smoke, and all ships were undamaged. Some forty torpedoes were launched against the enemy and the destroyers' guns were used for a short period whilst they were in range. One shell from the flotilla appeared to hit the battleship superstructure. This engagement came to be known as the Second Battle of Sirte.

Although the Italians had been driven off, the action had delayed the convoy, which instead of arriving off Malta at night did so after sunrise the next day. This had horrendous results as the German air force in Sicily threw in everything it had. Bombing started early in the morning, but *Talabot* and *Pampas* passed into Grand Harbour at 0900. *Clan Campbell,* astern was less fortunate and was sunk by aircraft before she got in. Conditions were made more difficult by the continuing heavy weather. *Breconshire* had a terrible time. A bomb exploded in her engine room and she came to dead stop and had to anchor very close to the coast. Eventually she was towed into Marsaxlokk Bay on the south coast of the island. There she was finally sunk during another air attack. Luckily though, the oil in her was later pumped out. The initial luck enjoyed by *Pampas* and *Talabot* ran out when they were sunk in harbour before they were even partially unloaded. Later *Legion* was sunk in harbour. Despite our victory at sea, not much got through to Malta.

A great welcome was afforded our ships as they returned to Alex harbour with much waving and cheering as they slowly moved to their berths. Many of the destroyers had received storm damage, so bad was the gale. This victory was a bit of a boost after our many setbacks in 1941.

By spring of 1942 the army was still holding out west of Tobruk and we continued to dominate the Italian fleet at sea, so things weren't altogether black. However, Malta convoys from Alex were just about impossible, given the enemy's access to airfields around the eastern and central Med.

As a result, things got so bad in Malta, what with the air raids and fuel shortages, that by early April we had to withdraw our last remaining cruiser there, the *Penelope.* This meant that we only had submarines and aircraft there to attack Italian convoys en route to Africa.

The Assault ship HMS *Glengyle* entering Grand Harbour, Valleta, Malta in January 1942.

Merchant ship *Clan Chattan* in Capetown harbour.

Hunt Class destroyer being refuelled by *Queen Elizabeth*.

The Union-Castle Royal Motor Mail Vessel *Stirling Castle*.

By this time Cunningham had been relieved as C-in-C by Admiral Sir Henry Harwood of *Graf Spee* fame. Pridham-Wippell was acting C-in-C for a spell during April and May.

From the Sirte battle on 22 March 1942 until I joined *Jervis* on 27 May, very little had transpired. Our betters were clearly cogitating whether to make another effort to relieve Malta.

On my third day aboard, all fighting ships went to sea for practises, sailing at 0800. First we carried out a mock torpedo attack, followed by a gunnery

Italian battleship *Littorio*.

shoot at a barge on a long tow. Then we practised an anti-aircraft barrage. In the afternoon all ships manoeuvred in unison to lay a smokescreen between an imaginary convoy and the enemy. The admiral was trying out some old tactics with a few new wrinkles.

During the first exercise we made a submarine contact and started to drop depth charges and the fleet dispersed in all directions. This was soon stopped as the contact was later adjudged to be false. We were still pretty edgy after the *Barham* sinking.

It was a hot day with a calm sea, and the bustle of so many sleek cruisers and destroyers cutting through the water was something to see. At one stage we steamed at right angles toward *Dido;* a somewhat dangerous exercise. She made a striking sight as she flashed across in front of us at full speed, her grey hull slipping easily through the waters with her bow foaming, while white-capped intent figures peered ahead on her bridge. Black smoke billowed from her funnels, covering her stern and part of her after superstructure, all the while creating a thick black wall astern of her. The next minute we were into the smoke, just like a London fog. Everyone on the bridge stared into the blackness, coughing and spluttering. And then we were out again in the clear Mediterranean, heading for the supposed enemy. We repeated this for several days until we got it right.

Then one day the first indication that a new operation was afoot reached us. A large envelope arrived, inside which was another one stamped "Top Secret" and sealed with the tell-tale red wax seal. It bore the injuction, "To be opened personally by the Commanding Officer." One look and I knew that it contained a set of operation orders. It arrived in the evening so I took it aft to the captain's cabin immediately.

He was clearly expecting it. He had been to several conferences onboard *Cleopatra* with the admiral. It was obvious that another Malta convoy was in the offing. I waited whilst he carefully slit it open and pulled out a thick wad of typed pages. My eyes were averted as he put on his glasses and began to read. After a few lines he looked up and told me to carry on.

He was not a man for small talk, although he was usually very polite with his officers and men. He was certainly not one to evoke a great response from his sailors, like Captain Barry. He had a temper which erupted from time to time as I well knew from direct experience.

So I wasn't to see the orders for a while. For a week he sat on them. Every now and then I brought down several cyphers outlining amendments, but unfortunately I couldn't glean much from them.

Every night I thought about those orders while the rest of the ship's company remained blissfully ignorant. They could only be about a Malta convoy. On the other hand, in my more optimistic moments, I speculated that they might concern a bombardment up the coast. Finally the captain thrust them at me together with the amendments with the comment, "Here, take these damned orders and bring them up to date!"

Looking as unconcerned as I could, I hurriedly retreated to my office and shut the door. My worst predictions were correct. All too unmistakably I read that the object of the operation was "To pass convoy MX 12 from Alexandria to Malta." My heart skipped a beat. I read on. The code name was "Vigorous." It amounted to a concerted effort to relieve Malta which, as the orders pointedly emphasized, was the pivot of our Mediterranean strategy. Unless the island was substantially reinforced with food and supplies it would be useless within a month or so. Intelligence had uncovered evidence of an intended airborne invasion of the island and every possible effort and sacrifice had to be made to get the convoy through.

To this end, the fleet was to be reinforced by two cruisers and two flotillas of destroyers from the Eastern fleet at Colombo in Ceylon. These units were to pass through the Suez Canal a few days before the convoy was set to leave. To give the impression that we were not without a capital ship, an old battleship and target towing ship, the *Centurion*, had been disguised as a King George V class battleship. For security reasons, the eleven merchant ships involved were to be loaded in the Red Sea ports of Massawa and Port Sudan.

At the same time, a large operation was also being mounted to pass another convoy from Gibraltar to Malta. Thus, an enormous concerted effort was afoot, with worldwide implications, to keep Malta alive.

The operation started when a dummy convoy sailed from Haifa toward Tobruk to try to deceive the enemy. The idea was to lure the Italian fleet to sea and attack it from the air and by submarine before our main body sailed. Clearly we needed something to offset our weak surface ship situation: we only had cruisers whereas the Italians had battleships. To this end, the RAF were going to help us with some bombers from Malta and there was now a new air element in the Mediterranean — United States Army Air Force long-range bombers in Egypt which would also be used to attack the Italian fleet.

The dummy convoy comprised *Coventry* and the 5th destroyer Flotilla, composed of the Hunt class destroyers *Dulverton*, *Exmoor*, *Croome*, *Eridge*, *Airedale*, *Beaufort*, *Hurworth*, *Tetcott* and *Aldenham* escorting the merchant ship *Rembrandt*. It set out on Thursday, 11 June 1942, and sailed about 350 miles to the west until it was slightly to the northwest of Alex. Then it reversed direction and met up with the main force on Saturday 13 June 1942.

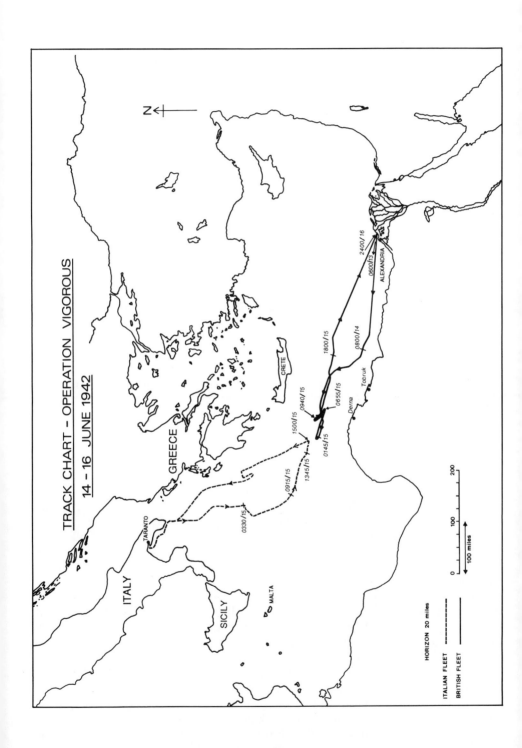

TRACK CHART – OPERATION VIGOROUS
14 – 16 JUNE 1942

ITALY

GREECE

TARANTO

SICILY

MALTA

CRETE

Derma

Tobruk

ALEXANDRIA

N

0330/15
0915/15
1345/15
1500/15
0940/15
0145/15
0655/15
1800/15
0800/14
2400/16
0600/13

HORIZON 20 miles

ITALIAN FLEET
BRITISH FLEET

0   100   200
100 miles

The latter force consisted of Vian's battlefleet comprising the 15th Cruiser Squadron, *Cleopatra* (flagship), *Dido, Hermione, Euryalus* and *Arethusa,* and the 4th Cruiser Squadron from the Far East, *Birmingham* (flagship under Rear-Admiral W.G. Tennant) and *Newcastle.* These two cruisers were slightly larger than the *Dido* class cruisers that we had in the Med fleet, and carried 6 inch guns as against *Dido's* 5.25-inch main armament. Lying in the middle of the fleet, as if she were being protected, was the *Centurion* (ostensibly the *Duke of York*) looking very much like a heavy modern battleship.

In total, the escort numbered seventeen fleet destroyers. From the 14th DF came *Jervis, Kelvin* and *Javelin;* from the Australian 7th, *Napier, Nestor, Nizam and Norman;* from the 12th, *Pakenham, Paladin* and *Inconstant;* from the 22nd, *Sikh, Zulu, Hasty* and *Hero* and from the 2nd, *Fortune, Griffin* and *Hotspur.*

As can be seen the Med fleet had been reinforced with more cruisers and destroyers from the United Kingdom as well as the Far East.

There were also two minesweepers *Boston* and *Seaham,* which were to sweep the convoy into Malta if necessary. And, finally there were four corvettes, *Delphinium, Primula, Erica* and *Snapdragon,* and two rescue ships, *Antwerp* and *Malines.*

Ten merchant ships were involved (eleven including *Rembrandt*), *City of Pretoria, City of Calcutta, City of Edinburgh, City of Lincoln, Bhutan, Potaro, Ajax, Elizabeth Bakke, Aagtekerk* and *Bulkoil.* Total tonnage was 72,000. Four of these merchantmen each had a motor torpedo boat (MTB) in tow in case of an expected German E-boat attack from North Africa.

Altogether, the force amounted to eight cruisers, twenty-six destroyers, four corvettes, two minesweepers and four MTBs — the largest British force that we had put to sea since Crete.

Nothing noteworthy transpired on 13 June except that *Elizabeth Bakke* was found to be too slow and had to be sent back to Alex.

Jervis lay ahead of the fleet in the centre of a screen of seventeen fleet destroyers, which stretched out four miles on either side. Well astern of us were the merchant ships in two columns, accompanied by their close escort of Hunt class destroyers. The cruisers — there were so many of them — and smaller vessels were disposed around them. This huge array, heading west, seemed to spread right across the horizon from north to south.

Throughout the operation I was very busy cyphering, keeping up with the busy traffic passing from Alex to the fleet, Malta, and Tobruk. I was the sole watchkeeper and had no one to spell me, and thus had very little sleep throughout the trip. Most of the time I was kept busy in my office in the after superstructure, so I only caught occasional glimpses of the action when I was walking on the upper deck forward to the bridge or the chart room. From the evening of Saturday 13 June to noon of Tuesday 16 June we were closed up at action stations almost without break, a period of two and a half days.

An encouraging sign on the Saturday and the forenoon and early afternoon of Sunday 14 June was the presence overhead of two or four fighters from our airfields in Egypt and Cyrenaica. This aerial coverage would continue until we were to the west of Tobruk. However, from Sunday afternoon onwards, after we were out of their range, we expected heavy attacks by German aircraft from Crete. We had turned north in the morning to get away from the Cyrenaican coast and the German aircraft there. But this put us closer to Crete.

C-in-C with Captain A.L. Poland on *Jervis*.

As it happened no air attacks developed during the day on the Sunday, presumably because the German air force in the desert was tied up in the fierce land fighting that was going on there, and the Crete aircraft were not yet aware of our presence. A major desert land battle, immediately to our south, had erupted as our naval operation was being carried out. It was taking place along the Gazala Line, which ran for fifty miles southwards from the coast, east of Derna and west of Tobruk, through fortified desert strong points until it reached the southern end at Bir Hacheim. Here, the Free French Brigade, after putting up very stiff resistance against a very large German force, was forced to evacuate and there was fighting raging all along the line to try and contain the Germans. Clearly Rommel had launched yet another major offensive.

During the day on Sunday the wind started to increase and a fair swell developed, thereby creating difficulties for the merchant ships towing the MTB's. So these were cast off and ordered back to Alex.

At about 2200 that night enemy aircraft — most likely from Crete about 175 miles away — dropped flares astern of us over the convoy.

This type of night bombing was something new and it was quite a sight to see the whole horizon astern lit up. The flares descended very slowly, clearly illuminating the sea below them before dying and then flashing alive again as they neared the water. The whole convoy was visible and all the merchant ships were clearly silhouetted against the horizon.

Two casualties resulted from this attack. *The City of Calcutta* was damaged and had to be diverted to Mersa Matruh with a Hunt class destroyer escort, and the corvette *Erica* was shaken up by a near miss, became too slow to continue and had to return to Alex.

On the morning of Monday the 14th, *Aagtekerk* developed engine room troubles and had to be diverted to Tobruk with escort. Later in the day Tobruk radioed that she had been sunk by Stukas off that port. Already we had lost three of our eleven merchant ships.

Around 1400, the expected daytime Stuka air attacks started in earnest. In some ways we were relieved that the suspense of waiting was past; the sooner they started the quicker they would be over. Also, we now had something to keep ourselves preoccupied. There had most certainly been a definite change in the ship's atmosphere as we approached the expected deadline for the attacks.

The first wave comprised a formation of medium-level Heinkel bombers which went straight for the merchant ships. Despite an enormous hail of gunfire from every ship, none was shot down but there were no direct hits on the ships. Then came the Stukas. I was on the bridge as the attack developed. They also left the warships alone and attacked the freighters. The sky was pockmarked with white puffs through which the black moving specks, which were the deadly dive bombers, could be seen. They came in groups from all directions. The total of all the formations must have numbered about sixty aircraft. They made a very concerted and brave attack, diving in right over their intended victims and swooping down low. This looked like a repeat of the fearful attacks over Cretan waters. By now they were also attacking the cruisers and I saw a *Dido* and a *Southampton* class cruiser being straddled but seemingly missed.

Three dived straight down on to the oiler *Bulkoil* which was carrying highly explosive aviation fuel. Sub-Lieutenant Nowson, my old QE buddy, was aboard her as the naval liaison officer, as I had noticed his name in the operation orders. One never knew what kind of appointment one would get next! I knew his parents, who lived in Alex, and had stayed with them on several occasions in their small flat near the Sporting Club. Luckily for them I was sure that they didn't have any idea of what danger their son was in. Equally luckily, the tanker steamed through the attack unscathed.

The air attacks continued nonstop throughout the afternoon, as expected, and at 1500 *Bhutan* was hit, sinking very quickly. The two rescue ships collected her survivors and headed for Tobruk at full speed, to get back to us as quickly as possible. *Potaro* was also struck, but was only slightly damaged and kept going.

Landing Ship Infantry *City of Edinburgh*.

Then at 1800 to add to our worries, we received a signal by light from the flagship *Cleopatra* that the Italian fleet had sailed from Taranto during the afternoon. After some quick figuring in the wardroom it was estimated that, at the closing speed of the two fleets, we would make contact with it by 1000 the following morning. That evening two more merchant ships parted company with us, having been damaged during the air attacks. Now we had only five merchantmen left.

At about 2200 after darkness had fallen, we started getting reports that German E-boats were around. All this was going on as the air raids of the previous night were being repeated. The flares, when they were on would easily light up the convoy for the German E-boats. A young VR Sub-lieutenant had joined us in Alex and was in charge of a special radio receiving set that had been installed in the chart room which could be tuned to E-boat frequencies. Fluent in German, his job was to advise Captain (D) about the intended movements of these craft. This equipment had been used quite successfully in the English Channel. Our man was a very quiet, scholarly chap who reminded me of my friend Frankie. That night I listened as he monitored the chatter. It was an eerie sensation to hear the German E-boat voices through the background static. The guttural sounds were distinctly threatening.

After the flare attack ended we could still hear the E-boats. *Kelvin,* near us in the screen, sighted one around midnight and there was quite a flap on the bridge as a result. From then on, all our lookouts were forever imagining that they had made a sighting, a forgiveable mistake given the gunfire that we kept hearing and seeing astern, near the convoy, where an E-boat attack was indeed taking place. The captain considered whether to fire star-shell to light up the immediate area, but decided against it as it would probably be more advantageous to the enemy than to us.

At around 0200 we received an inexplicable order from the flagship for the convoy to immediately swing around 180 degrees and head back east to Alex. This was a complicated manoeuvre since the extensive screen of destroyers had to redeploy itself astern of the convoy as quickly as possible and re-establish a new screen heading the other way. While this was going on the main body had to turn to place itself in position behind the new screen. In the interim, anti-submarine protection and defence against E-boats was not fully effective. The manoeuvre took about twenty minutes. I had taken a short nap at the time, but was awakened soon after to hear about it and given a cypher by a telegraphist.

By the time I took the decyphered message to the bridge we had already turned about but were still very much on the lookout for E-boats. *Newcastle* had apparently been hit by a torpedo from one of them but was able to keep up her speed, while the fleet destroyer *Hasty,* far out on the screen, a veteran of so many actions, had unfortunately been sunk by one. Her sister ship *Hotspur* picked up her survivors and despatched her with a torpedo as, although seriously damaged, she was sinking too slowly. The course reversal didn't seem to make any sense, particularly in the middle of an E-boat attack.

We had more cruisers on this occasion than when Vian had successfully fought the Italians in the two Sirte battles, so why turn tail on this occasion?

At sunrise on 15 June, the Stukas arrived back on schedule, and squadrons of them appeared thereafter at intervals of about twenty minutes. Just a little earlier at 0615, we had been ordered to turn around westward again and had fortunately completed this manoeuvre before the aircraft arrived. I wondered what on earth was going on. This type of apparent indecision was disturbing, and we had lost a lot of valuable time.

This day was clearly going to be another big one in the life of *Jervis* and, we hoped, a successful and safe one. Number One, Guns, and Torps moved around the ship, when they had a chance, to prepare her for the expected surface action. All of them had been through this sort of thing before and knew exactly what to look for and what to expect.

Air attacks continued with some near misses but apparently caused no serious damage. *Bulkoil,* a favourite target, seemed to be leading a charmed life. Even so, I could well imagine what Nowson was going through. Even the old *Centurion* was getting a lot of attention. By now the German pilots must have finally realized that there was something odd about her and that she didn't have the anti-aircraft guns of a modern British battleship. However, she too was coming through unscathed.

A few of the aircraft now started to bomb the fleet destroyers on the edge of the screen, where the concentration of fire power against them was not so great. The action was now getting close to home. Throughout the previous day and during the morning, we had had the relative luxury of watching proceedings from afar, hardly using our guns. This was because the Germans tended to come in from the north, east, or south, and we were lying to the west of the convoy. But now this was all changing.

After breakfast I decyphered a message from C-in-C stating that torpedo-carrying Wellingtons from Malta had unsuccessfully attacked the Italian fleet during the night. A later attack by Beaufort torpedo-bombers from Malta, however, had got a hit on an Italian cruiser. In the early morning Beauforts from Sidi Barrani and USAAF Liberators from Egypt — the latter being used for the first time over the sea in this command — carried out further attacks. The Americans, to their great credit, had got a hit on the Italian battleship *Littorio.* A later message stated that the damaged Italian cruiser *Trento* had been sunk by our submarine *Thorn* at 0700.

Warrant Ordnance Officer C. Simms, the Chief Engine Room Artificer (ERA) and Warrant Engineer N. Card, on *Jervis* during a lull in "Operation Vigorous" May, 1942.

As this good news was being conveyed to the crew over the SRE, we received yet another order from the flagship to turn around. This, despite the fact that morning air recce reports had indicated that the Italian Fleet was just over the horizon — about 80 miles, or an hour away.

A definite sense of anticlimax overwhelmed us as we headed away from the battle. In a situation like this, one steels oneself for the worst; that the ship could be sunk and one could end up in the water. Yet there were always positive thoughts to fall back on, such as the fact that the Italians never seemed to press home their attacks. The continued changes of orders from C-in-C were annoying everyone. It was depressing to think that we were not going to get the merchant ships through to Malta and the whole great venture was going to be a failure.

Just after we had settled down in the new direction, with the screen formed up in a proper order, there was a lull in the action for the first time in hours, and the captain had gone below to his cabin. Soon after, at 1015 I received an urgent cypher from C-in-C which set my heart racing again. The 14th DF with the Hunts under our command was to take over the remaining five merchant ships and attempt to fight our way through to Malta. I quickly attempted to work out the implications of this. The island was now about 400 miles, or twenty-four hours sailing away, eight hours of which would at night. Our estimated time of arrival at 1000 would be in broad daylight, and being so close to Malta, we could anticipate constant, concentrated bombing from dawn onwards.

I rushed up to the bridge with the decyphered message and, still in a state of some shock, knocked on the captain's sea cabin door. I realized, as everyone else would soon realize, that this would be an extremely dangerous mission. I had expected that the old man would be asleep, after nearly 24 hours on the bridge. However, he wasn't, and looked up at me from his bunk with a sort of distracted expression as if his mind was miles away. I handed him the message straight away. He looked at it for a long time without moving and, as was his habit in tense moments like this, said nothing. Fighting my inclination to discuss the subject, I kept my mouth shut. Finally he responded. I was to bring him anything new without delay. Then he slowly got up, put on his jacket, and prepared to make his way back up to the bridge, without a word.

I clambered back down to my office to await the next messages and, sure enough, they started pouring in. None was important, as they concerned some lighters going to Tobruk. Then after about fifteen minutes another urgent message came in and I immediately started working on it. To my amazement, it was C-in-C cancelling the last order for us to go to Malta. They certainly were in a quandary in Alex about what to do with us. I couldn't help thinking that none of this would have happened under Cunningham.

When I got back to the bridge with the latest orders, we were still in the screen with the convoy astern of us. Nothing had been done to carry out the order to proceed to Malta. The raids persisted with no let up and, if anything, the enemy was throwing in even more aircraft. This was hardly surprising, as we were now moving from the central basin back towards Crete.

At 1500 the Hunt class destroyer *Airedale* was seriously hit and had to be sunk. Later at 1800 the Aussie destroyer *Nestor* was also hit not far from us. She was seriously damaged by three close misses which lifted her almost out of the water with a great crash. *Javelin,* of our flotilla, took her in tow and three Hunts were detached to escort them to Alex. However, next morning C-in-C ordered her to be scuttled since the little force was being attacked by E-boats. She was finally sunk by depth charges.

The cruiser *Birmingham* was also damaged by a near miss. It was proving to be another depressing and scary afternoon with a mounting toll of losses as the air attacks continued. With some of the attacks still being carried out against the destroyer screen one wondered whether we would be the next victim. We were now firing our guns almost continuously; our 4.7-inch, our close-range pom-pom and Oerlikons.

Finally we were picked out for an attack and, all of a sudden, I heard a loud thunderclap overhead — the unnerving whine of Stukas — as they dived down at us, and the shouts of our gun crews and the staccato of our close-range guns as they tried to hit them. Then the ship shook violently but, to my great relief, still continued on her course. Thanks to God we had not been hit. The tremor had been from the force of a very near miss.

These attacks continued sporadically until sunset, by which time we were moving away from Crete. As darkness began to fall, one last torpedo attack developed. Instead of going for the main body of the fleet the attackers went for the destroyer screen. Before we realised what was going on, one singled out *Jervis*. In a very brave attack the aircraft came in close from astern dropping its torpedo before we could open fire. I knew nothing about the attack but was told later that it ran straight toward the ship on the starboard side, being deflected by our wake. It ran up the side of the ship disappearing in the gloom.

After dark there was a lull and we went to second degree of readiness and some of the crew were allowed to sleep or rest at their station while others were sent down to the galley to get a hot meal. Before long, however, the lull was past. The E-boats came back and their radio chatter could be heard from all over the place. There was an alarm in the convoy area and I heard later that the cruiser *Hermione* had been sunk by a submarine with a tragic heavy loss of life; so quickly had she sunk.

By the time dawn came up on 16 June we were well on our way back to Alex, about 200 miles or ten hours sailing away. Luckily, no other ships were lost during the rest of the night and we arrived at the Grand Pass by the late evening. The operation had been a bad setback for us, with one cruiser, three destroyers and two merchant ships sunk, as well as two cruisers damaged, one, the *Newcastle,* fairly seriously.

At the same time that we were carrying out our operation, a major convoy was sailed from Gibraltar to Malta. This was "Operation Harpoon." Of the original six merchant ships which sailed, two got through. So Malta had been given some relief, no matter how small, and I suppose we had indirectly contributed to this partial success.The "Harpoon" group lost four merchant ships and two destroyers, *Bedouin* and the Polish *Kujawiak* while the cruiser *Liverpool* was badly damaged.

The various changes of orders that we had received and that had been so confusing had resulted from C-in-C, Admiral Harwood's interference. Firstly, at around midnight on the 14th, Vian had signalled Harwood that it would be difficult for our force to fight off the superior Italian force during the day, given the excellent weather conditions. Harwood then ordered him to keep going until 0145 on the 15th. Then he was to turn back to allow our nine submarines, strung out across the path of the Italians, to attack, and to allow our aircraft to strike.[9]

Thereafter Harwood decided that the fleet should turn back toward the enemy at 0655 on the 15th, as the attacks had been accomplished with some success. Later he learned that they had not stopped the Italian fleet, which was still on course directly toward us.

As a result, at 0930, he decided to withdraw the fleet to await the results of the Liberator attacks at 0940. At 1345 on the 15th another signal was sent ordering Vian to turn back toward the enemy. This he ignored because our two large cruisers had been damaged and our ships, particularly the destroyers, were running out of AA ammunition. At the rate we were sacrificing warships, we would lose most of our fleet, especially if we ran out of AA ammunition. I suppose thoughts of Crete were in his mind. The number of German aircraft again on this occasion seemed limitless.

Harwood then gave his consent to Vian's action. Information was received later that the Italians had indeed turned north for home, and this prompted Harwood's suggestion that some of the destroyers try to get the four fastest merchant ships through. Vian urged that this was impracticable because of the poor AA ammunition supply situation, with the result that this order was also cancelled.

The difference between "Vigorous" and the two battles of Sirte was that the Luftwaffe was not such a factor in the sea battles and Vian had had freedom to attack the Italian fleet without the added problem of air attack. An additional difficulty was that the most effective AA destroyers, the Hunts, only had a third of their shells left in the later stages of the *"Vigorous"* operation.

The basic problem was that the delay of five hours, when we were heading back to Alex, had set us back and increased the distance that we had to steam. All in all it had been a bit of a fiasco. With the wisdom of hindsight, DF 14 should have fought its way with the convoy through to the beleaguered island because, unknown to us, the Luftwaffe in Sicily had just been moved to North Africa to assist Rommel in his major offensive. However, the "Harpoon" convoy had taken quite a beating despite this, and no doubt we too would have sustained losses.

CHAPTER TEN

The Evacuation of Alexandria

On our return to Alex, there was much gossip about the fighting in the desert around the Gazala line. Apparently it was very fierce and a typical desert melee. Reports on the radio and in the Alex press were sparse. At first the word was that we had Rommel on the ropes, although the fighting was touch and go. Our armour and the German armour were apparently moving swiftly from one area of action to another in an attempt to outwit each other. Then, on 20 June 1942 — a date not easily forgotten — we heard that the line had collapsed; we had suffered a terrible defeat and were retreating helter-skelter to the Egyptian border. Worse still, Tobruk had fallen.

Second-hand stories from the survivors of Tobruk pointed to a real shambles. British troops had been pulled out quite some time before and had been replaced by the 2nd South African Division, mostly Afrikaners, who had apparently made a very poor effort at stopping the Afrika Korps. Our naval forces, expecting that the port would be held as before, were not prepared for the sudden collapse, especially as Tobruk's defences, about seven miles from the harbour area, were very extensive and strong.

The German armour came in from the southeast in great strength. They had been expected from the southwest where the South African Division was

MTB 260 (U.S. PT boat) moving across Alexandria harbour, 1942. A *Mona's Queen* Class Isle of Man ferry fast troopship to the right.

Sub-Lieutenant Paul Pidcock, RCNVR sitting on "Bardia Bill" dud shell in Tobruk.

located. Before NOIC realized it, the Germans were descending on the harbour. He had been given no warning by the South African commander General Klopper, so Navy House and the small ships in harbour were unprepared.

Our MLs, MTBs, A lighters, and other small harbour craft tried to get out under cover of a hastily laid smokescreen. A number of them were hit and sunk right in the harbour. The smokescreen had been laid by MTB 260, an American built PT boat, in which Lieutenant Paul Pidcock RCNVR was serving.

He said that a heavier than usual bombardment plus heavy air attacks started early in the morning, and they knew that something was up. The skipper went ashore to Admiralty house and returned with bad news that the Germans had launched a major attack on the perimeter.

After several hours of continuous attacks, and with no instructions from ashore, it was decided to slip out of their camouflaged berth alongside *San Georgio*, and lay a smoke screen around the harbour to protect several ships which appeared to have been hit and were in difficulties.

As this was being done, they came across a schooner that had been hit and was sinking — not far from the main jetty. The MTB's bow was brought in to touch the schooner's stern and the crew and passengers, all army types, clambered aboard. They amounted to nearly a hundred souls who were packed in every nook and cranny of the tiny little ship and on the 150 foot long upper deck. He remembers seeing one lying on the deck with his legs missing.

As some craft were making for the boom to get out to sea, they decided to follow suit. The ship was damaged by shrapnel from a near miss and the steering compartment began to take on water. However, they were able to control this and keep going.

On the way out, they stopped to pick up a lone swimmer. He said that they went through the boom at full speed — 40 knots, and the passengers held on

Greek Caique used to supply Tobruk.

for dear life. Several miles out at sea they came across the boom defence vessel *Magnet* and the minsweeper *Aberdare*, so they transferred their passengers to the much larger *Aberdare*, and headed east.

On arrival at Mersa Matruh, they were told that Rommel was not far off, so immediately took off again. The skipper decided to celebrate their good fortune by "Splicing the Mainbrace" (an extra tot of rum for the passengers and crew), and they finally arrived safely in Alex.

The little minesweepers HMSAS *Bever* and HMSAS *Parktown* carried out their routine morning sweep off the entrance that morning. Later in the afternoon as they were alongside embarking the naval shore party and troops, they were fired on by German tanks. *Bever* was hit with some minor damage and one casualty. However, after a hasty cast off of their lines, they were able to escape to sea unscathed, mainly due to the smoke screen laid by MTB 260. Like the rest of the escaping ships they came under heavy shore fire as they cleared the entrance.

Parktown was the last allied ship to leave. Enroute west she had to tow a tug, filled with troops, which had broken down. After the next dawn came up, they were attacked by German E-boats from Derna. *Parktown* was severely damaged with a heavy loss of life and wounded. For some reason, the E-boats were attacked by their own planes, and retired.

The tug was assisted by one of our MTBs and eventually got her engines going again. *Parktown's* survivors were picked up and she was sunk by a torpedo from the MTB. The little force retreated east with no more mishaps, finally arriving at Alexandria.

Captain Frank Smith RNR, the celebrated NOIC, who had been in Tobruk from the beginning, was killed. Captain Walters, Senior Officer Inshore Squadron was wounded and taken prisoner. German tanks actually got around the

Albury class minesweeper HMS *Aberdare*.

harbour to the coast and shot up ships and craft as they tried to get out through the entrance to the open sea.

On receipt of this news in Alex, all leave was cancelled and the base went into a complete flap, with orders being issued right and left to evacuate the place as quickly as possible. If the front moved well to the east of the Egyptian border, which it showed every sign of doing, the city would fall within the range of the German desert air force. As we were confined to our ships, we had very little idea about what was actually happening ashore. Such information as we could gather from visiting boats indicated that many civilians were crowding the stations to get to Palestine. All our shore establishments were moving east to the Canal area.

Mrs. David Amoore of West Vancouver who was a wren there then, says that all the wrens were evacuated and placed on the troopship *Princess Kathleen* in Suez Bay. They were being kept ready for immediate transfer south to Mombasa in Kenya in the event that Alexandria and Cairo fell.

Some shop owners had apparently pulled down the pictures of our King and put up ones of Mussolini and Hitler. Others had actually boarded up their windows in anticipation of trouble. Until then I had always had the impression that the Egyptian non-belligerents were basically pro-British. Certainly I had never run into any problems and found the people to be helpful and friendly, despite the fact that perhaps our younger officers and men did not always behave in the best possible manner. Certainly one could hardly blame them for being against us, as we had taken over their country for all intents and purposes. Our fear was that they would make life very difficult for us at this critical time, by taking to the streets or creating a political crisis. But this did not happen.

On 25 June 1942 Mersa Matruh, inside the Egyptian border, fell, thereby confirming previous reports that the situation at the front was indeed serious.

Wren Edythe Dunn (now Mrs. D. Amoore) being promoted to Leading Wren at Parade at Port Tewfik, June 1942.

QE, which by this time was more or less ready to sail, was hastily floated out of the drydock and sent on her way. On the same day 14 DF sailed from Alex with two fleet tankers for Haifa, where we arrived the following day without mishap. This was a great relief for we had been very much on the lookout for U-boats, which were thought to be deployed in numbers in the area.

We were only in harbour for a few hours, but I managed to get ashore. Haifa lies on the southern end of the Bay of Acre, about twenty miles from the border. It faces north and is protected by a long mole on its seaward side with Mount Carmel — a high hill but not a mountain — dominating the harbour from the south. The town itself reaches up it from the harbour front.

The streets were almost empty and the houses and buildings were not particularly interesting, displaying little eastern influence. Most of them were flat-roofed and many were run down. The place seemed to be a bit of a backwater. There were few Arabs around; most of the people I saw were Jews. Quite a few of them were young; they were no doubt Sabras born in Palestine of European immigrant parents.

We sailed back to Alex, arriving there on 27 June. As we approached the harbour entrance, we received a warning that enemy aircraft had dropped a number of pressure mines in the harbour. We accordingly reduced speed as we went through the entrance gates, cleared lower decks, except for a skeleton crew in the engine room, and slowly and cautiously worked our way to our mooring buoys. We all stood on the upper deck fearing the worst. There seemed to be very few people about ashore.

The harbour was empty except for the French ships and a few of our own stragglers. At the time of our withdrawal to Haifa, Admiral Harwood had

requested Admiral Godfroy to join in with the evacuation. This the French admiral had, with characteristic obstinacy, refused to do, declaring that he would scuttle his squadron in the event of the Germans capturing the city. Knowing him, we had every confidence that he would have done it. Several MTBs were left behind to do the job if necessary.

Our present task was to escort our own stragglers to Port Said, leaving the French fleet to its own devices. By this time there were only a few ships remaining in Alex. *Woolwich* and *Resource*, two large maintenance vessels, and *Medway*, the submarine depot ship, had already gone. The only large ship left was *Glenroy* and we surmised she was being left to block the harbour entrance.

While back in harbour we learned that the Afrika Korps was less than fifty miles away and that a great battle to halt the German advance was in progress. How-

Wren E. Dunn (centre) on Alexandria Corniche with two friends, 1943.

ever, there were strong fears that the city could fall at any minute, and we had hardly moored ship before orders were signalled from the shore base at Ras el Tin that we take off again immediately.

This time we escorted a mixed bag of freighters and small ships of various types, leaving nothing behind except a few harbour craft. We made our way out of harbour very gingerly and arrived safely off Port Said on 30 June. All told the evacuation of Alex was executed without loss, except for *Medway,* which fell victim to a submarine on 30 June.

McGill saw a different side to the evacuation than we did. Once we got to Port Said, although we talked about what we would do if the Germans broke through, we tended to be optimistic that all would be well. McGill says that everyone in Alex expected the worst.

He wrote a letter to his girl friend — who later became his wife — and asked a friend, who was returning to England, to take it with him. He thought that it might be his last letter to her.

As the last convoy was leaving the port, damaged tanks, tattered lorries and columns of dishevelled and dispirited troops began to come into the city in a continuous column from the west. They moved through El Mex down the main road past Gabarri dock eastward, for all to see. They gave the definite impression of a dejected and defeated army in retreat.

We in *Jervis* never saw or heard of any of this, which was probably just as well.

McGill was part of a small naval rearguard party of officers and men who were to make a last ditch stand at El Mex to blow up the airport and main road as the enemy approached.

During this flap, he took part in one of the strangest incidents of his naval career. He had heard that a senior officer had given instructions to blow up the MTB base which was against the port admiral's orders and which, thankfully, was never carried out. There had been a number of incidents where naval shore units had taken matters into their own hands and packed up and left without proper permission.

This officer had been summarily tried by a quickly organised court martial and found guilty of disobeying orders in the face of the enemy.

All officers and men remaining behind at Ras El Tin were hastily assembled on the sandy parade quadrangle. The senior officer was marched in, under armed guard, into the centre of them. The charges and punishment were read and his ribbons, buttons and gold braid rank stripes were cut off his uniform as he stood at attention. He was then marched off. He was to be dishonourably discharged and sent back to England, and must have felt like a man who didn't have a country. It was the same ceremony — which is not mentioned in any book of regulations — that I had seen on the *Conway*.

To enter Port Said, a ship must turn south as the city appears on the horizon, and proceed down a two mile dredged channel beside a long breakwater. The Canal proper starts as soon as land is reached, with Port Said to the west of the entrance and Port Fuad to the east. It then continues south through the flat desert.

In those days, both ports were quite small and relatively attractive, possessing no large buildings except for one facing the Canal front on the Said side, the celebrated Simons Art department store. This emporium had long catered to the passengers of the P & O and other liners plying between Britain and India.

Once we had delivered our charges, we went alongside a jetty in front of Navy House. This had formerly been the Suez Canal Authority building, but had been commandeered by NOIC. The rest of the flotilla and the cruisers were moored further up the Canal. This was to be our permanent berth. It was handy to the offices of NOIC where I used to go ashore to get hand messages, and the downtown area. Port Said is located on a promontory of landfill on the east side of a large swampy lake, which is part of the Nile estuary — Alex being on the opposite side to the west.

In early July we learned that the army, reinforced with fresh troops and tanks, had finally stopped Rommel in his tracks about forty-five miles west of Alex, at a place called El Alamein. This was a good spot to make our last stand because the Quattara Depression (a quicksand area) to the south ruled out a German outflanking attack.

In mid-July, a naval operation was planned in support of the army to bombard Mersa Matruh, now 125 miles behind the front and the enemy's most forward supply port. On 18 July 1942, the cruisers *Dido* and *Euryalus* and three destroyers, *Jervis, Javelin* and *Pakenham,* set out from Port Said to carry this out. We sailed at 1700 to be off El Alamein by 2200 and off Matruh by 0200/19th. The return trip would be particularly dangerous because we would be off Alamein after dawn and liable to heavy air attacks.

The weather conditions were clear as we left but there was a fairly strong wind blowing and a slight swell. Although we wouldn't be off enemy territory until dark, we went to action stations at 1900 to be on the safe side. The destroyers provided an A/S screen for the two cruisers, but just before arriving off Matruh the formation was changed to line ahead, with *Jervis* leading the destroyers and the cruisers following behind.

There was always something exciting about fast destroyers moving at top speed in line ahead into a night battle. This was especially true if one was on the bridge. Firstly there was the noise of the sea crashing against the bows and, above you, the rattling of the rigging from the oncoming wind and the flapping of the huge battle ensign on the foremast. Looking aft, sparks flew out of the funnel and the heated air from it cast a blurred mist over the superstructure. The phosphorescent waves from the bow tumbled down the ship's side at great speed. On that night there were also small clouds which periodically blocked out the few visible stars in the sky. In the gloom astern one could make out the ships of the flotilla, straining to keep up with us.

Being the leader, our ship didn't have to keep station with the ship ahead. The flotilla had to conform to our movements. Everyone on deck was all attentiveness, eyes constantly moving from side to side, as we steamed off the hostile coast, where there was always the possibility of E-boat and submarine attacks.

The captain sat on his stool on the starboard side of the bridge. The officer of the watch, legs astride behind the centred binnacle, swept his glasses back and forth across the waters, periodically looking down at the dimly lit compass in front of him. Every now and then he would talk quietly down the voice pipe to the helmsman below. Guns, a little agitated, talked to the gun positions, the director (rangefinder) behind up the mast, and the TS (Transmitting Station) far below in the bowels of the ship. Everything had to be ready in the gunnery department before the deadline. Torps, as usual was out of a job; we did not anticipate firing torpedoes that night, although there was always a possibilty. He stood to one side peering through his glasses at some shore lights that were coming up in the distance. The navigator was very active, moving between his charts, under a canvas canopy at the front of the bridge and the bridge platform so he could look out for something on the land to take a bearing on. The approach to Matruh was a tricky exercise. We were about eight miles off the coast, within range of our guns and well outside the 100 fathom mark and, hopefully, well away from any minefields.

All eyes were turned to look ashore at the lights as they came up abeam. Enemy blackout procedures ashore weren't too good. Moreover, our navigator had done his job well, we were right in position. As we waited for the captain's order to open fire, there was a great air of excitement as we looked at the lights of the port and thought of the unawareness of the enemy that we were about to attack.

The first shots were star shells to illuminate the place, and then we were enveloped by noise and shaking as our nearby forward gun mountings flashed, rattled, and noisily detonated at regular intervals. The gun bells rang out before each firing and distant voices could be heard amid the din calling out the orders. The guns angled up and down so that we would cover as much territory as possible. We could see nothing ashore, even through binoculars,

Overhead shot of the bridge of the destroyer *Hotspur*.

except the odd light low on the horizon. No fires seemed to have been started. We could only hope that we were hitting ships, craft, railway yards, store sheds and port buildings, and not just churning up a lot of sand.

After fifteen minutes we turned and headed home as fast as possible. Our anxiety about air attacks in the morning was unwarranted, and we entered Port Said at noon, untouched, having not seen a single enemy aircraft.

Immediately afterwards, the ship was ordered to transit the canal to Port Tewfik drydock for a much needed boiler cleaning and repairs. *Jervis* was long overdue for this, having been at sea for two years virtually nonstop except for a short drydocking after being slightly damaged alongside *Sagona*.

The trip through the canal proved most interesting. The first leg of the transit from Port Said took us through a narrow man-made cut for thirty-seven miles to Lake Timsah. There are no locks in the Suez Canal, as the land between the Mediterranean and Red Sea is perfectly flat and level, and there is no marked difference between the sea level at either end. We sailed past Ismailia, located on this lake, which was where the new HQ for C-in-C and his staff was located.

After this, there is another short cut of twelve miles to the Bitter Lakes, which stretch for fifteen miles from north to south. Here one stopped to let ships moving north by, as only one line of ships could go through the canal at a time.

As we lay at anchor here, close to the shore, we witnessed the extraordinary sight of a camel auction in progress. One thing about the Middle East was that one never knew what one would suddenly come upon. Well over a hundred camels and their drivers were congregated on the hot desert dirt, near to where we were at anchor. The colourful garb of the men and women, the grunting of the restless animals, and the noisiness of the crowd, bespoke a way of life little changed since ancient times.

The last short canal portion to Port Tewfik, on the southern end, took no time at all, and we proceeded directly into drydock there. The city of Suez is located in a bay to the west, about a mile away. Tewfik proved to be a small, pleasant town which had been specially built to provide services for the canal. At the time of our visit it contained administrative offices, a small and attractive club overlooking the canal, as well as shops, modern housing and a small dockyard.

Flag Officer Red Sea and Canal Area (FORSCA), Vice Admiral R. Hallifax, had his headquarters here. All our seaborne reinforcements from England came around South Africa to this port, so it was a vital link in the supply line from the United Kingdom. Because there were no jetties in either Tewfik or Suez, all ships had to be unloaded by barge, an awkward and slow method. Not surprisingly, it had been the major target for air attack in Egypt and had been subjected to the heaviest of air raids, and bristled with AA batteries. Normally there was also one AA guardship there; either a Hunt class destroyer or a C class light cruiser.

For three weeks we were in a military backwater and could relax. Amazingly, there were no air raids while we were there despite the proximity of the enemy at El Alamein and the unloading of several cargo ships in the bay. No overnight leave was given because of the uncertain situation. However, we could go ashore and conditions could have been a lot worse. We were able to wander around the town, and frequent a bar and the open-air cinema. Suez city was an exclusively Egyptian town, rather run down, and we weren't encouraged to visit it.

Our doctor had heard that the Wrens, evacuated from Alex, were in a camp not far up the canal, near a place called Shallufa. After learning that a dance was to be held there, a group of us wardroom types decided to commandeer a car and attend. Finally we found the place, surrounded by a high barbed wire fence, and guarded by soldiers. We had quite a time talking our way in, but eventually found the dance hut. We blithely anticipated that, as navy types, we'd have no problem in getting a date or even a dance. Alas, we didn't fare too well. The numerous army officers didn't take too kindly to our gate-crashing. Neither did the Wrens, so we left in disgust.

After three weeks, *Jervis* left drydock and we moved back up the canal to Port Said and the war. Whilst we had been away, things had been quiet. However, on the day that we arrived a dummy Malta convoy sailed from Haifa and stayed at sea between 11 and 15 August. We concluded that a major convoy to Malta must have been mounted from Gib.

This, indeed, proved to be the case. By this time, mid-1942, Malta's defences were at an all-time low. Shorn of all surface ships, its harbour and

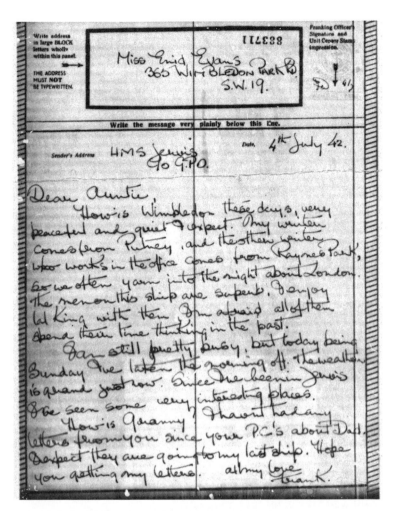

Actual size of lettergram from Jervis, which were photographed, reduced and sent back to England in the mail. Note censors stamp in right hand top corner.

airfields damaged, and lacking adequate supplies of food and fuel, the island was in grave condition. It had very little capacity to defend itself and the submarine squadron and our aircraft there would soon have to stop offensive operations unless they were resupplied.

By now the Germans and Italians were actively considering an invasion, to knock the island out of the war. To this end, four divisions, totalling 32,000 men, plus 1,500 aircraft and 80 landing vessels had been amassed in Sicily in preparation for "Operation Herkules," the code name for the invasion.

However, the scheme clashed with Rommel's campaign plans in North Africa. His offensive of June 1942 which had resulted in our hasty departure from Alex, necessitated the diversion of the aircraft based in Sicily to North Africa. Consequently Hitler and Mussolini decided to shelve "Herkules" for the time being.

Two developments led to its subsequent permanent cancellation. Firstly, the German armies, far away in Russia, had closed in on Stalingrad, thereby encouraging visions of German entry into Iran and the Middle East through the back door. Secondly, Rommel's progress in North Africa proved so spectacularly successful that it looked as though we would be swept right out of Egypt. That being so, Malta's capture lost its urgency in Axis eyes.

From our point of view, this was the major turning point in the Mediterranean war. Malta had been given a respite, and if it could hang on until we could properly resupply it then Rommel's chances of reaching the Nile basin could be profoundly undermined. We had to somehow make another major effort to reinforce it so that it could be used to cut off the enemy supplies to North Africa.

To this end, the dummy convoy, led by *Coventry* from Haifa in August, had been mounted to provide a diversion for a large convoy from Gib. This operation was code named "Pedestal," and was the biggest and most famous convoy ever sent to Malta during the war. Force H was augmented by ships from the Home Fleet. After a fierce two day battle, in which we lost a carrier, *Eagle,* two cruisers, *Cairo* and *Manchester,* and a destroyer, plus one carrier, two cruisers and one destroyer damaged, we were able to get three merchant ships and a tanker into Malta.

The rest of August proved relatively uneventful, except that we were sent to sea on several occasions to follow up aircraft sightings of submarines off Port Said. We did not, however, make any contacts.

But enemy submarines were undoubtedly present and active. On 17 August 1942, the *Princess Marguerite,* a Canadian Pacific coastal passenger vessel, was sunk by one of them while she was transporting troops from Port Said to Cyprus. She and the *Princess Kathleen* had been sent from the west coast of Canada as replacements for the Indian coastal steamers that had earlier been sunk off Tobruk. Both were used as fast troop transports. Fortunately, *Marguerite's* escort, the destroyer *Hero,* was able to rescue most of her crew and the troops being transported.

There was little to do ashore in Port Said except to visit the sole officers' night club which featured a rather plump belly dancer. The port was much more of an Egyptian town than Alex, and lacked the latter's fleshpots and cosmopolitan European atmosphere. But it did have something of a friendly small town air to it and was pleasant enough.

We were receiving very little information about developments at El Alamein. There had been rumours of battles in July, but as far as we could tell we seemed to be holding the line, if only because there was nothing in the papers about any successes or defeats one way or the other. And as there were no air raids, our air forces must have been doing a good job containing the Luftwaffe.

We also heard that in the early part of August, Churchill had been in Egypt. This was followed on 15 August by an announcement that General Auchinleck had been relieved by General Alexander as C-in-C Army and that a new general had arrived from England to take over command of the 8th Army — Lieutenant General Bernard Montgomery.

It wasn't long before things began to hot up again. Toward the end of August, I decyphered a surprising message to the effect that 14 DF was to transport marines to Tobruk for a night attack. This news dumbfounded me. I quickly figured that if we left Port Said at 0900, we could reach Tobruk by midnight. En route we would be off El Alamein by 1500, in broad daylight. From then on we could expect one Stuka attack after another for seven hours before nightfall. Even if we managed to survive this, on the return run we would be off Sidi Barrani, 180 miles behind enemy lines, at daylight.

Tribal Class destroyer HMS *Eskimo* with crew manning the sides.

What I felt we needed was the clear head of Cunningham to abandon this hazardous scheme. It would mean certain death for quite a few of us and the horrible sense of unease that I had experienced during Operation "Vigorous" returned. My predicament was made worse because only the captain and I were aware of the plans, and I could not discuss them with anyone. Several follow-up messages were received and the captain and the navigator went down the canal to visit headquarters; presumably to discuss the operation. I dared not even mention news of the impending operation to the navigator.

Then the luck that followed *Jervis* recurred. A message was received, changing the plans. Instead of using J and P class destroyers from 14 DF, it had been decided to use the larger *Tribal* class from 22 DF. 14 DF was to carry out a diversionary bombardment down the coast, a much safer operation. The reason for the change of plan was that not only did the ships going to Tobruk have to ferry the marines, but they also had to carry small flat-bottomed boats on deck, which would be towed by the ship's motor boats when the marines were put ashore. There was more upper deck space on the Tribals, so they were to be used.

Four naval forces were to participate in the operation: *Sikh,* carrying Captain St. J. Micklethwait, D22, and *Zulu,* the two *Tribal* class destroyers, to transport the marines from Alex; the AA cruiser *Coventry* plus eight Hunt class destroyers from Port Said, would provide AA support; a flotilla of MTBs and MLs, from Alex, was to carry up some army troops; and our own flotilla from Port Said would carry out the diversion.

The attack on Tobruk was to be conducted in the early hours of Sunday, 13 September. The date had been chosen because it was a moonless night.

Our flotilla, *Jervis, Javelin, Pakenham* and *Paladin,* and the cruiser *Dido,* sailed from Port Said at 1900 on 12 September to put us off El Daba, a station stop on the Alex-Mersah Matruh railway line, about thirty-five miles west of

El Alamein, around midnight. It was known to be a back-up area for the Afrika Korps, and filled with supplies and petrol dumps.

As with the Matruh bombardment, things went swimmingly. The operation was carried out like clockwork with no response from the enemy. This time, a few houses near the shore were illuminated by flares dropped by Fleet Air Arm Albacore aircraft. After this, we opened fire and kept up a barrage for about twenty minutes.

Then we retired at full speed, once again wondering whether we had done any real damage or had just stirred up the desert sand. Our return journey was uneventful. We were inside the breakwater at Alex by 0330, wondering what was happening at Tobruk.

Our first real news was received when two Hunts —*Aldenham* and *Belvoir,* came in during the next afternoon of 13 September with reports that the raid had not gone well. The remainder of the force returned during the night. It was only the next day that we learned all the bad news. The operation had been a total disaster, as expected. *Sikh* had been sunk off Tobruk and *Zulu* whilst she was returning. And the old stager *Coventry* had finally succumbed to air attack, as had numerous MTBs and MLs. Very few troops had got ashore. Captain Micklethwait and *Sikh's* crew had been left behind at Tobruk and we could only hope that those who survived were able to get ashore.

The Tobruk raid had evolved from an idea by the Middle East Commando Unit to mount a small-scale land attack on Tobruk to blow up petrol dumps. However, the plan was somehow expanded into a major tri-service operation with all the attendant problems of communication and co-ordination. The overall objective, however, seemed sound; the three services would provide relatively small contingents of ships, aircraft, and troops to attack the enemy's vital forward supply ports of Benghazi and Tobruk and the nearby airfield at Barce.[10]

Special Air Service troops were to attack Benghazi by land; the Long Range Desert Group, which operated behind enemy lines, was to attack Barce airfield; and the commandos would penetrate the Tobruk defences. The land forces would make their approach through the southern part of the desert, behind the Afrika Korps lines, before turning north to their objectives.

Off Tobruk, two destroyers were to land marines to the west of the port; MTBs and MLs would land army troops to the east. The commandos would come in from the south. These groups would then unite in a pincer movement into the harbour area. At that point the destroyers would force their way into the harbour, the petrol and supply dumps would be demolished and the land forces would be withdrawn by sea.

The commandos achieved their objectives undetected. Their daring entry into Tobruk reads like an adventure war novel. Dressed as Germans, they drove three German trucks, supposedly filled with British prisoners of war. After bluffing their way past the Italian guards, they ruthlessly shot up and seized the gun emplacements to the east of the harbour, and awaited the MTBs.

Initially the naval part of the operation proceeded well. *Coventry* with the Hunt class destroyers *Dulverton, Hursley, Croome* and *Belvoir* had left at midnight on 11/12 September 1942 from Port Said. At dawn they met up with the Alex force, composed of *Sikh* and *Zulu* and four more Hunts — *Hurworth, Beaufort, Exmoor* and *Aldenham.* The MTBs and MLs had left earlier and gone on ahead.

Excellent fighter cover was provided by Beaufighters, and VHF radio

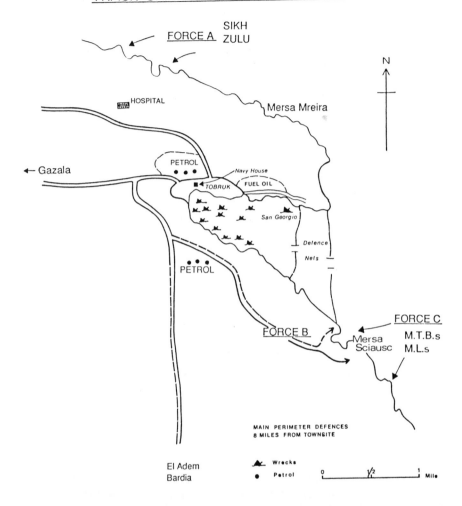

TRACK CHART - TOBRUK RAID 12-13 SEPT. 1942

SIKH
FORCE A ZULU

N

HOSPITAL

Mersa Mreira

← Gazala

PETROL

Navy House

TOBRUK   FUEL OIL

San Georgio

Defence

Nets

PETROL

FORCE C

FORCE B   M.T.B.s

Mersa   M.L.s
Sciausc

MAIN PERIMETER DEFENCES
8 MILES FROM TOWNSITE

El Adem   Wrecks
Bardia   Petrol   0   ½   1   Mile

telephone equipment was used for the first time in the Mediterranean fleet. It had been installed in our aircraft and in *Coventry,* thus enabling the ship to direct the fighters to some extent against any enemy bombers picked up by radar. (Radar, an American term for Radio Direction and Ranging had by now displaced the older British designation RDF). Our aircraft were also fitted with a black box called IFF (Identification Friend or Foe). This triggered a response in our own radar, and enabled us to distinguish between friend and enemy when firing our AA guns.

The expected enemy air activity during the day did not materialize except for shadowers. The force turned northwest for a while, to confuse the enemy, and then south. The *Coventry* group left the *Sikh* group at 2100 on 12 September and headed east. It would meet with the Tribals later, as they returned, and provide them with AA protection. The *Sikh* group rendezvoused as planned with the MTBs and MLs at 0200 on Sunday 13, off Tobruk. A total of 500 troops were carried by these two forces.

Now a very serious problem presented itself. Weather conditions were not ideal for the smaller ships. Strong winds were blowing, and the sea had been whipped up into a swell of about five feet. This was an eventuality that the planners had not taken into consideration mainly because the Mediterranean weather in September is normally good.

The submarine Taku which had been lying off Tobruk, moved close inshore, on the west side of the harbour near Mersa Mriera, to land specially trained demolition experts. These men were to go ashore in tiny canoes called folbots. Sea conditions were too rough for them, but *Taku* signalled *Sikh* that the troops could still be landed in larger boats. As it turned out, this was poor advice.

Once again the senior officer, Captain Micklethwait, had to make a key decision affecting many lives — as had happened so often in the Mediterranean during the previous two years — whether to proceed with or cancel the operation and pull out. He decided on the former. What else could he do? All the ships had come this far successfully, and there was still a chance that the marines might be put ashore. However, he could see for himself what the sea conditions were and knew the limitations of small boats — from his days as a cadet. And this was especially true, bearing in mind that the flat-bottomed boats that he had brought didn't look particularly seaworthy. However, notwithstanding even this, he must have felt that the risk had to be taken.

Whilst all this was going on the RAF and USAAF were carrying out a very heavy bombing attack on the harbour area, to distract the garrison. It wasn't altogether a success, as the German general suspected that something was afoot and ordered the garrison to stand to their guns.

Meanwhile, the MTBs and MLs heading for Mersa Sciause, to the east, were also in difficulty. Because of the weather, many of them did not make a good landfall but were dispersed along the coast. And those that were successful couldn't detect the contact signal from the commandos ashore. This was because an irresponsible commando officer had left his larger red Aldis lamp behind and was using instead a small white flashlight, which was utterly useless.

As a result only two MTBs got into the inlet at about 0400, two hours late. The forty men aboard made contact with the fifty commandos ashore. Unfortunately one of these boats ran aground on the way out and had to be abandoned. The remaining MTBs continued to flounder around looking for the entrance to the inlet, and were later ordered by *Zulu* to abandon the attempt to land their troops and return to Alex. This provoked angry protestations from the army types aboard who would rather have fought with their feet on land.

The net result was that the eastern force was not as large as planned. One of their main objectives was to blow up the petrol dump on the east side of the harbour. One of the ironies of the expedition was that this could easily have been done by the commandos when they first came down the road to Mersa Sciause earlier in the night.

As it was, this small force was attacked by superior German forces sent from Tobruk, and was quickly surrounded. An attempt was made to break out to the east in lorries, but many men were killed, including their leader Lt. Col. Haselden. Our Intelligence had let us down, as the operation had been based on the assumption that the town was lightly defended by Italian troops and that no major German forces were nearby.

Two miles off at the other side of the harbour, *Sikh* and *Zulu* unloaded their boats into the tossing waters punctually at 0300. To put it mildly, the light barges were loaded with troops with great difficulty, as can easily be imagined, given the poor weather conditions. Each motor boat was to tow three lighters, one behind the other — not a very efficient method in such sea conditions.

These boats were to land their loads and then return for a second trip, as there was only enough space for half the battalion to be transported at one time. This meant that the time of the landing had to be extended. Having loaded their boats and seen them disappear into the wild night, the two destroyers turned out to sea, to get away from the coastal batteries (range ten miles) which were known to be located onshore. They were to return later at a prearranged time to discharge the second flight.

It didn't take long before the tow lines between the motor boats and barges parted in the swell and time was wasted in an attempt to resecure them. A number of the barges drifted away in the confusion. Some were swept toward the shore and others floated aimlessly around in the sea. The ones that made the shore were far from the planned landing spot, and some even broke up on the rocks, with loss of life and injury. Finally, about seventy-five wet and shaken marines were able to get ashore.

Still in difficulty, the rest of the boats were found by *Sikh* and *Zulu* when they returned for the second landing. Instead of unloading more men, 100 Marines were brought back onboard. It was then decided that weather conditions were just too bad for further landing attempts.

In the middle of this operation, *Sikh* was picked up by shore searchlights and very quickly all the coastal guns in the area were directed at her. Initially, she received only minor damage, but she was eventually hit in the engine room by a lucky shot and came to a stop. *Zulu,* lying farther offshore, came back and made several attempts to pass a line to her to take her in tow. When one was finally secured, it was parted by shellfire. By this time dawn was coming up, and eventually both ships were hit. *Zulu* tried to lay a smokescreen, but by 0700 Micklethwait ordered her to leave. *Sikh* sank a half hour later, surrounded by survivors in the water.

It was as *Zulu* moved west that she encountered the MTBs and MLs and ordered them to head for Alex as best they could.

In the meantime, *Coventry* and the six Hunts were returned back towards Tobruk to help *Zulu*. Only *Aldenham* and *Belvoir* continued home as they were running low on fuel.

The German air force was not long in reacting to the attack. *Zulu* and the MTBs were an easy target for the Stukas from El Adem airfield, sixteen miles from Tobruk, and shortly after dawn they were being subjected to continuous bombing. Three MTBs and two MLs were sunk, but *Zulu* managed to escape further damage. Although the earlier hits had left her with a list, she could still make full speed.

The *Coventry* force fared much worse. Around 1100, whilst "Up Spirits" was being piped, it was attacked by fifteen Stukas coming in astern from out of the sun. Despite Beaufighter cover — the RAF were putting up a good show — *Coventry* was hit by two bombs, mortally wounding the ship. One blew her bow off as far as A gun mounting, and the other penetrated the engine room, leaving her stopped dead in the water. The ship was on fire and her magazines could blow up at any moment. There were many casualties. With the engines beyond repair, Captain Dendy decided to abandon ship immediately and not endanger the rest of the ships. The crew was taken off by *Beaufort* going alongside, while those who had taken to the water, were picked up by *Dulverton*.

After this the Hunts tried to sink *Coventry* with gunfire, to no avail. Not all ships of this class carried torpedoes. As this was happening, *Zulu* arrived at 1500 under air attack which caused no damage. After this there was a short respite whilst the force sorted itself out, and *Coventry* was finally despatched with two torpedoes. Then a very heavy air attack developed, one of the most concentrated ever, with sixteen enemy aircraft picking out *Zulu* as their prime target. Like *Coventry,* she was soon hit in her engine room and lost power. *Hursley* then took her in tow, and our own fighters massed over her in an desperate effort to get her back to Alex, now only 100 miles away. By dusk, however, she was awash, the tow line was loosed, and *Croome* took off her crew just before she rolled over and sank.

Thus ended the most inglorious action that I ever took part in. It was a fiasco from start to finish. As can be imagined, it was discussed at great length afterwards by all and sundry in the fleet. Everyone from boy seaman to admiral could have known beforehand that it was going to end the way it did.[11]

At the time no one really knew in detail what had happened. Even those who survived the action weren't too clear. Information was sparse for security reasons, but we all knew that the ships had been sunk. It was only after the war that a clear picture emerged.

Many thought at the time that spies in Egypt had divulged our plans to the Germans and that our security had been to blame. Certainly on *Jervis* nobody knew anything about it except the captain, the navigator, and myself. I never heard any rumours about the operation before it started, either on or off the ship.

Connell in his book *Valiant Quartet,* states that the Egyptian dhobimen (laundrymen) told the crew of *Coventry* that they were going to Tobruk, the day before they left. I find this hard to believe based on my own experience. Pitt, in his book *The Crucible of War, Year of Alamein, 1942,* claims that the Argyll and Sutherland Highlanders, who were in the small ships, had practised landing from the MTBs in front of the Royal Egyptian Yacht Club in Alex, under the eyes of the members. He goes on to say that army security in Cairo was reputed to be poor, with too much loose talk in the night clubs. However, an inspection of records after the war had revealed that the Tobruk garrison was not expecting an attack. It was the heavy air raid which had alerted the German commander that something unusual was going on. On the other hand, the Benghazi garrison did know of an impending attack and waited in ambush for our troops. The only consolation was that the attack on the airfield at Barce was very successful.

CHAPTER ELEVEN

Malta

After the disastrous Tobruk raid, the flotilla returned to Port Said and we went back to our old berth in front of Navy House. We remained there for the rest of September, only moving back to Alex in early October. Operational activity was reduced to a few local anti-submarine patrols.

During this respite there were rumours of a big build-up of troops and tanks through Suez. Huge liners were reported to be lying off the southern end of the canal disembarking thousands of troops. There were air raids down there, but we escaped them in Port Said.

On 15 October, after *Jervis* had returned to Alex, she went into drydock for a short refit. I went on five days leave to Cairo along with the doctor and our Aussie lieutenant. This was my first leave in almost two years.

Larger and more crowded than Alex, Cairo was much more a Moslem city. There were many large, remarkable western-style buildings but the Islamic mosques and edifices, some of them enormous, with their ornamentally decorated domes and towers and protruding balconies, were much more interesting.

Each day we were taken to see the sights by a dragoman. These men, attired in the traditional Egyptian nightshirt and fez, waited outside hotels to be hired as interpreters and guides. Ours was particularly good. He spoke English well, had a sense of humour, and was, as far we could tell, fairly knowledgeable about ancient Egyptian history. We used a horse-drawn gharry as our mode of transportation around the bustling city. Our first stop was at a museum, which was not something we wanted to see. However, our guide insisted that he was required by the military police to take us there first. It turned out to be a museum on venereal disease! Aussie and myself were not happy about this, taking one quick look around the display room and hastily departing to loud complaints from Doc, who had brightened up after entering the place.

We visited all the obligatory sights; the Sphinx, the Pyramids, the huge mosques, the extraordinary bazaar with its myriad narrow streets, Farouk's palace, and all the other fascinating public buildings, including the Museum of Antiquities. This latter was crammed with amazing artifacts of all desciptions, excavated from throughout Egypt. It was all a revelation to me, as I had never realised just how sophisticated ancient Egyptian culture had been and how fine the sculpture and jewellery. Aussie and Doc were not as interested, so unfortunately we did not stay there as long as I would have liked.

In between these outings we had a drink at the famous old fashioned Shephards Hotel, the only naval officers in a sea of army types. We had lunch at the Mena House Hotel, a beautiful place near the Pyramids, and visited the Gezira Sporting Club on an island in the Nile. There, pukka army staff officers took their pleasures just as we did at the Alex Sporting club.

Soon after returning to the ship, I went ashore on the evening of 23 October 1942, and ended up having a drink in the bar of the Cecil Hotel. Suddenly we started to hear a strange noise in the distance; the sound of guns rumbling in from the west. It got louder and louder and continued and continued. There was much talk that this must surely have been the greatest bombardment in the history of war. There was no doubt in our minds that it was from our own guns and not Germans, and that this was the start of our much discussed and sorely needed offensive.

The place was full of war correspondents and USAAF officers. Army types were conspicuously absent. American servicemen had first started appearing on the streets of Alex during the summer. At first there were only a few, but by October 1942 there were so many that we started taking them for granted. In their typical American way, they were full of life and a trifle too loud for us at times. They threw their money around, paying more than we considered necessary, which gave rise to a little tension. Their other ranks resented their exclusion by our MPs from the night clubs reserved for officers. It was heartening, nevertheless, to see them and know that the full might of the United States was now behind us. Their long-range Liberator bombers were very effective and their crews were well trained and adaptable so that they could operate in support of both land and sea forces.

As the barrage continued into the night, quite a party developed and there was much speculation as to where it would all lead. Relations between the two allies were well cemented that night. The optimism of the Americans was a welcome antidote to our rather cynical approach to things. We had been disappointed too many times.

The battle of El Alamein was a stunning victory for us and the Afrika Korps was thoroughly broken for the first time in its existence. Its commander, General von Thoma, plus a German divisional commander and three Italian divisional commanders were taken prisoner. Six Italian divisions and one German division were entirely written off and the remainder were in disarray. Their rout was complete and they retreated in total disorder, leaving behind 75,000 troops plus hundreds of tanks and guns. It was undoubtedly one of the great battles in British history and it turned our spirits right around.

It had come so unexpectedly and happened so quickly. Now we had some real hope that the battle for the Mediterranean might well be won. One of the big factors must have been the dominance of our air forces. Throughout October, there had been no air raids on Alex, yet the German airfields were only sixty miles or so away.

After that initial bombardment, the battle raged for ten days, but right from the start the news we got from the front was reassuring. A week after the end of the battle, Mersa Matruh fell to us on 8 November. Rommel had tried to make a last determined effort to contain us in Egypt but to no avail. We were at the border by 10 November.

Then we learned that a combined Anglo-American operation had been mounted from England to land troops in Vichy French Morocco and in Vichy French Algeria. The landings had taken place on 7 November 1942 and, after some initial fighting, were successful. The hated Admiral Darlan, the French leader in Algiers, had come over to our side.

Events were now happening fast and, for a change, in our favour. In retaliation for all this, Germany occupied Vichy France, thereby breaking the Franco-German peace treaty. Even so, there were no signs of the French ships at Alex joining us.

Even as the Battle of El Alamein was raging, plans were afoot to mount a fresh convoy to Malta. These came to fruition on 16 November, when the cruiser *Euryalus* and fleet destroyers from D14 *(Jervis, Kelvin, Javelin and Nubian)* and D2 *(Hero, Griffin and Queen Olga* (Greek)*)* sailed from Alex to rendezvous off Port Said with a Malta-bound convoy. This operation was code named "Stoneage".

We met four merchant ships — *Denbighshire* (UK), *Mormacmoom* (US), *Robin Locksley* (U.S.) *and Bantam* (Dutch). At noon the next day we rendezvoused off Alex with ten Hunts, *Dulverton, Hursley, Croome, Belvoir, Hurworth, Beaufort, Exmoor, Aldenham, Eridge* and *Tetcott*. They took over the screen and we put into Alex to fuel.

CS15, consisting of *Cleopatra* (the flagship of our new commander Rear-Admiral A.J. Power), *Dido, Arethusa* and *Orion* (recently returned after being repaired), sailed later in the day in company with the fleet destroyers. We were to catch up with the convoy early in the morning of the next day 18 November 1942, off Sidi Barrani. Before we left, we received the good news that the symbol of all our fighting in the Middle East, Tobruk, had been recaptured on the 13th. This gave us a further lift and meant that we would probably have fighter cover well into the central basin.

The improved quality of our air support was now much more marked; we hadn't seen anything like it since our aircraft carrier had left in 1941. We now had three or four Beaufighters or U.S. built Kitty Hawk fighters over us, controlled by a cruiser. Added to this were the anti-submarine aircraft — Bisleys, Hudsons and the old-stager Swordfish still in evidence (from our land-based Fleet Air Arm squadrons) — patrolling ahead of us. All our air forces, British, Australian, South African and U.S., were now providing us with the strong air defence so lacking in past years.

Operation orders indicated that we would still have to face the Italian navy and enemy air forces. However, after the beating that the German desert air force must have recently taken, we believed that the threat from this area would be minimal. But there was still the possibility of German aircraft from Crete, and the Air Division on Sicily to contend with. Our plan was to sail the convoy so that it arrived at Malta at dawn on 20 November, thus completing the last leg of its journey by night.

The Italian Navy was still a major threat, and given the recent Axis setbacks, this might be the time when it would be thrown into the fray, to reverse the tide of defeat. In case the Italian fleet did venture out, we had amassed a strong bomber and torpedo force from both Malta and Egypt, to carry out the heaviest air attacks we had yet attempted. The Italians had shown that they disliked this kind of thing. In addition, our Wellington and Baltimore photo reconnaissance aircraft from Malta were to keep an eye on the Italian naval bases at Taranto, Messina and Naples. And for good measure, our air forces at Malta were now sufficiently strong to carry out major air strikes on enemy airfields in Sicily on the night of the 19th.

All in all, the omens for a successful operation looked promising and our weakness in surface ships was offset by our impressive aerial plans. Not only were many more aircraft being devoted to naval operations, but interservice co-operation between the navy and air force was vastly improved. We were now beginning to draw on the massive resources of America which we had all hoped for in the past.

Our group met up with *Euryalus,* the Hunts and the convoy at 0700 on the next morning 18 November 1942. As usual, we lay ahead of the convoy which was surrounded by the Hunts. *Jervis,* as the senior destroyer, was in the vanguard of the antisubmarine screen, with three fleet destroyers spread out one mile apart on either side of us. Weather conditions were not too bad, with high clouds, a rising wind, and an increasing sea swell. A morning attack from the north by Stukas, had been beaten off by our fighter cover.

The rest of the day was uneventful. Every so often, if one was on deck, the small specks of our fighters and A/S aircraft could be seen weaving in and out of the clouds. No word had yet arrived that the Italian fleet had sailed.

Just prior to dusk, around 1800, CS15 and the fleet destroyers moved to the north, leaving *Euryalus* and the Hunts with the convoy. The purpose of this manoeuvre was to provide a distant screen between the Italian fleet and the convoy, should it decide to come out. With its high speed ships capable of 30 knots or more, it could have been in a position to engage us in the early morning, if it had sailed immediately.

Just as we had settled into our new formation, we received a warning from the flagship that an aircraft attack was developing from the north. It turned out to be the usual Italian dusk torpedo attack and this time it was pressed home with a great deal of daring.

The attack was over very quickly since only a few torpedo aircraft had taken part. They came in low over the sea and were very difficult to detect in the receding light. I was in my office working on a cypher at the time. We had been closed up at action stations for about half an hour when suddenly the ship shook as all three of our 4.7-inch positions opened up. We were firing an AA barrage. This lasted about ten minutes, and then things went back to normal.

I soon learned that *Arethusa* had been hit forward and must have received very serious damage as she had stopped, with smoke pouring from her forward section. Two destroyers, *Hero* and *Griffin* were detached to assist her and eventually she got going and they escorted her slowly back to Alex. By the time that I had heard about her, the little group was far astern.

The rest of the night passed peacefuly, and no urgent messages about the Italian fleet were received. By dawn, we were back in front of the convoy, which had also survived the night intact. The weather now had deteriorated considerably, with a full gale blowing with accompanying rough seas. We were now well into the central basin and out of range of our North African fighter cover, although we still enjoyed air anti-submarine protection.

To our amazement at 1000, as we pitched and rolled in showers of spume and spray, three Spitfires suddenly appeared overhead. They had come from Malta, which was still a long way off (250 miles). We hadn't expected them to arrive so soon because we were so far away from the island. We noticed that they were fitted with long-range wing tanks, which presumably greatly increased their range. But even with these tanks we were surprised that they should have come so far.

As the day progressed there were still no reports of the enemy fleet and, to our surprise, no air attacks developed even though we were still well within Stuka range of Crete and Sicily. Possibly the weather conditions were discouraging them. This was the furthest west that we had been since the spring and we had expected far more air attacks than we had received.

As I was on a short visit to the bridge with a message, the flagship signalled us that one of the Spitfires did not have enough fuel to return to Malta, and was ditching into the sea. This was tragic news as the seas were far too rough to lower a whaler. The old man was faced with a painful decision as to whether to order a destroyer to attempt a rescue, or not. We couldn't help wondering why the pilot didn't try his luck by flying on and landing in the desert. We could not be that far from our own lines, as we estimated that the 8th Army would now be closing in on Benghazi, to our south.

After some discussion, the captain finally decided that to attempt a rescue would only endanger the lives of the boat's crew. Consequently the order was given that no destroyer should go to the pilot's aid. An uneasy silence descended as a message was written out and given to the yeoman of signals to flash to the screen.

This pilot had spent as long as he could over us to give us invaluable coverage, and through an error was now faced with the awful option of having to bail out in heavy seas. And after all this, we were going to abandon him.

He kept on flying, as if undecided what to do, until finally a tiny white parachute could be seen descending slowly to the sea, a mile or so to our northwest, whilst the aircraft veered off to the north and then plunged into the raging waters.

Then, disobeying orders, the nearest destroyer, the Greek *Queen Olga,* raced toward the spot. The Greeks were now going to show who the real Mediterrranean sailors were. A few muffled exclamations arose on our bridge but the captain remained silent and did nothing but watch the proceedings.

An hour later the Greeks signalled that a boat had indeed been lowered and had gone to the rescue of the airman. Unfortunately, he had become entangled in his parachute in the heavy seas and drowned. They had recovered their boat with no loss of life. We had been shown up. The incident was then closed and Captain (D) never talked about it again. But few of us would ever forget the incident — the terrible predicament of the pilot and the courage and skill of the Greeks. Fortunately, being on a foreign ship, they got away with their disobedience.

Late in the afternoon, the 15th Cruiser Squadron and the fleets turned east and we left *Euryalus* and the Hunts with the privilege of escorting the first real relief convoy into Malta. We were right on time and unless the convoy ran into a catastrophe during the night, it would be in Valletta harbour in the early morning and the siege would be lifted.

Moving at almost full speed, we arrived back at Alex without incident and soon received a cypher that the convoy had arrived safely on 20 November 1942. This was just as well, for Malta had a mere three weeks supply of food left — this was how closely fought the Med battle was in its final stages.

There was no sign of *Arethusa* in port, but she returned the next day, looking most awkward and battered, as she was towed in stern first. This was a most humiliating position for any ship to be in, but one that had happened several times in the Med. Unfortunately she had sustained a considerable loss of life.

Before the end of the week, *Euryalus* and the Hunts were back unscathed. Five days later, on Wednesday 25 November 1942, the cruisers *Cleopatra, Dido* and *Euryalus* and our flotilla, under Admiral Power, again sailed for Malta to reactivate the famous Force K.

All ships were crammed with hundreds of cases of canned food to be stowed wherever possible without compromising their fighting capability. We had stacks of cases of canned goods blocking the passageways below and lashed down all over the upper deck. Our trip, extraordinarily enough, proved to be completely uneventful, without any air attacks or interference from the

S. 1320d.
(Established—May. 1930)
(Revised—January. 1933.)

To:

General.

FROM:

C. S. 15,

It is reported that all the Convoy and Escort arrived Safely.
This will mean that Malta will1 not only be able to Maintain
her gallant effort but the Island will be able to Greatly increas
that effort. In the last three days all Ships in Company can feel
they have played Their part Well and none better than the four
Merchant Ships trusted to Our Care.

(0609)

Light   P.L.   T.O.R. 0805.   20/11.

Flag Officer 15th Cruiser Squadron's signal to the fleet reporting the safe arrival in Malta of the operation "Stoneage" convoy on 20 November 1942. Thus ending the siege of the George Cross Island.

Italian navy — the first such operation since the start of the Mediterranean Sea war in 1940. Again we received excellent support and cover from our air forces who may have stopped some attacks without our knowing about it.

By now the German and Italian air forces were fully committed in the desert war and in a new area of operations for them — Tunisia. We knew from radio reports that our Algerian armies, along with French troops, were now fighting the Germans who had landed there.

Our force entered Grand Harbour, Malta, at dusk on 28 November. It is always exciting to make a landfall on an island. It suddenly appears in the distance on the edge of the sea, sometimes shrouded in a cloud, giving it an air of mystery. As we drew closer we could make out the contours of the place. It was bare and rocky with low rolling hills and about seventeen miles long. It was fully visible at a distance. We began to see the outline of Valletta, its capital and main port. Huge fortifications rose on either side of the entrance and great domes and church spires protruded behind them. As we moved slowly into the harbour we gazed in awe at these great battlements high above us on either side — surely one of the great sights of the world. There was no sign of anyone in the place, and no one looked down at us from the parapets. Instead, there was hushed silence as if we were entering a deserted medieval port.

Several inlets ran off the main harbour to port. Up the first, we could see

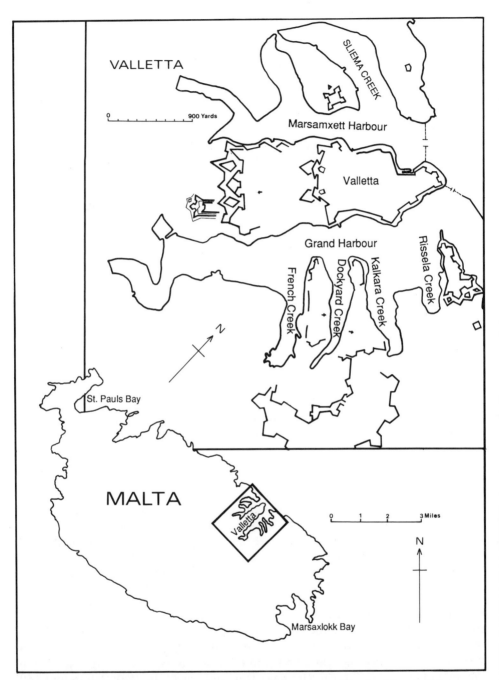

VALLETTA

0 ——————— 900 Yards

SLIEMA CREEK

Marsamxett Harbour

Valletta

Grand Harbour

French Creek

Dockyard Creek

Kalkara Creek

Rissela Creek

St. Pauls Bay

MALTA

Valletta

0   1   2   3 Miles

N

Marsaxlokk Bay

the tanker *Ohio* lying aground pointing to the south. She had battled her way in during "Operation Pedestal" in August, three months previously, and had provided our air forces with vital fuel and kept our aircraft and submarines in action. Up ahead almost completely submerged were the merchant ships *Pampas* and *Talabot,* with water lapping their upper decks. The smell of rotting grain from *Pampas* was still very strong. Both had arrived at Malta eight months earlier on 23 March, after the second Battle of Sirte, but very little of their cargoes had been removed before they had been sunk. The hulls of a number of other sunken warships and merchant ships littered other parts of the labyrinthine harbour. Up at the head of the inlet the ships from the recently arrived convoy lay alongside battered jetties.

Our flotilla turned up the last inlet, called French Creek, and tied up to buoys very close inshore to the foot of a high battlement. A concrete walk running out from the point of land opposite us appeared to be a landing stage for the several service boats tied up to a nearby floating pontoon. A large group of officers and men stood there as we entered, waving at us enthusiastically, and people began to scurry in and out of the rock fortifications. This seemed to be the site of underground stores and offices. In fact, we later found out this was the officer's mess for the naval shore establisment, *HMS St. Angelo.*

During the period of our relief of Malta, a number of new developments were occurring relatively close at hand. Following the "Torch" landings in North Africa on 8 November, the Germans occupied Vichy France, and three days later, had deployed two divisions around Toulon. Negotiations immediately began for the handing over of the large Vichy fleet based there; a fleet comprising three battleships, seven cruisers, thirty-two destroyers, sixteen submarines and eighteen smaller vessels.

Initially, the German forces agreed not to seize the ships. But Hitler was determined to claim this prize, and an attempt to do so was made on 27 November. However, the plan was thwarted by Admiral de Laborde who, recognizing that escape to sea was impossible, ordered the ships to be scuttled.

In a way, he was merely giving expression to a policy that had been formulated two and half years earlier. At a meeting on 18 June 1940, four days before France's capitulation, Admiral Darlan, later the despised Vichy War Minister, and his next in line, Admiral Auphan, had pledged their word to the British that they would never permit the French fleet to fall into German hands. The scuttling of the fleet in Toulon bore out that the officers of the French navy were honourable men in this regard and perhaps we had been too hard on them. In retrospect, our attack on Mers el Kebir in 1940, which Churchill had insisted upon against the advice of his admirals, was unjustifiable.

At the same time as the Germans invaded Vichy France, with their usual efficiency in reacting quickly to rapidly changing military situations, they began to airlift troops into Tunisia. They always seemed to have sufficient reserves and appropriate contingency plans to be able to put together an operation like this at the last minute. The French military hierarchy there, although basically pro-British, was torn between conflicting orders emanating from Algiers and France, whether to oppose or not oppose the Germans. Thus valuable time was wasted.

As a result, the Germans moved in by air unopposed, and the Italian fleet sent five MTBs and two small coasters off Bizerta, the naval base. The French army of 12,000 men had retreated into the mountains, separating itself from the base. In short order, the Germans were able bring in 35,000 men and 140 tanks by air, and eventually took over Tunis and Bizerta and the few Vichy ships there on 8 December 1942. The first elements of the British 1st Army arrived in Tunisia on 19 November, but by then it was already too late to dislodge the Axis forces.

Admiral Cunningham, now the Allied naval commander for "Torch", had much earlier pressed Eisenhower and others to extend the invasion to include a landing at Bizerta, but his suggestion had not been accepted. If it had been, it might well have shortened the war by a few months. As it transpired, the enemy was not driven out of Tunis and North Africa until early May 1943.

The French forces in Tunisia would have co-operated with us — they were only waiting for some kind of physical support — and our naval forces from the eastern Mediterranean could have assisted the "Torch" naval forces, especially as recent enemy air attacks on our shipping had not been as severe as we had expected. Our air forces in Malta were then starting to dominate the enemy air forces in Sicily and the Italian fleet had shown no sign of committing itself. Admittedly, the sea battles would still have been tough, and the German air force might have bestirred itself afresh. However, we would have had a very good chance of winning the day. It was unfortunate that the admiral, with his long experience and known expertise in Mediterranean matters, wasn't listened to.[12]

One of the questions which we kept asking ourselves during the latter part of 1942 was why the Italian navy hadn't made one last effort to engage in a major fleet action, particularly as they knew that we were weak in the eastern Mediterranean. The answer lay in their perennial lack of oil fuel.

At the beginning of the war they had quickly exhausted their oil reserves. Thereafter, they became entirely dependent upon the Germans for supplies. The Germans, however, never fully co-operated with the Italians, having little faith in their military capabilities. This was not entirely warranted in the case of the Italian navy, and German niggardliness was, in this case, a major mistake.

By mid-June 1941 the Italian navy had already begun to run into serious fuel problems and had to juggle supplies between its ships. As the war progressed, other problems, such as German needs on the Russian front, disruption of rail links from air attacks, and lack of tank cars, aggravated the situation. Moreover, by late 1942, American Liberators from Egypt — the Halverson force which had helped us in "Vigorous" — had started their bombing of the Ploesti oil fields in Romania with some success. Thus, the last time the Italians could use their capital ships was during "Vigorous" in June 1942. After this, they could only contemplate using them in very dire circumstances.

As soon as we were secured at Malta, dockyard harbour craft towed small barges alongside and all hands were put to work unloading our valuable provisions. The next morning it was decided to offload most of our ship's own stocks to add to the island's supplies. We had been told that the force would be sailing back to Alex in two days, to escort another convoy, and we could replenish stores then.

Later in the day, a number of officers from *St. Angelo* came aboard for a drink and lunch. They told us that they hadn't had a decent drink for nearly two years, the island had run out of spirits and beer long ago. The only drink available — and even that was hard to find — was medical grain alcohol. The island's food rations which everyone had been living off were terrible. They amounted to small amounts of canned bully beef, hard biscuits and tinned fruit. A few extras were thrown in, when available, such as the occasional loaf of bread and a few vegetables of poor quality. Meat, chicken, fresh fruit and eggs were unheard of. The officers were all smiles and kept gasping with surprise as they devoured each course. The outcome was that we agreed to sell them all our wine, spirit and beer stocks, knowing we could stock up at Alex on our return.

Next day we rued our spontaneous act of generosity as our orders were changed and the 14th Flotilla was to remain in Malta while the cruisers returned to Alex. After some soul-searching we all agreed that it was only fair that we should have the same rations as the Maltese. As to the spirits, we had been living very well in Alex all this time, while the poor beggars in Malta had been going through hell. From now on, our cooks had to devise as many ways as possible — which were very few — of disguising bully beef.

After the cruisers sailed the next day, 29 November, we were left in charge. We now started receiving many hand messages from the Admiral's office ashore about suspected convoy build-ups in southern Italian ports. Another naval strike unit, Force Q, had been set up in Bone, in eastern Algeria, and was to be used to attack convoys going to Bizerta. Our force would concentrate on those bound for Tripoli.

As the ship might have to sail at short notice, no shore leave was granted. On the morning of 2 December 1942 we were warned to stand by to sail in the afternoon. A convoy had been spotted heading south, near Pantelleria, north-west of Malta. Obviously, because of its position, it was not making for Bizerta. It had been picked up in the morning and had remained under surveillance. We were to sail at 1600 and make contact with it by midnight off the southern Tunisian coast.

The four ships of the flotilla, *Jervis, Javelin, Kelvin* and *Nubian,* duly set sail and proceeded south at full speed. There had been no air raids since we had arrived at Malta, and we were not attacked as we left the island. The enemy air force in Sicily, which was only twenty minutes flight time away, appeared to have been moved elsewhere. What a welcome change this was from conditions the year before, when so many ships had been sunk by aircraft within sight of the island.

We were getting hourly reports on the convoy's position and I was kept busy deciphering messages. As a result of this information, we were confident that we would able to intercept the convoy with no chance of error.

At 2300 we went to action stations. I was ordered by the old man to report to the bridge during the action and was supposed to take notes as best I could, to corroborate the reports of other officers.

At 2330 *Nubian* had the enemy on her radar. The night was clear with no moon. All eyes moved to starboard to find the ships visually. Shortly afterwards, flashes lit up the horizon. Our Albacore and Swordfish torpedo-bombers from Malta, fitted with equipment for night operations, had begun to attack them as planned.

There was quite a commotion on the bridge as we turned to lead the flotilla toward the enemy. This time, both guns and torpedoes were being prepared, and orders and reports were flying thick and fast. As usual, great tension was in the air. The skipper sat silently in his high chair, watching his young officers get on with their work. The officer on the watch had to be very much on his toes, but it was Guns and Torps who were the most active. Pilot was also very busy with his charts. I stayed as far out of harm's way as best I could.

Most people adopt an air of over-studied calm on these occasions, but not Guns and Torps. Both would become excitable as they tried to ensure that everything was ready. Torps twice reminded the old man not to forget to use the torpedoes.

The attack by our aircraft had obviously been successful, because we could make out a ship on fire in the distance. As we closed very rapidly, the stricken ship loomed larger and larger and we could soon make out its funnels, super-structure and masts partially covered by smoke and flames. It seemed quite unaware of our approach.

We were now tracking the convoy on our own radar and it was apparent that another group of ships was leaving the scene at high speed toward the coast. We were now about thirty-five miles off the port of Sfax, just off the Kerkanah bank — a string of islands and very shallow shoals — which we would have to avoid very carefully. We concluded that the Italian naval escort was abandoning the convoy to its own devices.

Within minutes we were within gun range of the convoy, about five miles away. Suddenly, the silhouette of a destroyer became clearly visible to us as it passed between us and the burning ship. Very quickly she passed out of view, but not before we had got an accurate true bearing on her. All our gun turrets were rapidly directed in her direction.

Then something extraordinary occurred. As Guns was orally preparing the turrets to open fire, we found ourselves steaming through hundreds of men in the water around us. They were so close that some of them could actually be identified as shadowy heads in the water. Farther away there were boats full of more survivors. They called out for help in Italian and German, their voices echoing pitifully over the sea. But on the bridge no one paid the slightest attention to them, concentrating instead on the imminent action. There was not even a comment, but those human voices calling for help in the night must have set other minds racing as they did mine. Would we have time after the action to pick them up? Would they ever make it to land in the morning, or would they be picked up?

Our first shot was a star shell which illuminated the whole scene. The destroyer and the sinking merchant ship were the only vessels visible in the area. After the illumination, all our ships directed their fire at the destroyer. We turned our searchlight on her and all the details of a small destroyer — similar to our Hunt class but even smaller — became starkly evident. Within three minutes, hot, glowing circles appeared on her superstructure and hull from the hits that she was sustaining. Things were happening very fast. The luckless destroyer, without any radar, apparently was quite unaware of our presence before the attack; she did not bring any of her guns to bear on us before she was a flaming wreck.

Within five minutes it was all over. Her mast soon collapsed and her superstructure all but disappeared, from internal explosions. What a terrible sight to see a ship being so brutally destroyed with such heavy loss of life. We were soon past her and we put the grisly memory out of our minds as best we could.

As we left her astern, she began to list heavily. Captain (D) signalled the last ship in line to despatch her with torpedoes and rejoin us as quickly as possible. There was no thought of picking up enemy survivors or following the other enemy warships around the Kerkanah Bank inshore. We immediately set sail for Malta at full speed, where we arrived as dawn came up. Torps never did get to fire his torpedoes.

Our victim that night was the Italian destroyer escort *Lupo*. She was a famous ship in the Italian navy, having taken part in a number of exploits under her captain, Commander Francesco Mimbelli.[13]

The famous Italian destroyer escort *Lupo*, sunk on 3 December 1942.

On 27 February 1941, she had landed troops on the island of Castelorizzo (located near the Turkish coast, east of Rhodes). Their objective was to expel our commandos who had recently landed there with a view to establishing an MTB base from which to harry enemy shipping in the Dodecanese Islands. Our land forces were no match for the Italians and had to be evacuated. Poor communications underlay our difficulties and this was not one of our better operations.

During the battle of Crete, *Lupo* was the sole escort of a convoy of small Greek coasters and caiques loaded with German troops and bound from Piraeus for Canea. This was the convoy that was attacked on the night of 21 May 1941 by Rear-Admiral I. G. Glennie in *Dido* with the cruisers *Ajax* and *Orion* and the destroyers *Janus, Kimberley, Hasty* and *Hereward*. All the merchant ships were sunk, but Lupo survived the night. She had fought gallantly; at first trying to lay a smokescreen ahead of the convoy before launching an incredibly courageous attack on one of our destroyers and a cruiser, during which she fired two torpedoes.

She actually pressed ahead right into our cruiser line between *Ajax* and *Orion,* and somehow miraculously escaped but not before being hit and suffering many casualties. *Ajax* claimed that *Lupo* had been sunk at point-blank range, an understandable error bearing in mind the confusion of the melee.

Looking back on these times now, we always tended to give the Italians little credit. Cunningham was perhaps wiser, in that he never underestimated them and later wrote that they were always professional seamen who often conducted themselves most capably.

After the great victory of 9 November 1941, when Force K from Malta sank the Duisberg convoy — so-called after the largest ship in the convoy — the Italian admiralty resorted to small convoys of no more than one or two ships. The idea was to present more targets to our forces in the hope that at least some of the convoys would get through.

On 23 November 1941 *Lupo* and another destroyer escort, *Cassiopea* escorted two small Italian merchant ships from Greece for Benghazi. It was this movement along with the simultaneous despatch of other Italian convoys, that had prompted our battlefleet to sail from Alex on the ill-fated trip which resulted in the sinking of the *Barham* on 25 November 1941.

Not that the *Lupo* force got off unscathed either. An Italian submarine had reported sighting Force K at sea, and the other Italian convoys at sea were turned around by the Italian admiralty. The *Lupo* convoy, however, failed to receive the message and was engaged by the cruiser *Penelope* and the destroyer *Lively*. Both merchant ships were sunk, but only after *Lupo* had made an abortive torpedo attack on *Penelope*.

In the Kerkenah action with us, she had stayed behind to pick up survivors from the burning merchant ship, whilst the other fast ships of the convoy made their way through the treacherous banks to the west. She was a fine ship with a gallant fighting record, and was certainly one that the Italian navy could be proud of. In a way it was unfortunate that we had to sink her, but such are the vagaries of war.

On 5 December another convoy arrived at Malta, and was composed of five merchant ships and, what was more important, a tankerload of aviation and bunker fuel. Again the trip had been completely unopposed. Malta was now in good shape to continue the war, and the enemy seemed to have been cowed into inactivity.

On 18 December I was transferred to the cruiser *Orion,* which had arrived to replace *Dido,* which in turn had been transferred to Bone. I was required to go to a bigger ship in order to take my exams to be promoted to the rank of sub-lieutenant.

Orion belonged to the Leander class which was composed of five ships, *Leander, Orion, Ajax, Achilles* and *Neptune.* They were built between 1931 and 1934 and carried four twin 6-inch gun turrets plus four turrets of twin 4-inch AA guns, and two quadruple torpedo tubes. They were comfortable ships with plenty of room, with a good-sized gun-room and cabins for midshipmen.

Ajax and Achilles, with *Exeter,* had taken part in the sinking of the *Graf Spee* in 1940. *Neptune,* as already described, was tragically sunk in early 1941. *Ajax* took part in many fleet actions in the Mediterranean including Matapan, Crete, Syria, and the original Force K in its heyday. Then she was badly damaged and returned to the UK.

To my surprise and great delight I found that Frankie David, my term-mate, was aboard. Also onboard was another Canadian, Mac Lynch, the radar officer. Lynch had joined the ship when she was being refitted in San Francisco, where she had gone after suffering her terrible damages off Crete. From Mac, I finally learned the reason why so many RN ships had Canadian radar officers aboard. Most electrical engineers in England had been signed up before the war to develop the RAF radar defence control network. As a result, the Admiralty was obliged to look to Canada for electrical engineers.

There were no trips to sea over the Christmas period, so Frankie and I were able to get ashore a bit. We took the opportunity to explore Valletta, and walked from the south of the harbour over the bare hills through stony rural villages to Marsaxlokk Bay. Here we encountered *Breconshire,* still lying half-submerged after being sunk in March.

Sliema Creek, Malta, June 1943.

I was shocked to see the incredible damage that the island had sustained. More than half of the handsome Mediterranean-style stone houses and buildings in Valletta appeared to have been damaged or destroyed. Many of the narrow streets were fully or partially blocked with rubble. Here and there an effort had been made to tidy up the mess, and many owners of damaged houses had salvaged one or two rooms, usually on the ground floor, and improvised repairs to them. Here they lived as squatters, waiting for the end of the war to make proper restoration.

The people looked listless and harried. Despite the recent arrival of two large convoys and the renewed presence of warships in the harbour, they showed no signs of optimism or relief. I suppose their rations hadn't been improved that much, and they had gone through so much that they still expected the worst. Their clothing looked worn and ill-fitting, and all the women and children had nasty scabies sores on their legs from malnutrition. There were few smiles and little animation, even on the part of the young.

Very little was on display in the few shops that had remained open, and there were virtually no bars and, obviously, no restaurants. The only other premises open, strangely enough, were two cinemas. All the government offices were underground in the tunnels beneath the battlements above the harbour.

When I had to take my oral exam in French from the Staff Officer Intelligence, I had to make my way to a miserable cubicle down a long rock tunnel which was lit by a few bare light bulbs. Fortunately, this cheerless environment had left my examiner's kindness untouched. He was very understanding about my efforts and marked me generously, with the note "bearing in mind the wartime situation."

The major feature on Malta is the extraordinary fortifications built by the Knights of St. John around Valletta and the adjacent towns in 1565, to defend themselves against the Turks. The Knights were driven out of Palestine, after the Crusades, to the island of Rhodes and then to Malta. The Turks, under Suleiman the Magnificent, couldn't take Valletta because of these fortifications. The island never won its independence over the centuries being under the Phoenicians, Carthaginians, Romans, Byzantines, Vandals, Arabs, Normans, the Knights, then the French, and finally the British.

Christmas Eve was spent singing carols in the narrow streets of Valletta; some of which were not streets but steps. Frankie, with his usual enthusiasm, organized this run ashore for a few of us midshipmen. It turned out to be an unforgettable night. We wandered around the colourful, ancient place singing carols, but basically in search of a pub — there was only one to our knowledge. No one was around in the darkened, blacked-out alleys, lit only by the new moon. We had the ancient town to ourselves. Frankie had introduced us to a marvellous new carol, the Coventry carol, which we had learned to sing in some sort of harmony. Finally we reached the pub, which was crowded with people. After we established that the only drink available was grain alcohol at exorbitant prices, we retraced our footsteps, getting lost in the bargain, back to the ship.

Christmas Day dawned without orders to go to sea or air raid warnings, so everyone got set for the Christmas spirit. One always remembers wartime Christmases vividly. The year before, I had celebrated Christmas dinner with an alleged Canadian cotton millionaire, with a very English accent, who had a magnificent house in the eastern suburbs of Alex. What impressed me most on that occasion was the sight of some twenty dinner guests being attended by individual servants in white tunics, red cummerbunds and fezzes.

This day in Malta was also memorable; the ships company went slightly crazy. I suppose, with the improving war news, they thought that they could finally let their hair down and the officers followed suit and did nothing to dampen their spirits. Anyone who could lay his hands on any kind of drink, attempted to get slightly tiddly.

There is a Christmas Day tradition in the navy that the most junior sailor be made captain for the day, and be allowed, within reason, to do whatever he pleases. He dons a captain's uniform and can order drinks from the officer's mess and have a special dinner. He goes around the ship being entertained by all and sundry. The senior officers always pay visits to the decorated mess-decks, where they swap jokes with the crew. On this occasion, every man onboard had been issued with a bottle of watery beer. I had a hand in getting the Malta brewery temporarily reopened to produce a bottle of beer for every soldier, sailor and airman on the island.

This day was particularly notable because our skipper, Captain Menzies, had a reception in his quarters for the denizens of the wardroom, gun-room and warrant officer's mess. His alcohol supply took quite a beating. I received a special invitation — presumably because I was a Canadian — to have Christmas dinner with him, along with several other officers.

Very early on in the meal it became apparent that his steward had over-imbibed and was barely under control. His Petty Officer Cook was not much better, as we could hear from an overloud conversation next door in the captain's galley. Apparently someone had made off with one of the captain's chickens or it had been eaten by his personal staff. As a result, we were each served with a tiny, cold portion. However, when I went to the festivities down below, I found similar problems. Nevertheless the day ended splendidly with a screening of the movie "Wagon Train" in the wardroom and we all lost ourselves in Hollywood's romantic picture of the old American West. The sight of the paint sizzling on the countertop in the saloon after a drink had been spilled, evoked laughter after our experiences of grain alcohol ashore.

The good cheer continued into the New Year, especially with the news that

Repaired *Orion* in Valleta harbour, Malta, January 1943.

the Russians had defeated the Germans around Stalingrad and had destroyed a complete German army. What an achievement! The threat to our rear now faded and we would presumably be able commit troops from Iraq to the Western Desert.

Force Q from Bone had also been very active. On 1 December, the day before the Kerkanah Bank action, it had decimated an Italian convoy headed for Bizerta. Three cruisers — *Aurora* (flagship of Rear-Admiral R. Harcourt), *Argonaut* and *Sirius* with the destroyers *Quiberon* and *Quentin,* had sunk four merchant ships and one destroyer off Cape Bon. Unfortunately *Quiberon* was sunk in the action. The enemy would now have to acknowledge that they would face great difficulties in supplying their North African armies by sea.

The main duty of *Orion* during this period was to escort convoys from Alex to Malta. From January to the end of March 1943 we, in conjunction with the Hunts escorted four convoys without incident. Even German submarine activity in the eastern basin seemed to have been reduced. The other cruisers at Malta were kept on standby in case the Italian fleet finally entered the fray or a large convoy to Tripoli or Bizerta was mounted. The remainder of the fleet at Alex was used to bring up convoys to Benghazi, and to Tripoli after it fell to us on 23 January 1943.

All the while, 14 DF was active in attacking small convoys. *Pakenham, Paladin* and the Greek *Queen Olga* also took part in these forays.

In late March, *Orion* transited the Suez Canal and took part in an experimental bombardment down the Gulf of Suez. I felt sorry for Guns who was responsible for putting this show on, as we had embarked a host of army top brass from Cairo as spectators. We were testing new naval land bombardment methods. The exercise fortunately went well. The army seemed quite pleased.

After returning to Malta I received a new appointment, to the staff of Flag Officer Red Sea and Suez Canal in Port Tewfik. I was confirmed as a sublieutenant and my pay was backdated to November 1942. On 10 April I packed

Eskimo **entering Tripoli harbour. Note blockships and narrow entrance.**

my effects and joined *Princess Kathleen* the fast troop transport. She was a comfortable ship with cabins on the upper decks and an open car deck below. Embarked with me were the heroines of Malta, the nurses, who were being sent back to Egypt after their experiences during the siege.

The officers made a bit of a fuss over me because I was a Canadian, and I was given one of the best cabins. We sailed south unescorted, at full speed, from Malta bound for Tripoli.

This port, like Alex, was not a natural harbour but was protected by a substantial concrete mole constructed between a series of small outer islands. Its narrow entrance lay between the outer mole and another one running out from the land. The Germans had done a thorough job in blocking it. Three merchant ships still lay across the entrance as we inched our way through a passage between them. A narrow opening about eighty feet wide had been forced through them. Inside the harbour, the wrecks of eight Italian warships and merchantmen lay scattered around, one right across a main jetty.

From the ship, Tripoli, with its ubiquitous domes amd minarets mixed with modern buildings and several old forts, was somewhat like Alex but on a much smaller scale.

After tying up to a buoy, we awaited orders. The purser was to go ashore on business and asked me to accompany him. From the harbour one could see many up-to-date buildings, and it looked as if the Italians had done a good job modernizing the city. However, on getting ashore I noticed that they had only built good buildings on the main streets, and had left the side streets to rot. This gave the place an appearance of a Hollywood movie lot; all show but with little substance.

The following day our next batch of passengers began to embark. These included the musicians and actors of the Kiwi Concert Party, which had been entertaining the New Zealand troops in the desert. But more interesting was the three bargeloads of German and Italian prisoners.

These men had been captured during the Battle of Mareth (150 miles to

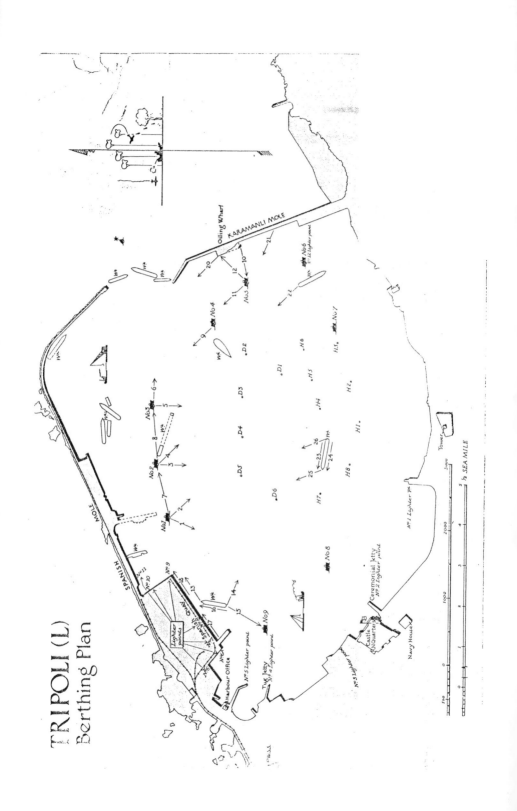

TRIPOLI (L)
Berthing Plan

The Canadian Pacific British Columbia ferry *Princess Kathleen,* in her wartime colours, operating as a fast troopship; sailing in the Gulf of Suez.

the west) which had ended about ten days earlier. Rommel had retreated to a position about a hundred miles inside southern Tunisia just south of Gabes and set up a defensive line, and had held us up for about two months before being driven back.

On each barge there was an armed guard of about twenty soldiers, each with a sub-machine gun. One barge held a mixed bag of German and Italian troops. Very obviously, the Germans were in much better condition than the Italians. Their uniforms were cleaner and they were better shaven. There was no communication between them, and I sensed from the behaviour of the Germans that they did not like Italians. They also gave the impression that they didn't think too much of us either.

The Italians were finally sent to another ship or returned back ashore and we loaded only Germans. They were marched directly onboard to the car deck, where they remained for the rest of the voyage under armed guard. They slept on the steel deck wrapped in a single blanket that had been given to each of them. A company of Royal Engineers had been entrusted with the task of guarding them. Each day groups of prisoners were brought up on deck to exercise.

Again we sailed unescorted. On the first day we practised abandon ship stations. This posed problems for the guards because half the complement of prisoners was brought up on deck at one time, when they were allocated their abandon ship position and a lifeboat. One had visions of the massed prisoners trying to take over physical control of the ship. They were commanded by their own officers and NCOs, while our troops nonchalantly looked on. Their officers shouted and carried on in front of them, carefully inspecting each man, making quite a scene, presumably for our benefit.

I was allotted a lifeboat with an engine room officer, a seaman, and thirty

Germans. We three were each to be given a pistol and ammunition to keep control of the prisoners. I have often wondered what would have happened if we had been forced to abandon ship.

The weather was excellent during the trip, and the company the same. What with the nurses, the Kiwis, who entertained us every night in the saloon, the congenial army types who were thoroughly enjoying themselves after the hardships of desert warfare, and the ship's officers, we had a wonderful time. The food was first class and there was no shortage of booze. The Germans staged their own concerts on the car deck below, being entertained by an opera singer. Some of us went down and listened to him and it was obvious he was a real professional. We asked that he come up to sing for us, but in typical German fashion, he refused. I believe that some of the Kiwis played for them. All too soon I was back in dear old Alex.

One last note on this period concerns the replacement of Admiral Harwood as C-in-C. In part this arose from the difficulties that were encountered at Tripoli in resupplying the advancing 8th Army. After the Battle of El Alamein and the fast follow-up of the retreating enemy armies, the naval Inshore Squadron was resurrected under the command of Captain I. Wauchope to carry out the job it did in the first push. Hunt class destroyers (when available), corvettes, minesweepers, MTBs and MLs, tank landing craft, small coasters, tugs and barges, netlayers and the salvage vessel HMSAS Gamtoos were used in this squadron. The difficulty facing the squadron was not enemy aircraft attacks, as before in 1941, but the speed of the advance and the terrible condition of the ports.

By and large, we did a tremendous job. Tobruk, which had only been captured on 13 November 1942, admitted its first convoy seven days later, after extensive clearance of the harbour and port facilities. By 1 December the railway link from Mersa Matruh to Tobruk (first opened in June 1942) was back in operation. In effect, the port was being used as a forwarding depot within two weeks.

Benghazi, which presented fewer clearance problems, was admitting convoys by 26 November, six days after falling into our hands. Tripoli, however, which we took on 23 January 1943, was another matter, because the entrance was tightly blocked by three merchant ships and a barge full of cement. It wasn't until twelve days later, 4 February, that the first sizeable convoy could be admitted.

By this time, the army's supply line stretched over 1,200 miles from the Nile, and our advance was temporarily halted for lack of fuel and ammunition. Montgomery complained about the navy's tardiness in clearing Tripoli harbour. This was not altogether justifiable as the clearance task was very difficult and the chief salvage officer was held up from getting an early flight into Tripoli through no fault of his own.

Churchill, who was in Egypt at the time, following the Casablanca conference, became involved in the dispute and took the army's side. He was not too happy at the time with Admiral Harwood, who had been criticized for the Tobruk raid and for not having exerted enough pressure on Admiral Godfroy to bring the Vichy French ships into the war. Consequently, Harwood was relieved of his command on 27 March 1943, to be replaced by Admiral J.H.D. Cunningham on 5 June. In the interim, Vice-Admiral Sir R. Leatham, who had been Flag Officer Malta, was acting C-in-C.[14]

CHAPTER TWELVE

Operation Husky:
The Assault on Sicily

"O Lord God, when thou givest to thy servants to endeavour any great matter, grant us also to know that it is not the beginning but the continuing of the same until it is thoroughly finished which yieldeth the true glory."

Drakes's prayer before Cadiz

I took the train from Alex, via Cairo, through the dusty desert to Port Tewfik where I reported to the staff of the Flag Officer Red Sea and Canal Area. Initially I was not too enthusiastic about being stuck in this backwater away from the action. However after about three weeks the place started to become a hive of activity. Something big was clearly afoot.

A huge Combined Operations tented base was being built on the bleak inlet south of Suez. Great numbers of ships of all types, from large liners to tugs, and all manner of sometimes novel, unfamiliar landing craft started to arrive. Unbelievable amounts of equipment and great numbers of men were being unloaded into these desert camps. The great bay of Suez (5 miles in width) was a forest of masts and the continuous line of hulls completely obscured the opposite bank.

Tunis had fallen on 7 May 1943 and the North African campaign was now over, so it was obvious that this build-up heralded a landing somewhere on the northern shores of the Mediterranean. At that stage the precise location was unclear; perhaps Greece, or Crete, or Italy, or the Balkans, or even Turkey to link up with the Russians. The 8th Army must have been moving back to the Nile delta and this great armada of ships was to carry it to attack Churchill's "soft underbelly of the axis."

Port Tewfik was as attractive as ever, and the weather and our quarters could not have been more agreeable. My job concerned the maintenance and construction of buildings and public works, a novel experience for me as it had nothing to do with ships or sailors.

One morning as I walked to work along the canal, I came upon an extraordinary sight. Long lines of soldiers were moving from out of the depths of the desert, on the other side of the canal. It could have been on the set of a Cecil B. de Mille epic. The nearest group was just beginning to arrive at the water's edge, where several Landing Craft Attack (LCAs, small armoured boats, about 40 feet long, which carried thirty soldiers) were beached, with their ramps down, waiting to embark them.

This was the first time that I had ever seen the army in such numbers. There were hundreds and hundreds of them; all in the same coloured uniforms and so indistinquishable that they were like a column of ants carrying twigs to their nest. They seemed rather helpless, as they slipped and stumbled in the heavy sand.

King George VI on *Eskimo* on 20 June 1943, off Tripoli.

The first party arrived at the shore and the leading files stopped and waited until the rest straggled up and fell into some kind of order behind them. Then an officer then began herding them into the craft. More and more columns arrived and waited patiently for further landing craft to come. I turned and saw an old Egyptian man further up the embankment, also intently looking at them. Then he too turned and we looked knowingly at each other. It was 7 oclock in the morning and we were the only people there.

This kept up for several days. The place was seething with pongos and ships and brasshats. On the third day of the embarkation, Montgomery visited the admiral. It wouldn't be long now. Headquarters was a hive of activity and alive with stories of new developments. More new, unfamiliar ships arrived, many of them smaller than coastal vessels and not designed for deep sea voyages. Yet some had sailed directly from the States, with tales of terrible storms.

Among this strange flotilla were ships designed to offload tanks directly onto a beach. They were built to steer straight for the shore, beaching themselves, and then letting down a big metal ramp from their open bows to admit or discharge their cargoes. These were Tank Landing Ships (LST) which had a tonnage of about 1,600 tons, and were armed with light AA guns and could carry eighteen tanks.

There were smaller ships, which carried more troops than an LCA and had special gangways on either side of their bows to disembark their charges quickly. They could carry 150 troops. What a tremendous effort must have gone into the planning, design and construction of all these new craft.

Most of us at headquarters were rather disgruntled that we wouldn't be taking part in this operation. Then the day came when the huge liners, loaded with troops and landing craft, could be seen from our office as they moved slowly and carefully, in line ahead into the canal. Getting these thirty-odd liners and some 200 merchant ships through the canal was going to be a tricky operation. They steamed north, one behind the other, at half mile intervals. If the enemy had only known what was happening, they could have stopped the movement with bombs and mines. No doubt we had a strong force of fighters on the alert.

While this was going on and we were commiserating with one another about the fact that we had to remain behind, the admiral's secretary sent for me. He was a cheerful soul who knew what we all wanted. Practically everyone had tried to get transfers to a ship or back to Alex.

Before I had even had time to take a seat in his office, he called out, "You've had plenty of staff cyphering work, havn't you my boy." I sensed his meaning. "Yes sir." I answered eagerly. "Well...." Before I knew it, I was bowling along the canal road in a lorry, happy as a clam. I was to join the Headquarters ship *Bulolo* as a cypher officer, on the staff of the Assault Admiral, Rear Admiral T. Troubridge. Away to my right was the spectacle of huge ships, moving in tandem across the desert. From my vantage point I could only make out the upper superstructures, not the hulls, which appeared to be moving over the land like toy ships on a thick carpet.

We sailed from Port Said on 5 July 1943 and formed up a convoy of twenty-nine Landing ships Infantry (LSIs, modified passenger ships carrying troops) escorted by the AA cruiser *Carlisle* and six Hunt class destroyers. As we moved out to sea, up the swept channel from the harbour in line ahead, the public address system clicked and the admiral began speaking to us. It was what everyone had been waiting to hear. He told us briefly that we were bound for the island of Sicily; that we must expect hectic and sleepless days and nights ahead of us during and after the landings, and candidly advised us to get as much sleep as possible during the five-day trip to the island.

This convoy was the most impressive of the many I had seen. Just about every ship was a liner, sleek and inspiring: something unheard of in the Med. But what a target for enemy aircraft! It seemed unbelievable to us old stagers that we could put ships of this type into these dangerous waters. All of them were well known worldwide; the likes of *Duchess of Bedford, Monarch of Bermuda, Orontes* and *Stratheden*. They were lying astern of us in three columns; their mighty bows dipping impressively into the slight Mediterranean swell. *Bulolo,* our ship was quite puny beside them. She was a small squat Australian coastal passenger vessel. Certainly she shouldn't have been leading these magnificent thoroughbreds into battle.

But where they had the beauty we had the brains. Our masts bristled with radio and radar aerials. The forward cargo hold had been modified to house a complete interservice headquarters. The hull in this part of the ship had been strengthened to withstand a direct hit.

The hold itself was divided into three decks. The lowest deck, where I would work, was given over to communications and housed army, navy and air force cypher and code rooms, and W/T receiving and transmitting rooms. The Main Signal Distributing Room was right in the centre. This was manned exclusively by naval personnel but from here messages were dispersed for all three services to the Operations Room on the next deck above. The whole deck area was manned by all three services on a watch basis, but everyone was to close up as required during and after the assault.

I was soon reading the operation orders, which were nothing like I had ever

Headquarters Landing Ship HMS *Bulolo*.

seen before (running to ten thick volumes). I soon learned that the estimated traffic which we would have to handle would be enormous. We would be listening on sixty-two wave lengths, and on D-Day could anticipate 1,500 messages in and out a day, roughly one a minute. Not all messages would be short, so we would be hard pressed to keep pace at times.

The Operations or Support Control Room deck, as it was called, contained three signal filtering rooms, one each for Navy Ops, Army Intelligence and the RAF filter room, with the main Support Control Room in the centre. The main room was what I had always imagined a huge operations room to be. It was dominated by a large map of Sicily, about twenty feet square, parallel to the deck and raised off the floor like a huge table. Around it would stand the plotters moving little markers showing the disposition of the three forces. Large notice boards were mounted on the bulkheads, containing lists which constantly had to be updated. High above was a balcony which gave the senior officers a panoramic view of the place. The purpose of this deck was to co-ordinate reports from the three services and portray them in one clear picture as simply, correctly and as up to date as possible.

There was also an adjacent room behind a glass wall which served as the Fighter Control Room compartment. Our fighter aircraft cover was to be directed from here until a control centre could be be set up ashore. Likewise, the generals would control their forces ashore from this room until they could land their own headquarters staff. It was estimated that these rooms would be used for three or four days after the assault, depending upon how well the landings went.

The top deck contained rooms for the senior officers. We carried our own admiral who would direct all naval forces in our sector. There were also two generals aboard with their staffs. Lieutenant-General M.C. Dempsey who commanded the 8th Army 13th Corps which consisted of two infantry divisions, the 5th Division commanded by Major-General H.P. Berney-Ficklin,

Canadian Pacific Liner *Duchess of Richmond*.

Ellerman City Line S.S. *City of Canterbury*.

who was also onboard, and the 50th Division commanded by Major-General S.C. Kirkman, who was on another ship. We were responsible for landing this corps plus an additional brigade, the 231st Infantry Brigade. This brigade was part of the the 51st Highland Division, which was to land in the sector to our south. Each infantry division comprised three or four brigades, and each brigade, three battalions.

The famous regiments that we would land included the London Irish Rifles (my father's regiment in the First World War), the Green Howards, the Durham Light Infantry (three battalions) and the Inniskilling Fusiliers amongst others.

Navy's Part In Sicily Invasion Described

THE first letter to describe action in Sicily was received in Winnipeg this morning by Mrs. Frank Wade, 206 Ethelbert st., from her son, Sub-Lieut. Frank Wade, who was serving aboard the Royal Navy ship which lauded part of the 8th Army.

"Our ship had the job of landing part of the famous 8th Army in Sicily," he wrote.

There were heavy air attacks during the landing and the ship had been instrumental in shooting down 150 enemy aircraft.

"Our ship directed the fighters on to them (the enemy)."

"I spent a few days in Syracuse. It was an interesting experience, but, unfortunately, I did not see any of the Canadians," he said.

Sub.-Lieut. Wade has been stationed in the Mediterranean for two-and-a-half years. His letter was dated July 23 and was mailed from his home port in Egypt.

His father, Capt. Frank Wade, is serving overseas with the army.

SUB.-LIEUT. FRANK WADE.
Helped land 8th Army in Sicily.

Winnipeg Free Press cutting, 9 August 1943, on Sicilian landings.

There were about 1,600 men in each battalion, 5,000 men in a brigade, and 15,000 in a division. Thus we were transporting 35,000 troops in 19 LSIs, each of which held about 1,800 men. As each LSI carried a number of LCAs, thousands of men could be put ashore in the first wave.

Also aboard was an RAF Group Captain who was to liaise between the air force headquarters in Malta and the other two services. One of his main responsibilties would be to arrange for the transfer of our aircraft to the airfield at Pachino, on the south east tip of Sicily, at the south end of our sector, once it had been taken.

The ingenuity and imagination which had gone into the design and modification of this ship were extraordinary. Somehow the old prejudices and competition between the three services had been buried and now we were working in close harmony. Every conceivable contingency had been anticipated in the operation orders.

In a nutshell, *Bulolo's* job was therefore to direct the landing; accomodate the army staffs until they could get get ashore; direct the fighters over the beachheads; and arrange for the opening of Syracuse harbour before the beachhead was shut down.

Therafter we would leave the army and the air force to do the job of winning Sicily. To carry out our functions we had to rely entirely on our communications capability. We were nothing more than a glorified signal ship.

The morning of 7 July 1943 dawned calm and clear. What was unexpected, however, was that there were no enemy aircraft about. As with all convoys during 1943, we kept very close to the North African coast until we left it north of Benghazi. As a result, were able to have continuous fighter coverage throughout the day and even some night fighters at night, as well as excellent A/S air coverage. To the north of us a powerful fleet protected us in case the Italian Navy came out and made a direct attack, which was a possibility. This force consisted of three veterans of the Med naval war, the battleships *Valiant* and *Warspite* and the aircraft carrier *Formidable,* plus the cruisers *Aurora* and *Penelope* and nine fleet destroyers. This force would follow us right into the landing areas.

The proverbial pessimists were prophesying that the German air force was biding it's time until we got into a tight spot, closer to land. Many of the officers onboard had never been in the Med or seen what had happened a year before. They laughingly dismissed these anxieties and talked glibly of a walkover. We were now south of Crete and could expect attacks from the German air force there. However, nothing transpired. There appeared to be no change from the situation we had been experiencing during the spring, when air attacks from the north had been very sparse. Even so, at the time, I looked at these huge ships and shook my head in wonderment at what was happening.

We were soon steaming almost due north of Benghazi. Earlier that afternoon, my misgivings about air attacks were reawakened following the sighting of a very high-flying enemy recce aircraft trailing white vapour behind it. We wondered what had happened to our fighters, and even anticipated the worst. All the while, the Cyranaican hills were clearly visible on the horizon to the south, and we could even make out the occasional small village on the coastline.

Later in the day (7 July) a meeting of all naval signals staff was called and the whole of the afternoon was spent familiarizing ourselves with what to expect when the messages started pouring in. Our senior signals officer, a tired-looking lieutenant Commander went over the major aspects of the operation, pointing out every likely emergency and change of plan that might arise and the appropriate responses.

He explained that we were not the only force taking part. Three countries were participating, Britain, United States and Canada. The U.S. 7th Army, under General G. Patton was to land on the southwest of the island, whereas we would land on the southeast coast. The American forces were slightly smaller than ours, consisting of one corps of three divisions. Our force, by contrast, totalled two corps and three armoured brigades. The American organistion and plans were similar to ours, but did not directly concern us.

Our task was to land 13th Corps about fifteen miles south of Syracuse on the east coast. At the same time, Special Air Service (SAS) troops were to land by sea in the bay were the landings were to take place, to destroy Italian defence batteries. Also a commando unit was to do the same thing further south of them. The 1st Air Landing Brigade was to land by glider further to the north of these two groups, to take a very strategic bridge over a river, north from the beaches, just south of and leading to Syracuse.

The 231st Brigade of 30th Corps, aboard *Strathnaver* and *Otranto* in our convoy, which I have mentioned, was not really part of our force, was to land to our south, in the sector around Cape Passero, where *Keren* would serve as the local HQ ship.

We also learned that the 51st highland Division and a supporting tank brigade had sailed in another convoy from Sfax in Tunisia, while the 1st Canadian Infantry Division was coming direct from the United Kingdom. The Americans divisions came from the States and North Africa.

Ahead of us lay an enormous supply convoy comprising sixty merchant ships and five tankers, and another later convoy of LSTs carrying tanks and motor transport. These we would soon overtake and they would follow us into the beaches. Both convoys would be unloaded after the initial assault. All these convoys, including ours and the Yankee ones, had sailed at differing dates, depending upon the distance to Sicily, and all of them were to be south of the island by the morning of 9 July. They would stay close to the North African shore, so that they could enjoy fighter cover until the last minute. Further convoys were expected to arrive later to complete the drop.

Thus, on the night that we landed, there would be hundreds of ships, both large and small, massed together in an area about fifty miles square around Malta. Flags (Senior Signal Officer) told us that the critical factor which had held up the operation was neither the outcome of the Tunisian campaign, nor the amassing of sufficient troops, nor even the training of the army in seaborne landing techniques, but the time needed to adjust worldwide shipping so that sufficient ships would be available. Thousands of ships were involved, approximately one third of the total allied merchant fleet.

He continued that he had been at the Casablanca conference, back in January, and had been party to the first discussions which culminated in the decision to invade Sicily. Consequently he had seen the operation develop from its inception to its implementation. The broad strategy and the detailed plans were entrusted to the Allied Chiefs of Staff because the field commanders — Eisenhower, Alexander and Montgomery — were too busy finishing off the Tunisian campaign.

Initally, the Americans were to have landed around Palermo, on the north west end of the island, with the British going in around Syracuse. Monty immediately objected, because the two armies would be split: thereby flying in the face of one of the main principles of war: never separate your forces. He wanted the main effort to be concentrated to the south and the south east, so that all our forces could land together, before fanning out to the north and west. British troops would move up the eastern side of the island to cut off the enemy from Italy, and the Americans would mop up the rest of the island. The Americans were not happy with this because they wanted the port of Palermo to supply their army.

Finally, after a lot of wrangling, it was agreed that we would land south of Syracuse and the Americans would land closer to us, on the beaches on the south coast. It was expected that ours would probably be the more difficult area because intelligence assessments indicated the German army was concentrated around Syracuse.

However, this fitted in with Monty's preference for striking at the enemy at his strongest point and destroying him as quickly as possible. Instead of taking territory, extending lines of communication and avoiding the issue. This plan also ensured that we would achieve one of our main objectives early on, namely the capture of the important airfields at Pachino and Gela, in the south.

The 8th Army was to endeavour to reach Messina, at the northeast corner of the island, in about a week to isolate the island from mainland Italy and bring the campaign to a rapid end. Flags continued that they had had a terrible time with the detailed planning because of arguments about basic deployments. More than once they had to scrap everything they had done and start over again. No wonder he looked so tired. By the time he had finished speaking, all of us had a much clearer picture of the operation and our part in it. We had just two more days to wait before the massive undertaking came to fruition.

Following the admirals's advice, I had been taking it easy, as cyphering traffic had been purely routine and we were on reduced watches. The best course was to retire to your cabin with a book, as the wardoom was chock-a-block with army types. Most of them were members of corps and divisional HQ staffs and they didn't have too much to do either. Most were very senior officers; brigadiers and colonels were ten a penny.

They were all seasoned veterans of the desert war and Lord knows what exciting and dangerous battles they had been through. They were a very impressive group. But for the most part, they were quiet and friendly, and, although they were in the majority, and of senior rank, they hadn't taken over the mess but deferred to the ship's officers and the admiral's staff. There was no side to them and they certainly didn't stand on their rank. Even the two generals, who occasionally came into the mess for a drink were unassuming.

They were certainly not like our admiral, who was danced attendance on at all times by his subordinates. He was quite a character. Portly and never without a smile, he was full of energy and drive. One of his distinquishing marks was a tiny set of Zeiss prismatic binoculars which he always wore across his chest instead of the larger navy issue.

July 9 was D-1, and a day of mounting excitement. Dawn came up slowly to reveal us in company with several more convoys. There were ships all around us as far as the eye could see. We were now roughly due north of Tripoli and heading north. Many army and air force personnel were standing on the promenade deck gazing in awe at the wonderful sight of this great armada.

Wallowing in the swell astern was the old *Erebus*, a 15-inch gun monitor; an unwieldy looking relic of the First World War. She would be used for inshore bombardment. There were also two Dutch gunboats, *Soemba* and *Flores*, steaming between the destroyer screen and us, along with the old China river-gunboats, *Aphis* and *Scarab*. These colourful flat-bottomed ships looked more like armed houseboats than warships. One monitor and two gunboats were allocated to each sector.

Lying far out on the horizon, two cruisers *Newfoundland* and *Mauritius* were discernable on the horizon. They were to remain with us throughout the landings to provide AA protection, inshore shelling in support of the army, and to protect us if we were attacked at anchor by the Italian fleet. Just as well, because although this eventuality was highly unlikely, I had never really felt secure in *Bulolo*. Although she flew the white ensign, she was only a merchant

201

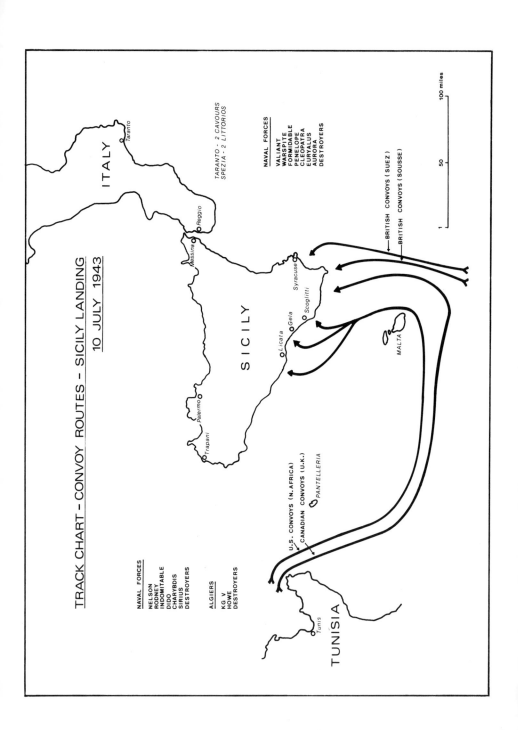

TRACK CHART – CONVOY ROUTES – SICILY LANDING

10 JULY 1943

ITALY

Taranto

SICILY

Messina

Reggio

Syracuse

Scoglitti

Gela

Licata

Palermo

Trapani

MALTA

PANTELLERIA

TUNISIA

Tunis

NAVAL FORCES

NELSON
RODNEY
INDOMITABLE
DIDO
CHARYBDIS
SIRIUS
DESTROYERS

ALGIERS

KG V
HOWE
DESTROYERS

U.S. CONVOYS (N. AFRICA)
CANADIAN CONVOYS (U.K.)

TARANTO – 2 CAVOURS
SPEZIA – 2 LITTORIOS

NAVAL FORCES

VALIANT
WARSPITE
FORMIDABLE
PENELOPE
CLEOPATRA
EURYALUS
AURORA
DESTROYERS

BRITISH CONVOYS (SUEZ)
BRITISH CONVOYS (SOUSSE)

1   50   100 miles

ship with a few light AA guns. I began to realize what it must have been like on a merchant ship in a Med convoy. Certainly one felt safer with a few warships around.

As the day progressed we began to join the convoys from Sfax. Then two small English Channel ferries swung in from astern and steamed up at about 25 knots between the columns of the convoy. They raised quite a bow wave, and were presumably putting on a bit of show for our admiral who, at this point, came up on the bridge. He levelled his tiny binoculars on them, and I imagined some devilish signal brewing in his mind, ordering them to take position with less speed. This seemed likely because several of the small ships, LCIs, and the tiny Harbour Defence Motor Launches (HDMLs), that we had picked up during the night, were having a rough time in the wash of these "Johnny come latelys." But no, he turned and smiled. He, too, was caught up in the excitement. The two speeding ships were carrying the Commandos, and would be the first to go to the shore.

What an unforgettable sight it was; so many ships of all shapes and sizes, from all parts of the world and from so many nations, pressing eagerly ahead northward for enemy shores with the wind rattling their flags and rigging. One thought of Henry V leading his mounted knights and yeomen into battle amid colourful flags and armour.

"I see you stand like greyhounds in the slips.
Straining upon the start. The game's afoot:
Follow your spirit; and upon this charge
Cry — God for Harry! England! and Saint George!"

Soon the LCIs from Sfax were attached four to an LST and began clustering around their mother ships like a brood of wandering ducklings around an annoyed duck. The two MLs attached to us seemed to be having trouble keeping up with us. Both rose and plunged in our wash about a cable (200 yards) astern, and were taking quite a beating as they tried valiantly to get abeam. The seas were definitely getting rougher and the wind was rising. We could only hope that the landing would not be jeopardised.

Lying astern of the entire convoy was a flotilla of fleet minesweepers, which were to clear a path for us to the beaches if necessary. Most of the new ships had rendezvoused with us in the night, and it was a wonder that there hadn't been any collisions. The entire horizon was now circumscribed with ships. Three miles to our starboard was a long line of freighters in convoy, which we had finally caught up with and would soon be passing. To port there was a convoy of LSTs, easily distinquishable by their ugliness; big whale-like barges which stuck high out of the water. When the sun peeked through a gap in the clouds, the whole armada glistened and sparkled, especially the barrage balloons bouncing in the sky above the LSIs and cargo ships. A patch of low cloud astern blocked out other ships far away for a while and the winds continued to increase ominously.

Up on the promenade deck, in the lee of the bridge, stood four boxes of pigeons. I noticed a soldier, in his shirtsleeves, removing them from their compartments and inspecting them. Presumably they were to be taken ashore by the army. I also noticed that many people were now self-consciously wearing their life-jackets.

Some hours later, at 1700, I was ensconced in the cypher room where work was still very slack. I'd just returned from a rather depressing tea in the wardroom. The place was almost empty as most of the army types were getting their heads down in preparation for the landings later in the night. The few people there discussed the deteriorating weather. There was now a very strong northwest wind blowing up quite a swell. The little ships were having a bad time of it. They were not designed for this kind of weather. The troops in the LCIs must have been sick as dogs and in no shape to land. The LCAs, the smallest landing craft of all — carried in the LSIs in place of lifeboats — could not operate in this weather. If it continued, the build-up on the beaches would probably be delayed, with dire consequences.

Our two HDMLs had by now caught up with us, one on each side directly abeam, and were having a terrible time trying to keep up. It was something to see these little ships riding out a storm with the spray going clean over them. They were being tossed around like leaves. It must have been murder below decks. As they nosed into the seas, half of their hulls disappeared under water and the next minute, as they came up, they seemed to be almost airborne.

Someone mentioned that we would probably be okay because our beaches were on the southeast side of Sicily and would therefore be in the lee of land from the northwest wind. It was suggested that the Americans would be the ones who would be taking the beating because they would be landing on the west coast open to the wind.

But we wondered what would happen to the airborne operation. Our gliders were due to drop in another six hours, and wouldn't the wind blow them off course? I had raised the problem with a young Lieutenant-Colonel, who was the airborne liaison officer. It was too late, he said, to cancel the airborne operation now. The latest hour that this could have been done was noon. At that time he had advised the Corps commander that the weather was good enough, but he was not too happy by the time I spoke to him. However, he stoically accepted the situation, and every time someone tactlessly asked him what was going to happen, he replied "Wind or no wind they'll do it."

As the afternoon passed, the weather continued to worsen. The ship started to develop a marked slow roll and the upper deck began to be swept by spray.

Later at 1900, cyphering was still very light — the calm before the storm. I managed a quick look around on deck before returning below to prepare for the night. Dusk was now falling and Mount Etna could be seen coming up over the horizon ahead. The island itself was not visible: just this unexpected, strange mountain appearing out of the clouds. We were now north of Malta, and it was quiet on deck, with little talk. The sea seemed to be easing a little, although the wind was still blowing quite strongly. A small group of LCTs nearby disappeared in the waves from time to time almost like submarines.

Throughout the day and evening there had been no air attacks and no reports of the Italian fleet leaving port. Despite the enormous size of our forces, covering a front of 150 miles so close to Sicily, it appeared that the enemy were quite unaware of our movements. This seemed beyond belief to us. Either the pre-invasion bombing by our own air forces had thoroughly neutralised their air affort, or they were expecting the invasion somewhere else. Possibly the Germans were too tied up in their Russian adventure — which, from recent news, hadn't been going too well for them — and had withdrawn all their Air Divisions. They must have not had the air resources to counter our strong air component. We had all believed that by this time we would have been under continuous and heavy air attack.

The plan for the night ahead was that, at fifteen minutes past midnight, each leading convoy would steer for a marking submarine, located at a prearranged position about five miles off the beaches. Then the LSIs would stop and lower and load their LCAs with troops. HDMLs would then start herding these little craft together to escort them farther inshore toward sonic buoys which had been laid by submarines. These buoys, which dropped to the bottom when first laid, had been set to rise to the surface at 0200. By then, it was expected that the landing craft would be approaching, and from here they would be in position to proceed to their correct beach. After the LCAs had left the LSIs; the LCIs — which carried a greater number of troops — would follow them in.

All the beaches had been carefully inspected beforehand by specially trained crews operating from submarine-launched tiny folbots at night. They had checked that the beaches were suitable for landings: that they were open to the sea, not too rocky or narrow, not too steep and not blocked by obstructions. This dangerous work was kept very secret. No mention had been made of it in the operation orders; because of its sensitive and furtive nature. No one knew anything about it prior to the landings. In fact, during the first night after the landings, a very tanned and rugged-looking Sub came aboard who was reputed to have spent two weeks in Sicily before we arrived and had been picked up by one of our ship's landing craft which had brought him aboard to be debriefed by corps intelligence.

By 2200 the landings were ready to go ahead. All our ship movements had gone like clockwork and there was no sign whatsoever of the enemy. Soon signal traffic began to increase. The latest air recce reports of the Italian fleet timed at 1600 indicated that there were two *Littorios* at Spezia and two *Cavours* in Taranto, and they were showing no signs of activity.

Our battleship force from the west, *Nelson* and *Rodney* and the carrier *Indomitable* plus cruisers and destroyers had joined our *Warspite* force to take care of the *Cavours*. At this point both forces were lying not far off our sector to the east. Another battleship force consisting of *Howe* and *King George V* plus cruisers and destroyers was stationed off Algiers to deal with the *Littorios*. We had mustered a fleet greatly superior to that of the Italians and this probably accounted for their reluctance to come out.

All air dispositions had been made. Every bomber in Malta had been withdrawn and the island filled with fighters. As a result, fortunately, none of the landing sectors would be out of fighter range from Malta. There were even enough fighters to provide a standing patrol of twelve aircraft over all sectors.

At 2200 precisely I went on deck briefly to watch for the big transport planes, which each towed two large gliders, to go by. They were due to be over the dropping zone at about 2215. We didn't see them, but someone mentioned that they heard the sound of aircraft engines in the distance. It was pitch-dark on deck, and even when our eyes became accustomed to the darkness, it was difficult to see the closest ships around us. But I could make out the phospherescent wake of the ML abeam of us. Happily by now the seas had dropped considerably. *Bulolo* had reduced speed and practically stopped and the water could be heard lapping our sides. Just then I felt the presence of someone behind me, and turned. It was my glider friend, the worried Lieutenant-Colonel.

Then suddenly a voice cried out, "Look!" The assault had begun. We could see one thin white line of tracer bullets shooting up into the sky for about two seconds before dying out. Gradually the tracer grew heavier and heavier and more widespread, until the night sky was gashed with coloured lines. The glider boys were being attacked, and were clearly taking quite a pasting. The Lieutenant-Colonel smiling a little self-consciously, remarked, "We don't mind, it lights up the ground and shows us where to land."

Before I returned below, I dropped into the army signals section. The major in charge simply shook his head. As yet there had been no signals from Airborne Brigade HQ ashore. By this time they should have landed and established their transmitter. In fact, we never received a message from them.

Later at 0130, Saturday 10 July 1943, D-Day, I went on deck for another quick look around. The night was still very black, and the convoy by now was practically stopped. Ships were moving slowly and carefully to their lowering positions. We were now about eight miles offshore and about 25 miles south of Syracuse. I joined the groups on the promenade deck waiting for the aerial bombing of the beaches to begin just before we went in.

The sea was now much calmer but was still slightly choppy; we were out of the worst of the wind. This must have been a relief to our admiral and the generals, who had clearly been fretting during the afternoon about the rough weather. Then the bombers could be heard droning in the night. Soon they were overhead and within minutes the attack began.

I am ashamed to say that we all took great satisfaction in watching someone else taking a beating for a change. The ship shook slightly with each bomb thud. In the direction of Syracuse the Italian Anti-aircraft guns threw up little white flashes, which died very quickly, like shooting stars. But the barrage was sparse and irregular. Their light guns were much more active; and shots were coming from both Syracuse and the beach-heads. Glowing tracer lines were clearly visible all over the place, and there were even a few searchlights sweeping the sky back and forth. The enemy was obviously well armed in this area, which didn't bode too well for our troops. Then something really caught our fancy; bursts of tracer were tearing downwards from the sky as our bombers returned the fire. There were more explosions, fires broke out on the distant horizon and the faint whine of falling bombs could actually be heard. I went below feeling happy.

I was on duty below throughout the night and could imagine the troops as they approached their respective beaches after 0200, in the wake of the commandos and glider-borne troops. Our immediate sector was around the town of Avola, and was code named ACID. It was divided into four beach sections, Fox, George, How and Jig. These were again sub-divided into stretches of the coastline approximately four miles wide. Not all areas were suitable for landing so it was very important that the landing craft get to the right location. It was for this reason that the beaches were broken down in such detail.

The operation had reached a critical phase, and in between breaks from our work we constantly wondered how the attack was progressing. Would the defences be too much for our troops? Would the sea be calm enough? Would they find the right beaches? I remembered the frightful confusion during the Tobruk raid. But this could be even more disastrous. If the huge numbers of men became congested and entangled, they would be a splendid target for the enemy. And, from what we had already seen, the beach areas were well defended.

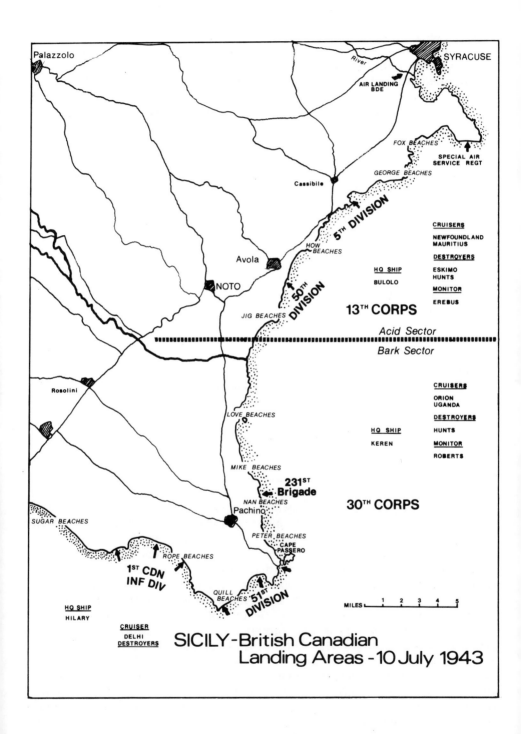

SICILY-British Canadian
Landing Areas -10 July 1943

As the night progressed, signal traffic built to the point where we could hardly cope. Finally at 0800, I was able to go for a quick breakfast and find out what was happening. Three black-faced commando officers in battledress stood out menacingly from those finishing off their breakfasts. How they got aboard, I did not know. But I could imagine the horrific attack that they must have been involved in during the night, capturing the Italian heavy shore gun batteries to our north.

At this time we were lying well off the coast. Through binoculars, the beaches looked nice and flat and were thronged with all types of craft. Behind the beaches were rolling hills with olive groves and greenish fields. What a sight! Green fields again after two years of desert. One could practically smell the grass even though it was probably a bit dried out. And beyond the hills were stark, brown jagged ridges which stretched north and south as far as the eye could see. Etna had disappeared in the haze to the north.

Meanwhile, in the foreground tiny landing craft buzzed between the beaches and the transport ships. The bay was peaceful and calm and the sun shone brightly, just what we wanted. Another two hours was all we would need to get everyone ashore.

Around us the anchored liners continued to disgorge their troops. The nearest was the modern, streamlined Polish ship *Sobieski.* An LCI and LCAs could be seen alongside her three starboard disembarking ladders, each one leading to three open doorways clearly numbered 1, 3 and 5, in white painted numbers so as to expedite disembarkation. Her boat and promenade decks were already deserted, indicating that most of her troops had already left.

Our two cruisers and a monitor were lying well out to sea. In between us and the shore, several destroyers were busily steaming up and down. There was no sign of activity ashore, so the landings must have been successful.

Suddenly a Tribal, the *Eskimo,* opened up and clouds of dust could be seen rising from a blue ridge on the north end of the bay. The army must have encountered resistance on their way north to Syracuse and had called in naval fire for support.

Coming over the horizon, the slow supply convoy of ninety ships could be seen followed a convoy of LSTs. At the same time, I noticed that two of our own landing craft had left their davits. Obviously, some army people had already gone ashore to find out how events were proceeding.

At 0900 all ships lifted anchor and majestically edged inshore, followed by the freighters, heading to a smaller anchorage area which could be better protected. It was a magnificent sight, as each vessel went to its designated anchorage position. And best of all there were still no signs of any enemy aircraft. What havoc they could have wreaked on this vast assemblage of shipping! Within forty-eight hours all these ships would discharge their cargoes and leave.

As we steamed in, we passed a floating glider with six bedraggled soldiers perched on its wings: their legs dangling in the sea and the water lapping their bottoms. We lowered a motor launch to rescue them. Many other gliders had shared the same fate because we could see them protruding from the water around us. Even so, the glider troops must have achieved some success, as we had been receiving reports of fighting around the target bridge near Syracuse.

Just then a small American-built BYMS minesweeper flying the white ensign came up close and a Scottish voice boomed at us through a loud hailer,

Eskimo **going into action.**

asking directions to BARK North sector. After we had told him he turned his ship and headed off south. Soon after, a little ML came up asking for orders. A very youthful sub, the skipper, and an unkempt youthful crew looked up at us. From their appearance, it was clear that they had had a terrible time in the rough weather in the night. The ML was told to lay off and come alongside after we were anchored.

Once our ship was anchored inshore, one had a much better view of the land. Avola, a fair-sized town, lay slightly to our south, just behind the beaches up some hills. It looked incongrously peaceful and appeared to be completely deserted. It reminded me of the little towns and hamlets I had seen in Malta, with its church steeples and hodge podge of tiered streets and stone houses. There was no sign of any damage; it must have been taken without any fighting. But what a shock for the inhabitants to awaken to the tumult of of bombs, gunfire and masses of troops suddenly arriving right on their doorsteps. No wonder they had taken to their basements or to the hills.

Below the town, the foreshore was still crowded with craft. The beaches were crammed with tanks, motor vehicles and crowds of khaki soldiers, patiently waiting orders. LCMs (Landing Craft Mechanised) and LCVs (Landing

Craft Vehicles), from the freighters were now arriving and waiting their turn to land.

Further to the north were "George" beaches; the best in our sector. Not only was the terrain behind them flatter, but the beach shelf was such that the larger LSTs could nudge right up on to the dry sand without running aground, before opening their huge bow doors. This was the first operational use of these strange ships and they had already proved their worth. From where I stood, I could make out the squat impressive forms of the Sherman and Churchill tanks as they nosed their way up the beach and trundled off to battle.

We hadn't been bombarded by the powerful Italian shore batteries near Cape Morro di Porco to the north, so there was no doubt that they must have been captured by our SAS troops. Resistance from the air so far had been inconsequential. So, once the beach opposition had been overpowered, there had been no disruption to our movement of troops, tanks, guns and equipment ashore.

By the time that I got another short break on deck in the late afternoon, the situation ashore had strangely livened up. The enemy was recovering from its initial surprise, and seemed to have been able to regroup its forces and begin to put up a better fight. The sound of heavy gunfire could be heard clearly from somewhere toward Syracuse. If everything had gone according to plan, we should already have been in control of the city.

Out to sea, near the anti-submarine screen, our two cruisers were blasting with their 6-inch guns at some target ashore. Spirals of dust could be seen on land to the north as the shells reached their targets.

As I watched, I saw our river gunboat trundling along slowly in a haze of smoke from her stovepipe funnels, toward the cape. She was furiously firing her 6-inch gun and clearly meant business. Then a splash of water erupted about 500 yards from her from an enemy shore battery. This shore fire intensified indicating that the enemy still had some heavy guns to command the bay. The gunboat was finally straddled but continued on her course undeterred and we began to fear she might receive a mortal hit. After a while the enemy shooting faltered and finally died down. Perhaps our army had overrun their position.

The gunfire continued elsewhere, however, with the occasional "whoomph" from seaward as *Erebus* let rip with her 15-inchers. Bombardment co-operation between the army and navy seemed to be working well, and hopefully we were helping them clear the way into Syracuse before nightfall.

This procedure had been improved by the presence on each warship of an artillery officer, who was in radio contact with a forward observation oficer at the front. Fire could be pinpointed using a grid map, ensuring that the fall of shot was kept well away from our own lines. Improved communication equipment had made this possible. Prior to this, the army have been very leery of naval shore bombardment support and there had been several nasty incidents when we had fired into our own troops. Nevertheless, after considerable experimenetation in the Gulf of Suez, new tactics were perfected.

Our guns were now firing at shore targets and we wouldn't have been doing this without a request from the army forward observers, so the new procedures must have been working.

By late afternoon, just before the great liners weighed anchor and steamed away, the number of ships in the sector reached its zenith, surely one of the great sights of the history of naval war. The long gulf was full of all manner of shipping: tall passenger ships, workmanlike cargo steamers, coughing tugs, shapely destroyers and hordes of busy landing craft. Spitfires patrolled above us, and the horizon was dotted with cruisers and destroyers. Twenty miles to the south the misty shapes of many further ships in the BARK sector were also visible. Surely this panorama was on a par with the Armada approaching the shores of England at sundown, or the escorted German high seas fleet sailing through the grey Scottish mist into Scapa Flow at the end of the First World War.

Not long after the LSIs had left, we started to receive our first air attacks. Finally the enemy had come to life. They were mostly fighter-bombers which flew in low over the ridges behind the beaches from the west and dived down on the anchorage. One or two high-levellers also dropped sticks of bombs among the freighters. The fleet closed up to action stations and an enormous AA barrage was put up whenever it was needed. Every craft, down to the smallest, which had any sort of weaponry, including rifles, had a go at the low flying planes. Inflicted damage was negligible, and a few enemy aircraft were actually brought down. Presumably many more were destroyed or driven off by our more than adequate fighter cover which was being controlled by *Bulolo*.

As dusk fell, many ships began to make smoke to enshroud the bay. This somewhat questionable action was taken presumably to protect us from air and surface attack during the night. Inshore, small landing craft plied up and down trailing white mist over the beaches and the small craft clustered together for protection. As I watched them, I wondered how they had fared so far. They were living on bully beef and biscuits.

Our own ML circled around and around us making a filthy dirty-looking smoke which completely covered the ship. It was much worse than a London fog and seeped into the inside of the ship and irritated our eyes.

As anticipated, just before night came, low-flying torpedo-bomber attacks did develop from seaward from the east, but no ships were damaged or sunk. From this point on, high-, medium-, and low-level air attacks were almost continuous, but there few signs of Stukas, presumably because of our strong fighter cover.

Below decks, the routine continued as before. The lull would be periodically shattered by the clatter of our guns. Conversation was useless and it was difficult to do anything else while this was going on. Sometimes the ship would shake so hard that the pencils would tumble from the desks. At first everyone would be very tense waiting for something to happen, but after the firing had persisted off and on for hours, we simply became annoyed and ignored it.

By the end of the first day of the operation we had reason to congratulate ourselves. Considering how bad the weather had been, it was amazing how well things had gone. Some LCA officers told me later that the long trip to the beaches had been very rough indeed and the reception ashore considerable. In some parts the battle had not been as easy as we had surmised. Because of the weather, most of the troops in the LCAs were drenched to the skin by the time they went ashore. They had to forget about their uncomfortable condition and immediately attend to the business of fighting the enemy.

There was enemy resistance on the beaches practically everywhere and it was particularly bad where the Italians had machine-gun, mortar and heavier field gun emplacements. There were no Germans in the area; we were dealing

**Landing Craft Attack (LCA) passing by in the anchorage
off Sicily during the landings, July 1943.**

with purely Italian troops, which was probably to our advantage. With some stalwart and herioc work by our seasoned desert infrantrymen, we soon overcame their defensive positions and had the beaches well cleared by early morning.

Several LCAs had been holed by machine gun and mortar fire and a number of LCIs were damaged by artillery during the landing, two being sunk with the loss of most of their crews.

By now we were receiving word about the fate of the glider troops during the initial attacks. They had taken quite a beating, mainly because of the weather. This was the first major glider attack ever undertaken by our side and no doubt mistakes were made. But the few who got through were able to take the important bridge over the Anapo river, about a mile south of Syracuse — their main objective — and prevent it from being blown up by the enemy. Then they held it until the arrival of forward elements of 13th Corps. Many had been killed, drowned or injured when their gliders crashed into the sea or on the rocky shoreline.

One hundred and forty-four gliders had taken off from Tunisia, towed by half as many Douglas DC-3 aircraft. They flew low over the sea, and immediately ran into high 45 m.p.h. gale force winds, the sea often being sprayed on them. The high winds confused the inexperienced navigators and, along with the heavy enemy AA fire around the beaches and the mist which obscured their shore landmarks, only fifty-four gliders (36 percent) got over land. The rest ditched in the sea or crashed into the rocky coastline, killing or injuring their occupants. Many landed well away from their target area.[15]

Major General G.F. "Hoppy" Hopkinson, their commander was picked up by a destroyer from the sea and was taken to *Bulolo*. It was he who had talked Monty, against his better judgement possibly, into allowing the operation to go ahead. I remember Hopkinson clearly on the first morning, before he went ashore to his battered troops. He was a small man and was distinquishable because he didn't wear battledress, like the rest of the 8th army brass hats, but was immaculate in his regular uniform with all his campaign ribbons. He stood near me on the promenade deck whilst an air attack was developing. Suddenly we could all hear a whining bomb which sounded as if it was meant for us and everyone headed for the nearest cover — everyone, that is, except "Hoppy." He stood his ground, without a tin hat, and watched the bomb fall harmlessly into the sea, not too far away. His foolhardiness didn't make us navy types look too good.

The fifty-four gliders that made the coast were spread out all along the forty mile long beach area. Only four were able to land near the bridge. A young platoon lieutenant was able to gather thirty men from two gliders, and these thirty did the trick. They took the bridge, disconnected the demolition charges, and held it until reinforced by other glider troops. By evening the main body showed up, with "Hoppy", and the bridge was secure.

The 1st Air Landing Brigade paid a heavy price; out of around 3.000 who left Tunisia, 252 were drowned, 61 killed and 87 were wounded, and very few gliders were left intact.

We were also able to form a clearer picture of the overall progress on the battlefront. By the evening of D-Day 10 July 1943, heavy fighting had reached the outskirts of Syracuse, which fell during the night. We had heard that the crack Hermann Goering Division was in the vicinity to reinforce the Italians but it didn't arrive until well after Syracuse fell. The ridges behind the beaches had also been taken, with troops pushing on to Floridia, a town ten miles inland, and to Palazzolo, twenty miles to the northwest. Within twenty-four hours the battle had moved out of our area, and in general our part in the operation had gone magnificently with few hitches.

Finally, after midnight on D-Day, I was able to get a few hours sleep. As I turned in, a raid was in progress but I was too tired to care. I fell asleep to the distant sounds of guns — the raid was apparently farther down the coast. During the night I was disturbed by what I took to be women's voices, but soon drifted off again.

At 0330 I was shaken by a messenger from the cypher office. The cabin was hot and stuffy because the ship had been battened down with all watertight doors closed, because of the raids. Suddenly our guns opened up. I tried to gather myself together and shake off the sleep and get dressed. I noticed that my two airforce officer cabin mates had left.

Then I heard them again, women's voices, only this time I was sure they

213

were definitely real. Pushing back the curtain to the cabin door and looking out, I saw a woman wrapped in a blanket standing in the narrow passageway. Around her head was a bandage and she stared at me impassively as I gazed up and down. Then a blonde nurse in uniform appeared from a cabin. She told me that they had just been taken off a hospital ship that had been sunk. The two of them must have been quite shaken, and a frightened look came over their faces as our guns started to fire again. I felt that I should stay, but a doctor, whom I had never seen before, arrived and I left them.

That was the last I saw of them for they were gone by breakfast time. I later found out that they had been picked up by a destroyer which had gone alongside their burning hospital ship *Talamba* at night, after it had been dive-bombed. The ship had been lying outside the screen, about three miles offshore, and was embarking wounded at the time of the attack, which was launched despite the fact that the the big Red Cross on her funnel was clearly illuminated.

On the second day, 11 July 1943, the beaches could be seen humming with activity and I noticed that yet another new crop of cargo ships had arrived during the night. Just then an LCA came alongside, bearing a very dirty looking crew and a bearded RN sub whom I immediately recognized as one of my term. I called out to him and he knew me right away and came aboard and we exchanged news. He looked utterly dishevelled and tired out. He told me that he had been living in an open LCA for nearly two days, subsisting on canned goods, washing out of a bucket and sleeping on a rug on the bottom of the boat.

The rest of flotilla had been embarked in the LSIs and had gone, but his boat had been left behind to do what it could around the beaches. The worst part had been during the dusk attack when fighter-bombers had tried to drop bombs on the beaches and the landing craft anchorages. I took him down to my cabin, showed him where the bathroom was and told him to get some sleep. I promised to wake him later and take him to the wardroom for a drink and a decent meal. I didn't see him again. He had left by the time I was able to hunt for him.

Late in the forenoon of the second day the admiral returned onboard in the middle of an air raid. The admiral's barge came alongside just as our guns opened up. The officer of the watch and the quartermaster, at the top of the gangway were undecided as to what to do, whether to wait and pipe the old boy aboard or take cover. The admiral took the initiative, squeezing his portly frame through the door of the after cabin of the barge, and tumbling up the ladder, tin hat and all, to the sound of the boatswain's pipe. Before this incident, a rumour had gone around the ship that he had been killed.

He had been away since early morning, having embarked on the destroyer *Eskimo* to reconnoitre Syracuse and find out at first-hand whether action could be taken to open it up immediately. *Eskimo* hadn't moved far out from the screen when it was attacked by aircraft and seriously damaged aft. X turret had been knocked out, with the loss of thirty men. This was well away from the open forward bridge, where the admiral was located, so he survived the attack.

Not to be deterred, however, he called for another horse in the shape of a Hunt class destroyer and proceeded onwards. The entrance to the port was subsequently found to be swept of mines and he was able to steam around the

harbour inspecting the facilities. The port had got off lightly in the battle although there was still some desultory street fighting going on in the old city, on the eastern seaward side. The port facilities, docks and cranes, on the inner western side, which had been taken early in the attack, were in good condition. At one point the destroyer got too close to land and was swept by rifle fire, with everyone on the bridge ducking for cover. Our smiling Falstaff of an admiral was proving to be quite a fire-eater.

I had taken a few very urgent cyphers up to him from to time and always found him to be very pleasant to deal with. He didn't seem to be too concerned about details and paperwork, or about the incompleteness of his messages. As long as he could get the gist of the communication that was all that mattered. Once, I gave him an urgent message about an expected E-boat attack on our sector which I thought he would be very interested in. After waiting for some time before interrupting his

Rear Admiral Troubridge RN with Cdr. MacLachlan RCNVR, his aide, on the bridge of *Eskimo*, off Syracuse, July 1943.

conversation, much to my surprise he quickly read it and handed it back to me without a comment. I gave it to the duty operations officer who went into a great flap. Unlike Cunningham, who was very fussy about his messages and liked to see everything and give personal direction, this admiral left most things to his staff officers unless he thought they were extremely important.

People on the admiral's tour brought back a story of the success of the 13th Minesweeping Flotilla comprising *Seaham, Boston, Poole* and *Cromarty*. The flotilla had been given the job of clearing mines from the entrance to Syracuse harbour. These ships were very experienced, having cleared harbours of mines from Mersa Matruh to Tunis during the 8th army's long advance from Egypt to Tunisia.

As dawn came up on the first morning of the invasion, they were strung out in a diagonal formation, heading towards the harbour mouth, with their sweep gear out. Around breakfast time when all eyes were focused on a mine which had been cut to the surface, something else bobbed up astern; an Italian submarine. They were quick to identify the hapless enemy ship and, casting off their sweeps, turned on it with all guns blazing. The submarine captain wasn't long in surrendering and abandoning ship, but unfortunately not before some of his crew were killed or wounded as they climbed out of the conning tower under a hail of fire. The sub was quickly captured and a prize crew put aboard. The unfortunate Italian skipper had been completely unaware that Sicily had been invaded.

On the second day, corps and divisional headquarters were transferred ashore and the ship became much quieter. The wardroom was almost empty. The air raids still continued and intensified in numbers and size. The Germans had obviously transferred more squadrons to Southern Italy. Possibly we were finally taking a little pressure off our Russian allies.

The ships in the bay were not the only ones being attacked. I watched a group of men on the beach run a hundred yards and dive for their slit trenches as a fighter-bomber dropped a stick of bombs in the olive groves just behind them. The bombs threw up clouds of dust but there didn't seem to be any casualties or damage. Another plane flew up and down several times just above the blue hills, hedge-hopping and weaving to avoid the ground fire, all the while casting its shadow across the beaches. It dropped no bombs and I wondered what it was trying to do. Maybe it was machine-gunning a ground target. Finally it turned and attempted to fly over the anchorage, but the Ack-Ack fire seemed to be too much for the pilot and he turned and flew off inland.

At dusk that evening an excited cry arose from the promenade deck; someone had spotted two small dots moving above the horizon out at sea. Then more dots were spotted moving from right to left. It looked like a torpedo-bomber attack was developing. Then we could see that the enemy aircraft were going after one small Hunt class destroyer on the outer screen, instead of coming in over the anchorage to attack us. The destroyer appeared oblivious of the attack at first and appeared to be taking no countermeasures.

It was only when the planes climbed up to position themselves for a concentrated attack and one torpedo could be seen dropping that the ship finally came to life. Then she opened up with everything that she had in an effort to defend herself. We laughed, in spite of the danger that she was in. She looked like nothing so much as an awkward puppy fighting off the attentions of a swarm of angry bees. After a while her fire subsided and the dots disappeared in the gloom, apparently leaving her none the worse for wear.

The second full night was a replica of the first. Intermittent raids but little damage inflicted on us. Presumably our night fighters were doing a magnificent job in stopping many of them. And those that did get through were thwarted by our concentrated AA fire.

By breakfast on D plus 3, 12 July, several MTBs lay alongside. A close inspection revealed that some of them were quite seriously damaged. I deduced that they must have been in some kind of action during the night. There were two jagged holes in the bridge superstructure of one of them, and the gun of the other appeared to have been blown off its base. These little ships were terribly vulnerable to any type of gunfire, no matter how small the calibre. The sight of them lying there in such a state brought home to me just how hazardous life in them must be.

But these thoughts soon passed as ML 565 came alongside, tying up outside one of the the MTBs. Its skipper on the tiny bridge was full of smiles and very cheerful, making Vee signs and mimiking the shooting of a gun. I

Admiral Troubridge and Monty on Bulolo off Sicilian beaches, 13 July 1943.

heard him shout, "Shot down an aircraft." What an astonishing achievement for such a small craft; he had reason to be proud.

Back in the wardroom, everyone was discussing the E-boat and torpedo-bomber attacks of the previous night. All of them had been unsuccessful. Although none of our MTBs had been sunk, some, as I already had seen, had suffered severe damage and a number of their crew had been either killed or wounded. I told them of the young Fairmile skipper and his aircraft.

The third day off the beaches was similar to the others; more air raids and more ships leaving as they completed their unloading. The highlight of the day was a shipboard visit by General Montgomery. Decks were cleared of all the ship's company to the forward well deck to hear him give a talk. He was shorter than I had expected him to be, shorter than our admiral who wasn't too tall; who led him through a crowd of cheering soldiers, sailors and a few airmen. He was taken up to the forecastle, where he could turn and look down on us. He was smartly dressed in khaki army shorts and a shirt with a tie, with knee stockings and stylish suede desert boots. On his head he wore his famous tank beret with its various army insignia. After the admiral introduced him with a big grin, he quickly took over the proceedings and silence descended as he started to speak. We had done a good job, he declared, the army had been safely landed and was moving up the coast hitting the Jerries for six.

He liked to use colloquial or cricket terms, which I suppose he thought the troops enjoyed. There is no doubt that he had been something of a genius in turning around the fortunes of the 8th Army and winning every battle since he arrived in the Middle East. He conveyed an air of brisk authority and it was obvious that he would not suffer shirkers gladly. He was like a tough little bantam cock; quite in contrast to the senior officers of the desert army whom we had transported and who had so greatly impressed me. But it takes all kinds of leaders and you couldn't argue with his success.

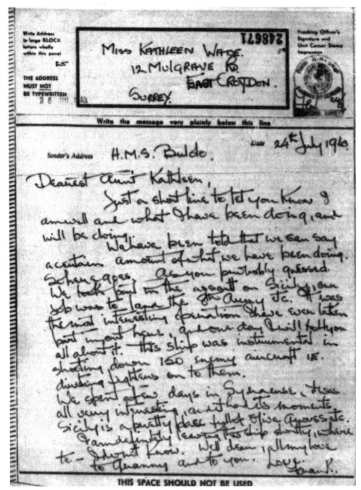

**Lettergram from Bulolo. Note that censor restrictions were not
so tight since the news was better.**

Before he could end his talk, an air raid started, but we ignored it and
waited until he had finished. As soon as the raid had ended, he departed by
launch back to his army.

Shortly afterwards we suffered our first serious loss when a Dutch
freighter carrying ammunition was hit by a bomb from a lone undetected
bomber. She began to burn fiercely, with thick smoke and flames billowing
from her forward and after well-decks where her hatch covers were located.
The smoke rose to an enormous height and drifted north over the anchorage,
blotting out the sun and casting gloom on the bay. Fortunately her crew had
been able to take to her boats. After several violent explosions, she was
despatched by a torpedo to prevent any further damage to nearby ships.

Meanwhile our forces ashore were moving well. Augusta, an Italian naval
base about twenty miles north of Syracuse, was ours. Other troops from our
sector, the Highland Division and the Canadians, had all taken small towns
twenty or thirty miles inland and were swinging north. The American divisions
were making similar progress, and had taken Gela and Licata and were moving

north and west. They had had a much tougher time than us during the landings on the first night because of the rough weather. They had lacked the protection from the wind that we had received from the land.

By the next day, D plus 4, the anchorage was just about empty so we weighed anchor and moved into Syracuse, stationing ourselves in the centre of the harbour. It was normally an excellent, well protected harbour, with the colourful ancient Greek town on the protecting promontory and the new city on the mainland. It had been the scene a famous Greek naval battle between the Syracuse and Athens city states. But our sojourn there was far from peaceful. Enemy air raids were now being concentrated on the port and we were under almost continuous attack after our arrival. We had very little AA protection so things didn't look good. With a number of cargo ships and *Bulolo* in the harbour, the enemy was presented with a concentrated target.

We had not yet taken the port of Catania, just over thirty miles north, and the four important airfields around Gerbini on the Catanian plains near it. However, they must have been taking a pasting from our own bombers and it was doubtful whether they were being used by the enemy.

The following night we went through our most unpleasant experience of the trip. The continuous air attacks made sleep impossible as the ship rattled from gunfire and from the impact of bombs exploding on the water nearby. During my night watch the ship shook as if she were in her death-throes, and rocked back and forth after a tremendous bang which sounded as if she had definitely been hit. Hastily we looked around for our lifejackets and awaited instructions. No word came over the sound system, the captain of *Bulolo* was not one to use it much. The ship did not appear to be sinking or listing after she had settled down. Later we learned that a bomb had exploded within thirty feet of the ship. Luckily, very little damage was sustained and no one on the upper deck had been killed or wounded.

It was with some relief that we sailed back to Egypt the following day. The port had become too hot and our objectives had been achieved. There was no need for us to stay longer and risk being sunk. A naval party had landed ashore and would look after the cleaning up of the beaches and the reactivation of the port.

One of the most extraordinary intelligence hoaxes of the war had been organised to confuse the enemy about our invasion plans for Sicily. As is well known, a naval Intelligence officer had dreamed up the bright idea of planting false papers on a dead Royal Marine officer who was to be floated ashore off the Spanish coast. On the night of 30 April 1943 the submarine *Seraph* had executed this task off the southern Spanish coast near Huelva, about 140 miles west of Gib near the Portuguese border. The secret papers on the body were ostensibly from the Imperial General Staff to General Alexander, outlining a plan to invade Sardinia and western Greece.[16]

After the war, evidence was found in the German military files that these papers had indeed made their way to Berlin and that German intelligence had fallen for the ruse. A German Panzer division was moved from France to Cape Araxos in Greece and a squadron of German R-boats (light gunboats) was transferred there from Sicily as well. Troop reinforcements were also sent to Corsica and northern Sicily.

To give substance to the hoax, our two battlefleets, *Nelson, Rodney* and *Indomitable* from the west, and *Warspite, Valiant* and *Formidable* from the east, had rendezvoused north of the Gulf of Sirte on 9 July 1943, and made a short sweep towards Greece. On the same day, *King George V* and *Howe* moved from Algiers towards Sardinia.

Other German reports indicated that in reveiwing their loss of Sicily they very much regretted their decision to move their R-boats from Sicily to Greece.

Another feature of the invasion was the absence of the Italian fleet, a fact which excited much wardroom discussion at the time. The explanation lay in their lack of destroyers to escort their fleet, and not because of oil fuel shortages or, as some writers have suggested, because they wished to keep their fleet intact for the purposes of bargaining with either the allies or the Germans. We knew from our own experience in the past that valuable battle-ships could not be risked at sea without adequate anti-submarine protection. Indeed this consideration had forced Cunningham to keep our battleships out of the second battle of Sirte the year before.

By this stage in the war, Italy was down to ten serviceable destroyers to cover all their commitments, including fleet duties and the supply of Sicily, Sardinia and French Corsica, which they had taken over from the Vichy French in November 1942. Their losses of destroyers had been particularly heavy in the previous six months during the Tunisian campaign.

Also, they had no guaranteed air cover from their own air force or from the Luftwaffe, whereas we had two fleet carriers, properly outfitted with modern naval aircraft, and many more air force squadrons earmarked for naval operations. Their air recce capability was practically zero and they were unable to keep track of all our naval forces. In retrospect, it is understandable that they did not put up a better fight, although, at the time, the lack of Italian seaborne and air opposition seemed incredible to us.

The last enemy stronghold on Sicily, Messina, fell on 17 August, 1943, just a month after the start of the landings. However, the one big mistake which we made was in allowing the enemy to evacuate five divisions across the Straits of Messina back to mainland Italy. Approximately 50,000 German and 60,000 Italian troops plus some tanks and equipment were transported by barge and small steamers at night in a five day period before the fall.

Our air forces kept enemy movements across the straits during the day down to a minimum, and our MTBs and MGBs (motor gun boats), operating from Augusta, battled German naval coastal forces in the straits at night. However, their efforts were not nearly enough.

The straits were heavily defended on either side by German 90mm field guns (3.5 inch) and Italian 6-inch coastal guns, which had ranges that totally covered the area, making daylight approach by our ships very dangerous. Possibly we should have saved some of our airborne troops to deal with these coastal batteries and then forced the issue from the sea.

The invasion of Sicily was the largest amphibious operation in the history of war, with about 2,600 seagoing vessels being involved — 500 warships, 1,700 landing craft and 400 merchant ships landing around 180,000 troops plus tanks and equipment. It was an immense venture with worldwide international and interservice implications, and had been an extremely well planned and successful operation.

CHAPTER THIRTEEN

Epilogue

With operations finished in Sicily, *Bulolo* in company with two Hunts returned to Alex. On arrival, the efficient posting system of the Med fleet had already picked out a new job for me. I was to report to a Combined Operations camp at Adabiya on the Gulf of Suez. So I was to return to Suez, a place I thought I had got out of for good.

With a railway warrant in my hand, I took the train across the delta and was finally delivered by lorry to a neat encampment on the dusty shores of the gulf, dominated by a barren grey escarpment lying behind it. Tents were laid out in neat rows down to the beach; some strung together for the sailors quarters, offices, workshops, sick bay, galleys, and mess halls. Two large tents formed a very comfortable wardroom complete with a bar, dining and sitting area, stuffed chairs, radio and well turned out stewards. Each officer had his own comfortably equipped private tent. These quarters were as good, if not better, than those on a battleship.

The ship's company were a mixed lot. We had our own sailors to look after the base plus a Palestinian Jewish Royal Engineers detachment to look after the maintenance of our landing craft. We also had an Indian army motor transport pool.

The Jewish mechanics were a constant problem and were forever before the captain as defaulters. They hailed from the ghettos of Europe and no doubt were excellent tradesmen. One could sympathise with their distaste at the thought of the possibility of their possible return to Europe. They would take off without leave at the drop of a hat, being picked up by the shore patrol in Suez or even as far as Cairo. They could only speak yiddish and defaulters parade was a slow and, at times, comic process as their officer translated everything into English.

My job was as adminstrative secretary to Lieutenant Commander "Loopy" Lowndes who was in charge of this base. We were obviously a mobile port organisation, waiting to be moved somewhere at a moments notice. Commander Lowndes was very close with his secret papers, which he carefully locked away in his safe. I was not allowed to open any secret envelopes, so had no idea where we were going. But I had been around long enough to guess that I was part of some planned secret mission. Later I found out that this was a naval port authority party and that it was to be sent to an enemy port, possibly Leros, as part of a planned invasion force to the Dodecanese islands.

For the month of August 1943, I worked in this rather odd naval establishment. There wasn't much to do except look after routine matters and wait for our marching orders. It was extremely hot there and we worked tropical routine, starting work early, taking the afternoon off, and then going back at 1600 for a couple more hours. Usually some of us would drive down the coast a few miles to a good swimming spot. The bay was reputed to be shark-infested but this didn't deter us. Sometimes we could see huge manta rays flapping their wings on the surface. One day we were lying on the small pier that we

Lieutenant-Commander Lowndes and officers of the Dodecanese naval party, September 1943.

swam off and looked down to see an enormous shark resting on the sandy bottom, a foot or so underwater, right under us.

In the evening we would don uniform trousers, tropical shirt, black cummerbund and a black bow tie, for dinner. An English officer was expected to keep up appearances, no matter what. The South African regiment, camped next door, must have thought we were quite mad. However, they were envious of our comfortable quarters and were always inviting themselves over for free drinks. Their appearance and dress indicated that they preferred to live rough.

Someone told us that there was a golf course in Suez, so we drove over one day to take a look at it. Laid out on a sand shore-ledge by the bay, it had to be one of the most unusual courses in the world. The fairways were nothing but pancake sand leading to greens of rolled, hard mud. There was a pathetic little clubhouse, really a shack, with faded photos hanging on the wall over the bar of old club members dressed in their plus fours.

Outside the camp, across the road, was a Shafto open air cinema. Mr Shafto was well known to thousands of soldiers in Egypt for providing these theatres outside camps in both wars. For a few piastres one could watch an ancient movie in the cool of the evening. The cinema was nothing more than an enclosure with a canvas wall, benches and chairs, a screen and a projector.

One night the place was full of troops from the famous New Zealand Divisions which were encamped around us, waiting repatriation. The film was the usual English country-house mystery, with the butler being one of the prime suspects. Unfortunately, the projector broke down about three minutes before the end of the film without revealing the indentity of the murderer. We waited for the machine to be repaired but were informed by the Egyptian attendant that the show was over. The New Zealanders, who had been in just about every action in the desert war and were probably the finest troops in the 8th army, would have none of this. They began to complain vigorously, and before long chairs were flying through the air. The navy persons present made a quick tactical exit. A bit of a riot ensued before the military police arrived, by which time there wasn't much left of the theatre. Nevertherless, it was soon rebuilt and back in business within a few days.

On 20 August 1943, I received some unexpected information. The Canadian naval authorities had finally caught up with me and I was ordered to leave immediately and report to a holding camp and await passage back to Canada. I had never dreamed that I would be transferred from the Med before the end of the war and was in two minds about having to leave. But the move did make a certain amount of sense, bearing in mind that I was a career officer and should be starting to learn about my own navy. I found out later that Canada had been trying to retrieve me for over a year. But it was very hard trying to pry personnel away from the Med command, which was a law unto itself and short of officers.

I never found out what happened to the Lowndes naval party and if it did indeed go to Leros. The Greek Dodecanese islands were invaded by our forces on 10 September 1943, three weeks after I left the party, when the islands of Leros, Samos and Cos were easily captured. The armistice with Italy had been signed two days before on 8 September and Mussolini deposed and imprisoned. So there was not much fighting during the attack as the Italian island garrisons quite quickly threw their lot in with us and became our allies, once they found out about the armistice.

Churchill had always wanted to mount a major operation into the Balkans, but the Americans were dead against it because they didn't want any ships, troops or aircraft taken away from either the Italian front or the build up of forces for the planned cross-channel European invasion. Also, they suspected, quite incorrectly, that the British were pushing the plan for their own post-war political purposes.

Thus, a greatly reduced operation was to be mounted by our then limited Eastern Mediterranean service commands; just the capture of a few Greek islands from where Axis shipping could be harassed by our sea and air forces. The navy at Alex had a few light cruisers and destroyers. The army used the 234th Brigade comprising four unseasoned battalions which had sat out the war in Malta. The islands were too far away for fighter air coverage from Egypt or Syria and, in any event, there were few air squadrons available.

As it turned out, the Germans had a crack army division backed up by other troops in Greece and Crete, as Hitler had expected a major Allied incursion into the area. With typical Teutonic efficiency, initiative and daring, using makeshift convoys of old coastal ships and barges, plus airborne troops, the Germans quickly retook the captured islands. The venture had ended by 16 November 1993 in just over two months.

A South African fighter squadron on Cos was quickly eliminated by German aircraft from Rhodes and the island was the first to fall. Our troops and our Italian allies on Leros fought fiercely but were no match for the Germans who had the major advantage of unopposed air supremacy.

In a little known battle that had all the earmarks of Crete, we incurred heavy losses, mostly from air attack. Four destroyers were sunk, *Queen Olga* (which had been so daring in attempting to rescue the downed spitfire pilot during a Malta convoy), *Intrepid, Panther,* and *Eclipse.* As well five cruisers were damaged, *Penelope, Carlisle* (which was towed back to Alex but was never put back in service, the last of the famous Med C class AA cruisers), *Aurora, Sirius,* and *Dido.* Two destroyers were also damaged, the Greek *Adrias,* and *Rockwood.*

The operation had failed because inadequate forces had been deployed to do the job, due to American instransigence in not allowing sufficient transference of land, sea and air forces from Italy.

I have often wondered whether any of my shipmates in the Lowndes party were able to escape in small boats to Turkey, which was only fifteen miles away from Leros.

I was duly transported to El Fayid Naval Air Station, about midway up the canal, just south of Ismailia. By now this station was not very active and was being used as a holding base for naval personnel awaiting passage back to England.

The facilities at the station were excellent. The group in the wardroom were very congenial. All of us agreed that, in some ways, we were sorry to be leaving Egypt but were very happy to have somehow survived our Middle East adventures unscathed. There was little for us to do as we waited, but sit around and reminisce about our experiences and play the odd game of tennis.

I was, however, able to pay a final visit to Alex. A few naval aircraft stood on the tarmac and a sub-lieutenant asked me if I would like to fly up to Alex for the day, for one last fling. He had to get in so many hours flying a month to keep his hand in and get his flight pay. So we boarded a Fairey Fulmar and took off over the Nile delta. As we flew over Cairo, we could make out the great buildings and squares of the city, and the nearby pyramids lying to the west. From the air, a definite demarcation line could be seen between the greenish arable land of the delta and the brown sand of the Western Desert.

After we passed Cairo and turned north for the coast, my friend got carried away and started to do aerobatics. I was scared stiff and was extremely glad when we landed at el Mex airport and headed into town. We planned one last lunch at the Cecil Hotel and relive the old days for an hour or so, and then quickly back to the airfield. The bar was as warm and friendly as ever. There were the usual "small eats" of potato chips and other delights, provided free with your drinks — so novel to us when we had first arrived. Then we stuffed ourselves from the hors d'oeuvres cart before going on to the main course. We relished every minute of it, knowing full well that we would never see anything like this again.

As we took off for home, my heart was saddened by the thought that I probably would not see Alex again. I knew this city from end to end, better than any other. I thought of all the good friends that I had made and of all my experiences in the city and at sea. What a pleasure it had always been to return to Alex after a difficult operation. The city and its inhabitants had always been so friendly and there was so much that a young officer could enjoy. Canada seemed remote and cold and I knew that I would never see these friends again — the best that I would ever make.

Eventually we received our marching orders and I moved one last time down the canal to Port Tewfik. I was put aboard the Cunard White Star liner *Britannic* but later transferred to the P. & O. liner *Stratheden.* She had come from India and was partially filled with Indian army types, some with dark handsome Indian wives.

Several days later the convoy sailed into the canal. As we passed through the Bitter Lakes, I caught my first and last glimpse of the adversaries which had so dominated my life these past two and half years; two Italian battleships plus some cruisers and destroyers lying at anchor. They were as sleek and as good-looking as I had imagined them to be, with their long low bows and sterns and streamlined superstructures. What more obvious sign that the naval war in the Mediterranean was just about over! It was the right time to leave.

The surrender of the Italian fleet had been the final dramatic act in the Mediterranean naval war. After the fall of Sicily, Italy started to negotiate a secret armistice. The country was in a great state of turmoil and practically everyone wished that the war would end. The Germans were gradually asserting total control, while the hated Fascists waited in the wings to resume power. Communications were difficult, but the Italian navy proved that it was still a loyal and disciplined force to the very end.

One of the conditions of the armistice was that all Italian naval and merchant ships should sail immediately to Allied ports. The negotiations had been kept very secret and the Italian naval chief, Admiral de Courten, was told only two days before the armistice was about to be signed. Right to the last minute some of the commanders thought that they were to be ordered to sea for one last fight.

Within minutes of General Eisenhower's radio announcement of the armistice, on the afternoon of 8 September 1943, de Courten issued his orders to the fleet. In Spezia, Admiral Bergami sailed at 0300, early next morning, on the 9th, as the Germans moved in to take over the port. Aboard *Roma,* a brand new battleship, he led out the battleships *Vittorio* and *Italia (ex Littorio),* three light cruisers *Eugenio di Savoia, Montecuccoli* and *Duca D'Aosta* and eight destroyers. They rendezvoused with three light cruisers from Genoa *Duca Degli, Garibaldi* and *Regolo.* They were to head south and meet up with a British battlefleet off Tunisia and be led to Malta. During the morning of the 9th, the force was attacked by the Luftwaffe off Corsica and, sadly, the *Roma's* magazines were hit by a glider bomb. The Italian navy now suffered its last and most tragic loss of the war. The great ship blew up, with the loss of most of its crew, including the admiral. *Italia* was also damaged.

The surviving ships were met at 0600 on 10 September 1943 by our force which, fittingly, comprised so many veterans of the Med naval war; *Warspite, Valiant* and the destroyers *Faulkner, Fury, Intrepid, Raider, Queen Olga* (Greek) and *Le Terrible* (French). Cunningham, since 21 January 1943 an Admiral of the Fleet, General Eisenhower and Commodore R. Dick witnessed the dramatic scene from the destroyer *Hambeldon.*

At much the same time, Admiral da Zara had sailed from Taranto with the battleships *Andrea Doria, Caio Duilio,* and the cruisers *Cadorna* and *Pompeo Magno* and one destroyer and was met off Malta by *King George V.* The Italian battleship *Guilio Cesare* and the depot ship *Miraglia* and two destroyer also escaped from the Adriatic, as did numerous submarines and destroyer escorts. The cruiser *Bolzano* and three destroyers had to be scuttled in Taranto harbour.

Thus it was that on 11 September 1943, Cunningham was able to make his famous signal "Be pleased to inform their Lordships that the Italian Battle fleet now lies at anchor beneath the guns of the fortress of Malta."

Cunningham gave orders that every respect should be afforded the Italian ships. Consequently their surrender and disarmament proceeded without dif-

Cunningham's bust in Trafalgar Square, along with Nelson, Jellicoe and Beatty.

ficulty. Several of the ships, the battleships *Italia* and *Vittorio Veneto,* four cruisers and four destroyers were later transferred to the Suez Canal. It was these vessels that I had seen as I sailed up the canal for the last time.

All the ships that I served in survived the war. *Queen Elizabeth,* after major repairs following the Alex attack, passed through the Mediterranean on its way to the far east in January 1944. She took part in the later stages of the war in the Indian and Pacific oceans as flagship of the Eastern fleet. She was scrapped in 1948 after thirty-three years' service, and must surely rate as one of the more famous ships in the history of the Royal Navy.

Jervis, briefly took part in the Dodecanese operations before being damaged by a German glider bomb off Anzio on 25 January 1944. Later that year she participated in the Normandy landings. Not long after the war she was sent to the scrap-yard. Without doubt, she saw more action than any other destroyer in the Mediterranean, with the possible exception of *Hotspur,* having been present from almost the beginning to the very end, from 1940 to 1944. Her survival was all the more remarkable, for in total forty-eight of our destroyers had been sunk during the Mediterranean war.

Orion took part in the capture of Pantelleria after I left her, as well as the

226

Admiralty,

London, S.W.1.

1st June, 1942.

Dear Madam,

Thank you for your letter
of 28th May and for the interest
that you took in my recent broad-
cast.

I well remember your
grandson, Paymaster Midshipman
Wade, who served on my staff for
three months in the middle of last
year. He is still in the QUEEN
ELIZABETH where, you will be pleased
to hear, he is shaping well and
shows promise of becoming a fine
officer.

Yours truly,

Andrew Cunningham

Letter from Cunningham to my grandmother.

landings on Sicily, at Salerno and at Anzio. Thereafter, she took part in the
Normandy landings and, in October 1944, was the flagship in the liberation of
Greece. She was scrapped in 1949.

Bulolo was built in 1938, in Glasgow, as a 250 passenger cargo ship for the
Australian Burns, Philp Shipping Company to operate out of Sydney to South
Pacific ports. She was converted to an Armed Merchant Cruiser in 1939; later
being modified to a Landing Ship Headquarters in 1942. She directed landings on
North Africa, Sicily, Anzio and Normandy. The Normandy D-Day invasion fleet
was reviewed from her bridge by King George VI. She was scrapped in 1968 after
thirty years service under many merchant captains and six admirals.

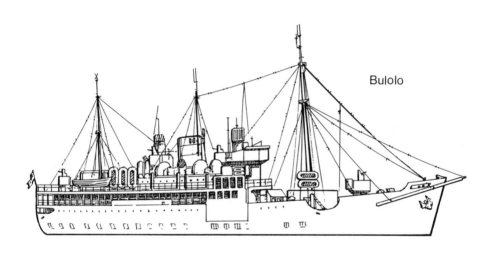

Bulolo

APPENDIX i

Two Speeches by Captain Claud Barry of HMS Queen Elizabeth

Our captain Claud Barry who looked and spoke like Churchill liked to talk to us and encourage us from time to time, in an effort to motivate us and get us to think about what we were fighting for. These two talks of special interest, reproduced verbatim, were given to the ship's company over the public address system.

"A commentary" dated 18th April 1941, given before the ship entered the Mediterranean.

"Britain, thank God, is a democracy and is therefore governed by the will of her people. But when you are faced with a total war this form of government may well prove a handicap. For a country as a whole is slow in peacetime to realise the full extent of any menace to their existence, and therefore the country lags behind in its preparations for war.

"On the other hand, a country governed by a dictatorship, such as Germany, is in the strongest possible position to make ample preparations in peace for war, for the dictator decrees this and that and the dumb masses obediently turn to and get on with the preparations, regardless of anything.

"If that dictator is as capable, ruthless and determined as is our great enemy Hitler then there is no limit to the preparations that can be carried out in peacetime to prepare for a war.

"Thus for the six years prior to this war Germany made preparations to fight on a scale that had not even been imagined in the whole history of the world. Britain did not realise the full extent of these preparations for some time and then, through being a democracy, was slow in getting off the mark with her preparations to meet the menace to her very existence which the German re-armament represented.

"So the war came with Germany strong and prepared and with Great Britain ill prepared but strong in her determination to defeat Nazism, which presented everything alien to her principles and ideals and, what was more important still, which threatened the whole existence of the British Empire.

"Except at sea the war started in a rather half hearted manner, in fact the first few months of the struggle are often called the "Phoney War". This suited Germany admirably, for although well prepared she was not quite so well prepared as she could have wished. She was thus able to push further ahead with her preparations. We pushed ahead with ours but still suffered from the time lag of Democracy and possibly from a certain lulling to security by the phoney nature of the War.

"You all remember the events of the early part of the last year, culminating in the defeat of our ally, France, and the brilliant withdrawal of our Expeditionary Force from Dunkirk. This saved Great Britain, and gave Hitler the biggest shock of his life. We then realised just what we were up against and with true British determination, and lead by our magnificent Prime Minister, Mr. Winston Churchill, we set our teeth and decided to show them really what we could do.

229

"Since then, you have all seen the spectacle of our Empire absolutely united, organising itself to fight for the cause of freedom almost single handed. And you have seen the superlative courage and morale of our nation under heavy air attack from our ruthless enemy. Never have I been so proud to be an Englishman.

"But it takes time to gain the necessary strength and it was almost more than even we could do single handed. But all this time, our near relation, the United States of America, had been watching events and soon they discerned in the swallowing up by the Nazis of one country after another that behind it all lay an unbounded ambition to gain domination of the whole world. And they realised that the only thing that stood in the way of the attainment of this ambition was the British Empire, fighting so gallantly. From that it was a natural step to realise that our cause was their cause, so that now, under the leadership of their President, Mr. Roosevelt, they have placed themselves side by side with us in the fight. I say they are side by side with us in the fight, for although they are not actually at war with the Axis Powers, they are supplying us without limit with every form of material assistance, and it would take little to bring them into the actual war.

"So now, added to our own tremendous war effort, we have the whole resources of the other great democracy, the United States of America. There is, therefore, no end to what we can achieve, but as I said before, the building up of the necessary strength needs time, and although immeasurably stronger now than we were, we are not yet anything like at our full strength, but we are progressing rapidly the whole time. So it is now rather a case of holding our enemy at bay, so that we can wear him down as we grow stronger.

"Well does Hitler realise all this and his whole plan of campaign appears to be aimed at trying to finish us off quick, before we attain the tremendous strength that will be ours before long.

"The Nazis collared most of Europe, thereby gaining great economic resources, but because of our blockade they are not yet self-supporting for a long war, especially is that so in the matter of oil. So, at this moment, you see them reaching out towards the Near East and Asia with the double object of trying to cut our Empire at its waist and to seize the oil resources of Asia.

"At the same time they are going for our industries at home, with intense aerial bombardment, which so often results in terrible loss to harmless civil property and population and little loss to Industry.

"But where perhaps they are making their biggest effort is here at sea by their strong submarine, surface craft and aerial attacks upon our trade routes, in a great endeavour to stop the ever increasing flow of American assistance, which is arriving in England across the Atlantic.

"The spirit of our people at home is magnificent and he is not going to get us or our industries by bombing. The position in the Near East may well be critical and may get more so, but that won't get us down. We are a brave and determined nation, and we'll hang on to his throat like a mongoose to a cobra. But what could get us down is to lose the Battle of the Atlantic, for that would stop the flow of supplies from America, upon which the ultimate success of our campaign depends.

"But he is not going to win the Battle of the Atlantic - our Navy, our Air Force and the indomitable spirit of our Merchant Navy will see to that. Admiral Sir Percy Noble backed by the ablest Staff the Navy can produce is in charge of our operations against the "U" Boats and Focke-Wolfes in the North Western approaches. Daily our forces there grow stronger and the results they are obtaining in destroying the enemy are now excellent. It is going to be a hard and bitter struggle there, but I have no doubts whatsoever of our success.

"So if we defeat him in his drive against our sea-borne trade, the great supplies being made ready in America will arrive in Great Britain and so allow our strength to mount to invincibility. In the meantime should we receive a knock or two from our strong and crafty enemy we shall know how to take it, knowing full well that he won't get any stronger whilst we shall immeasurably so, so that in the end we shall do the Bugger down.

"Now to look again at the Nazis, certainly they have conquered most of Europe, but what a commitment has that left them! All these races to be kept in subjection must be a tremendous strain on the strength of our enemy, and most of these nations hating the Germans like Hell, afraid now to do anything, but longing to turn on them when the going is not so good.

"Now just a word or two on the present situation in the Eastern Mediterranean. That so gallant nation, the Greeks, having done so magnificently against the Italians, were menaced by the far stronger Germans and the only earthly thing we could do in justice and decency was to send them military assistance as well as the air assistance we were already giving them. But in the present state of development of our strength this could only be done at the expense of our forces in Egypt. Strategically, perhaps it would have been better to have left the Greeks to their fate and remained strong in Egypt, but morally this would have been indefensible and a course that the British Empire could never adopt."

Captain Barry made another such speech in early June 1941, after the fall of Crete. He said,

"It is only natural that we should feel very disappointed with the German successes in Crete, especially after the valiant and determined efforts of the fleet to help our comrades in the army there and the heavy losses that we have thereby sustained.

"Under the circumstances it is inevitable that the picture of the war as a whole should be obscured by a cloud which temporarily hangs over our own theatre of operations. At the moment we cannot disperse the cloud but we can get behind it, see its silver lining and the blue sky beyond. To begin with, it is quite obvious that in their attack on Crete, the Germans put in all their resources, called up their reserves of aircraft from all over Europe and threw them, regardless of cost, into the battle in order to secure victory in this one small area. That at once proves that there is a limit to German resources and the number of aircraft they possess, and, in the course of the battle, we have undoubtedly eaten into those reserves to an enormous extent. If we knew the number of aircraft we have brought down and damaged during the past ten days we would be encouraged, for it must amount to several hundreds.

"With the successful invasion of Crete by German air-borne troops, it is only natural that we should consider the threatened invasion of Great Britain. In this connection, I feel that the results of the battle of Crete should give us the greatest encouragement. With virtually no air opposition and inadequate A.A defence, we have managed to destroy hundreds of German aircraft and exterminate thousands of Germans. Though they had complete mastery of the air from the beginning, they have only conquered after twelve days of the fiercest fighting they have probably ever faced.

"It is, I feel sure, no exaggeration to say that had we been able to put into the air over Crete a tenth of the aircraft used by the Germans, the story would have been very different. We know that at home we have a very large airforce capable of operating from a number of widely separate bases. For an invasion of England to stand the slightest chance of success, the Germans would have to launch an attack on a scale at least twenty times heavier than they delivered at Crete. Are they capable of it? It is reasonable to suppose they are not capable of it.

"I am going to make a bold statement, that the battle of Crete, though a temporary defeat for us, marks the final defeat of Germany as nothing has marked it before. I have already explained that it must have shaken their confidence in an ability to invade Great Britain, but I am prepared to say more. I believe that the opposition the Germans have encountered both in Greece and Crete has possibly called a stop to their eastward advance in the Mediterranean and most certainly has upset their programme. This will undoubtedly have a most important effect on the whole course of the war and thoroughly justifies the strategic policy in this theatre of war. Naturally I cannot enlarge on this point without giving away secrets, but it is no secret to say that we'd be happier if we were stronger, especially in the air, and that we know - in time - we'll have sufficient men and material to throw the Germans back to where they belong."

APPENDIX ii

Memorandum issued by the captain's office, Queen Elizabeth, May 1941

List of Officers Serving On HMS Queen Elizabeth
with
The Vice Admiral Commanding, First Battle Squadron
Vice Admiral H.D. Pridham-Wippel, C.B., C.V.O.

PERSONAL STAFF

Secretary	Paymaster Commander H. Prevett
Flag Lieutenant	Lieutenant I.H. McDonald, R.A.N.

STAFF

Staff Officer (Operations) & Squadron Navigating Officer	Commander R.H. Craske, D.S.C.
Squadron Gunnery Officer	Commander G.P.U. Morris
Squadron Wireless Officer	Lt. Cdr. D. Grove-White

FOR DUTY IN ADMIRAL'S OFFICE

Paymaster Lieutenant J. Charles (Assistant Secretary)
Temporary Paymaster Lieutenant G.M. Peake, R,N.V.R.
Temporary Paymaster Sub-lieutenant J.C. Robertson, R.N.V.R.
Acting Paymaster Sub-Lieutenant D.M. Lawler
Temporary Paymaster Sub-Lieutenant A.J. Allserbrook, R.N.V.R.
Mr. J.G. Warren, Signal Boatswain

EXECUTIVE BRANCH

Captain	C.B. Barry, D.S.O.	
Commander	R. Gotto, D.S.O.	Executive Officer
Lieutenant Commander	T.L. Alkin	First Lieutenant
Lieutenant Commander	G.M. Stitt	Navigating Officer
Lieutenant Commander Rt.	G. Whitefield	
Lieutenant Commander Rt.	V.I. Mylius	Top Divisional Officer
Lieutenant Commander	P.G. Langley	Torpedo Officer
Lieutenant Commander	H.S. Hopkins	Gunnery Officer
Lieutenant Commander RNVR	R.T. Taggart	
Lieutenant Commander	J.K. Wright	Fxle. Divisional Officer
Lieutenant	N.D. Campbell	Lieutenant (G)
Lieutenant, RNR	R.J. Fox	Q.D. Divisional Officer
Temp. Lieutenant, RNR	T. Cooper	
Lieutenant, RNR	M. Hughes-D'Aeth	
Temp. Lieutenant, RNVR	D.F. Landale	Ventilation & A/G Officer
Lieutenant	J.R. Jamieson	Boy's Divisional Officer
Lieutenant RAN	B.M. Macfarlane	
Lieutenant	R.A. Wright	
Sub-Lieutenant	A.G. Davies	
Temp. Sub-Lieut., RNVR	P.G. Farwell	
Temp. Sub-Lieut., RNVR	D.C. Peacock	
Temp. Sub-Lieut., RNVR	S.T. Nowson	
Midshipman	D.G. Goldsmith	

Midshipman	L.K. Oliphant	
Midshipman	R.B. Watson	
Midshipman	L.D. Temple-Richards	
Midshipman	B.E. Bray	
Midshipman	J.W. Pertwee	
Midshipman	M.D. Smith	
Midshipman	T.P. Hubbard	
Midshipman	R.F. Drake	
Midshipman, RNR	P. A. Chubb	
Prob. Temp. Mid., RNR	J.F. Bloxham	
Midshipman (Polish)	Z. Plesniak	
Midshipman (Polish)	T. Noworal	
Midshipman (Polish)	G. Plewako	
Midshipman (Polish)	M. Wosniak	
Midshipman (Polish)	J. Dobrodsicki	
Midshipman (Polish)	O. Glinski	
Commissioned Gunner (T)	F. Chard	
Commissioned Gunner	F.W. Ings	
Gunner	G. Wynn	
Boatswain	W.H. Leaman	

FLEET AIR ARM

Sub-Lieutenant (A)	J.A. Hopking	Senior F.A.A. Officer
Sub-Lieutenant (A)	R.L. Bigg-Wither	
Sub-Lieutenant (A)	M.J. Baring	

ENGINEERING BRANCH

Commander (E)	W.E. Davy	
Lieutenant Commander (E)	A. Kirkonnel	
Lieutenant (E)	J.P. Sandbrook	Ordnance
Lieutenant (E)	H.T. Lewis	
Lieutenant (E)	G.F. Samllridge	
Temp. Lieutenant (E)	J.D. Percy	
Lieutenant (E)	F.W. Batley	
Lieutenant (E)	J.B. Morrison	
Temp. Sub-Lieut. (E)	W.D. Hutty	
Warrant Engineer	L.W. Green	
Warrant Mechanician	R.H. Neal	
Act. Warrant Engineer	A.C. Rolfe	

MEDICAL BRANCH

Surgeon Commander	C. Kirker, MB., BCh.	Principal Medical Officer
Surgeon Lieut., RNVR	R.M. Marshall, MB., BCh	
Surgeon Lieut. (D), RNVR	W.C. Kenrick, LDS	
Temp. Surgeon Lieut., RNVR	W.J. Patton, MB., Ch.B.	

ACCOUNTANT BRANCH

Paymaster Commander	A. D'O. Morse	Accountant Officer
Paymaster Lieutenant	H.E. James	
Paymaster Sub-Lieutenant	A.K. Pallot	Captain's Secretary
Temp. Pay. Sub-Lt., RNVR	T.L. Frost	
Paymaster Midshipman	J.G. Tyndall	
Paymaster Midshipman, RCN	F.E. Wade	
Act. Warrant Supply Officer	S.E. Cloke	

ROYAL MARINE OFFICER

Captain, RM	T.P. Honnor	Senior Officer, R.M.
Lieutenant, RM	L.W. Fisher	
Lieutenant, RM	K.W. Smale	

MISCELLANEOUS

Temp. Chaplain, RNVR	Rev. W.L. Fleming	Chaplain
Temp. Instr. Lieutenant	A.J. Peters, BA	
Temp. Lieutenant, RCNVR	L.B. Leppard	R. D/F. Officer
Senior Master	H. Fowler	
Warrant Shipwright	F.L. Butler	
Warrant Electrician	H. Syms	
Warrant Ordnance Officer	D.A. Follows	
Act. Warrant Telegraphist	S. Willoughby	

End Notes

1. *Page 60 On page 385* of Cunningham's book *A Sailor's Odyssey,* he writes, "A signal was made to the admiralty setting out the evacuation up-to-date... we further asked if we were further justified in accepting a similar scale of loss and damage to that already incurred to our already weakened fleet. We were ready and willing to continue the evacuation so long as a ship remained."

2. *Page 63* Cunningham, *A Sailor's Odyssey, page 374.*

3. *Page 71* Cunningham, *A Sailor's Odyssey, page 392.* "I have seen it stated that the delaying effect of their attack upon Greece and Crete not only interfered with their designs on Syria and Iraq; but eventually proved disastrous in their attack upon Russia. The German army reached the outskirts of Moscow in October 1941, by which time the early frost had begun to interfere with its movements. Its arrival in front of Moscow five weeks earlier would have probably led to the capture of the city, with fatal results."

4. *Page 78* Cunningham, *A Sailor's Odyssey,* pages 246 to 254.

5. *Page 82* Cunningham, *A Sailor's Odyssey,* page 398.

6. *Page 125* Schofield and Carisella, *Frogmen First Battles,* pages 119 to 132.

7. *Page 129* Smith and Walker *Malta Striking Forces,* page 100.

8. *Page 139* Seth *Two Fleets Surprised - Cape Matapan,* pages 158 to 160

9. *Page 153* Vian, *Action This Day,* pages 94 to 97.

10. *Page 168* Pitt, *The Crucible of War, Year of Alamein 1942,* pages 236 to 262.

11. *Page 172* Roskill, in his *Churchill and the Admirals,* writes at page 191, "In September Harwood tried to restore the situation by launching a sea-borne raid on Tobruk combined with a surprise land attack (Operation "Agreement"). It accomplished nothing and heavy losses were suffered. Churchill's opinion of Harwood at once slumped. He said "I was not favourably impressed... we suffered very heavy losses for little or no result."

12. *Page 181* Cunningham, *A Sailor's Odyssey,* page 501.

13. *Page 183* Bragadin, *Italian Navy in World War II,* pages, 80, 108, 109, 138, 239, 268 and 307.

14. *Page 192* Roskill, *Churchill and the Admirals* pages 211 to 214.

15. *Page 213* Dank, *The Glider Gang* pages 63 to 91.

16. *Page 219* Cave Brown, *Bodyguard Of Lies,* (New York: Bantam Books 1976, pages 282 to 289 (Operation "Mincemeat").

Glossary of Naval Terms

AA	Anti-aircraft.
A/S	Anti-submarine.
Abaft	Toward the stern.
Abeam	Beside; in line abreast.
Ack	Anti-aircraft.
Aft	At the stern.
Asdic	Anti-submarine detection equipment (Sonar).
Astern	Behind the ship.
Battleship	Warship with 13 inch armament or larger.
Binnacle	Compass holder.
C-in-C	Commander-in-Chief.
Carley float	Lifesaving raft with slat deck hung inside a floating ring.
Commander	Second-in command of a ship the size of a cruiser or larger.
CS	Cruiser Squadron.
Destroyer	Warship with 4 inch armament.
DF or D	Destroyer Flotilla.
Dhobi	Laundry.
FAA	Fleet Air Arm.
Flag officer	Senior officer above the rank of captain.
Divisions	Parade by departments.
Flags	Communications officer.
Flotilla	Formation of destroyers or smaller ships under the command of a senior officer.
Fleet, Force, Group	A combination of squadrons or flotillas or individual warships under the command of a flag officer or senior officer.
GOC	General Officer Commanding.
Gun-room	Sub-Lieutenants' and Midshipmen' mess.
Guns	Gunnery Officer.
HMS	His Majesty's Ship.
HMAS	His Majesty's Australian Ship.
HMSAS	His Majesty's South African Ship
Hands	Seamen.
Heavy Cruiser	Warship with 8 to 12 inch armament.
Lee	Downwind sheltered side.
HO	Hostilities Only (called up for war only).
Light Cruiser	Warship with 5 or 6 inch armament.
MGB	Motor gun boat.
ML	Motor Launch.
MT	Motor Transport.
MTB	Motor torpedo boat.
NOIC	Naval Officer in Charge, usually of a port.
Number One	The first (senior) Lieutenant who is the second in command of a destroyer or smaller ship also "Jimmy".

Oerlikon	Light rapid-firing manually operated AA gun.
Other Ranks	Sailors who are not petty officers or officers.
Pay	Paymaster-Commander in charge of the Accountant Department.
Chief or Petty Officers	(CPO, PO), Non-commissioned Officers.
Paravane	Minesweeping gear.
Pipe the Side	Ceremony using a Bosun's pipe for senior officers coming aboard ship or passing another warship.
Pilot	Navigating Officer.
Pom-Pom	Single or multi-barrelled power-operated rapid-firing 1.5 inch AA gun.
Port	Left.
Pongo	Soldier.
Pusser	Paymaster or carried out in accordance with Queens Regulations and Admiralty Instructions.
Ratings	Seamen.
Recce	Reconnaissance.
RDF	Radio Direction Finder (Radar)
RM	Royal Marine.
RNR	Royal Naval Reserve.
RNVR	Royal Naval Volunteer Reserve.
Snottie	Midshipman.
SRE	Sound Reproduction Equipment (Public Address System).
Starboard	Right.
Starshell	Illumination shell which releases flare suspended from a parachute.
Squadron	Formation of battleships or cruisers under the command of a Flag officer.
Sub	Sub-lieutenant, senior to midshipman, junior to lieutenant.
Torps	Torpedo Officer.
VR	Volunteer Reserve.
Whaler	Twenty-five foot clinker built seaworthy yawl-rigged sailing boat with a drop keel, which can also be rowed.
Wardroom	Mess for officers above the rank of Sub-lieutenant.
Wren	Womans Royal Naval Service
W/T	Wireless Telegraphy.
24 Hour Clock	1 a.m. = 01:00, 2 a.m. = 02:00 etc., 12 noon = 12:00 etc. to 6 p.m. = 18:00 etc to midnight = 24:00.

Photograph List

The author would like to recognise the following people or organizations for their contributions of the following photographs and illustrations numbered against their respective names:

Commander Phil Booth RCN, 167, 186, 189, 194, 209, 212, 215

Conway Club of Vancouver, 11

D. McGill, 85, 90

H. Tiesenhausen, 110

Imperial War Museum, 44, 65, 78, 109, 123, 138

K. Gibson, 115

Malta National War Museum, 141

Museo Storico Navale,Venice, 143, 184

Naval Historical Society of Australia, 87

Paul Pidcock, 48, 92, 117, 121, 132, 155, 156, 157, 158

Royal British Columbian Museum, 191

South African Naval Museum, 86

World Ship Society, 141, 149

E. Amoore, 159, 160

Burns, Philp Shipping Co., 196

All other photos are from the author's personal collection.

Map List

Miscellaneous List

Index

245

Ship Index

BATTLESHIPS
King George V Class
King George V, 29, 205, 220, 225
Prince of Wales, (sunk) 122
Howe, 205, 220

Nelson Class
Nelson, 24, 27, 29, 205, 219
Rodney, 205, 219

Queen Elizabeth Class
Queen Elizabeth, (severely damaged), 9, 20, 21, 22, 23, 24, 26, 45, 46, 54
    63, 65, 66, 70, 76, 93, 103, 105, 107, 109, 111, 115, 119, 121, 123, 124
    126, 132, 134, 159, 226
Warspite, (severely damaged), 45, 51, 53, 57, 66, 70, 138, 199, 225
Valiant, (severely damaged), 45, 46, 48, 51, 53, 57, 70, 77, 93, 105, 106, 119,
    121, 122, 123, 124
    126, 131 132, 133, 134, 135, 138, 199, 225
Malaya, 26, 45, 46
Barham, (sunk), 45, 46, 51, 53, 63, 65, 70, 103, 105-118, 122, 138

Royal Sovereign Class
Royal Oak, (sunk) 23

BATTLE CRUISERS
Hood, (sunk), 23, 24, 25, 26, 27, 28, 29, 30, 70
Repulse, (sunk), 24, 29, 37, 123
Renown, 26, 34, 39, 40

AIRCRAFT CARRIERS
Eagle, (sunk) 166
Ark Royal, (sunk) 26, 29, 30, 31, 34, 39, 40, 41, 104, 122

Illustrious Class
Illustrious, (severely damaged) 43, 44
Formidable, (severely damaged) 45, 46, 47, 60, 62, 63, 64, 111, 138, 199
Indomitable, 205, 219

CRUISERS
London Class
London, 25

Exeter Class
Exeter, (sunk), 15, 185
York, (sunk), 62

Leander Class
Leander, 81, 185
Orion, (severely damaged), 45, 50, 54, 62, 66, 67, 68, 69, 175, 184, 185, 188
Ajax, 15, 45, 54, 55, 56, 62, 66, 67, 81, 105, 126, 131, 184, 185
Achilles, 15, 185
Neptune, (sunk), 105, 126, 128, 129, 185

Arethusa Class
  Arethusa, (severely damaged), 146, 175, 176
  Aurora, (damaged), 104, 127, 128, 188, 199, 224
  Galatea, (sunk), 89, 105, 127
  Penelope, (sunk), 104, 127, 128, 131, 140, 185, 199, 224
  Perth, (HMAS) (sunk), 45 69, 70

Southampton Class
  Southampton, (sunk), 43
  Gloucester, (sunk), 45, 51, 54, 57, 58
  Manchester, (sunk), 166
  Newcastle, (damaged), 146, 150, 153
  Birmingham, 146, 152
  Liverpool, (damaged), 153

Dido Class
  Dido, (damaged), 54, 62, 66, 67, 68, 70, 131, 143, 146, 148, 162, 168, 175
      177, 184, 185, 224
  Phoebe, 69, 70, 81, 88
  Cleopatra, 143, 146, 149, 175, 177
  Euryalus, 105, 126, 127, 131, 146, 162, 175, 176, 177
  Sirius (damaged), 188, 224
  Argonaut, 188
  Hermione, (sunk), 146, 153
  Naiad, (sunk), 39, 42, 43, 54, 70, 81, 105, 126, 127, 131, 139

Colony Class
  Fiji, (sunk), 45, 51, 54, 57, 58
  Mauritius, 201
  Newfoundland, 201

C Class
  Carlisle, (damaged beyond repair), 44, 56, 70, 127, 131, 195, 224
  Cairo, (sunk), 166
  Calcutta, (sunk), 44, 56, 69, 70, 71, 72
  Coventry, (sunk), 44, 69, 70, 72, 81, 166, 168-172

Cruiser Squadrons
  4th., 146
  7th., 88
  15th., 88, 125, 146, 175, 177, 178

MINELAYERS
Manxman Class
  Abdiel, (sunk), 62, 63, 65, 70, 88
  Latona, (sunk), 88

DESTROYERS
V & W Class
  Vampire (HMAS) (sunk), 129
  Vendetta (HMAS), 86, 88, 92, 129
  Voyager (HMAS) (sunk), 129
  Waterhen (HMAS) (sunk), 86, 87, 88
  Wolverine, 32

ENEMY WARSHIPS
ITALY
BATTLESHIPS
Cavour Class

Littorio Class

CRUISERS
Zara Class

Bibliography

Attard, J., *Battle of Malta* (London: William Kimber 1980)

Auphan, Rear-Admiral P. FN & Mordal, J., *The French Navy in World War Two* (Annapolis: U.S. Naval Institute 1959)

Blundell W., *Royal Navy Warships 1939 - 1945* (London: Almark Publications 1971)

Bragadon, Commander M. It.N, *The Italian Navy in World War Two* (Annapolis: U.S.Naval Institute 1957)

Chapman, Paul, *Submarine Torbay* (London, Robert Hale 1989)

Connel, G., *Valiant Quartet - H.M. Anti-Aircraft Cruisers Curlew, Cairo, Calcutta and Coventry* (London: William Kimber 1979)

Connel, G., *Mediterranean Maelstrom - HMS Jervis and the 14th Flotilla* (London: William Kimber 1987)

Cunningham, Admiral of the Fleet Viscount A.B. RN, *A Sailor's Odyssey* (London: E.P.Dutton, 1951)

Churchill, Rt. Hon. Winston, *The Hinge of Fate-1941 & The Grand Alliance-1942* (Boston: Houghton Mifflin, 1950)

Dank, M., *The Glider Gang* (New York: J.B.Lippincott, 1977)

Dover, *The Sky Generals* (London: Cassel, 1981)

Goosens, Commodore John South African Navy *History of the South African Navy, South African Ships in the Mediterranean*, Chapter 5 (Capetown: Publisher not known)

Hezlet, Vice Admiral Sir A. RN, *The Electron and Sea Power* (London: Peter Davies 1956)

Jones, G.P., *Battleship Barham* (London: William Kimber 1979)

Lind L.J. & Payne M.A. *Scrap Iron Destroyers, The Story of HMA ships Stuart, Vampire, Vendetta, Voyager, and Waterhen* (Sydney: The Naval Historical Society of Australia 1976)

Lind L.J. & Payne M.A. N Class, *The Story of HMA Ships Napier, Nizam, Nestor, Norman and Nepal* (Sydney: The Naval Historical Society of Australia 1974)

Lund Paul and Ludlam Harry, *The War of the Landing Craft* (Slough, England, W. Foulsham, 1976)

Lynch, Captain M. RCN, *Orion - Story of a Radar Officer in a British Cruiser* (Toronto, Lugus Publications 1992)

Pack, S.W., *Cunningham the Commander* (London: Batsford 1974)

Pitt, B., *The Crucible of War - Year of Alamein* (London: Jonathan Cape, 1982)

Rohwer J. & Hummelchen G., *Chronology of the War at Sea-1939 to 1945 2 Volumes* (New York: Arco, 1974)

Roskill Captain S. RN, *Churchill and the Admirals* (London: Collins 1977)

History of the Second World War - The Mediterranean and the Middle East Volumes 3, 4 and 5, from Sept '41 to Mar '44 (London: HM Stationery Office 1960)

Schofield, W. & Carisella, P., *Frogmen First Battles* (New York: Avon, 1987)

Seth, R., *Two Fleets Surprised - Cape Matapan* (London: G. Bles, 1960)

Shrubb, R.E.A. & Sainsbury, A.B., *The Royal Navy, Day by Day* (Fontwell, England: Centaur 1979)

Smith, P. & Walker, E., *War in the Aegean* (London: William Kimber 1974)

Smith, P, & Walker, E., *Malta Striking Forces* (Shepperton, England: Ian Allan, 1974)

Stitt, Commander G. RN, (Navigator *Queen Elizabeth* 1941 - 1942) *Under Cunningham's Command-1940 to 1943* (London: Allen and Unwin 1944)

Vian, Admiral of the Fleet Sir Philip, RN, *Action this day* (London: F. Muller, 1960)

Winton, J.(ed), *The War at Sea - The British Navy in World War 2* (New York, William Morrow, 1967)

The Mediterranean - World War II (New York: Time Life Books 1981)

East of Malta West of Suez, The Admiralty Account of The Naval War in The Eastern Mediterranean September 1939 to March 1941 (London: His Majesty's Stationary Office 1943)

The Mediterranean Fleet, Greece to Tripoli, The Admiralty Account of Naval Operations April 1941 to January 1943 (London, His Majesty's Stationary Office 1944)

Booth, Commander P. RCN, *HMS Eskimo.* Personal interview, West Vancouver, May 1988.

Gibson K., Engine Room Artificer 4th Class, *HMS Barham,* personal interview, West Vancouver, October 1989

Tiesenhausen H.D. von, Oberleutenant, GN, Captain *U331,* personal interview, November 1987.

McGill D., Lieutenant RCNVR, personal interview, August 1992.

Yuill, Dr. B., Senior Medical Officer, LSI *City of Canterbury,* Ellerman Lines, which took part in the Sicilian landings, personal interview, Vancouver, May 1988.

Public Records Office, Kew, Richmond. UK, Admiralty Files ADM 1/ 9923, 11948; ADM 53/ 310, 116398; ADM 199/ 11728, 2067, 2070. Ship Index - *Bulolo, Jervis, Orion,* and *Queen Elizabeth.*